Brent B. Benda
Nathaniel J. Pallone
Editors

Rehabilitation Issues, Problems, and Prospects in Boot Camp

Rehabilitation Issues, Problems, and Prospects in Boot Camp has been co-published simultaneously as *Journal of Offender Rehabilitation*, Volume 40, Numbers 3/4 2005.

Pre-publication REVIEWS, COMMENTARIES, EVALUATIONS...

"A WELL-RESEARCHED, WELL-WRITTEN, AND WELL-PRESENTED collection of chapters by the leading experts on the subject. REQUIRED READING for policymakers and scholars interested in discovering what works (and what doesn't) in corrections. This book collects some of the best and most recent empirical research on boot camps, along with several excellent summaries of the extant research. It is timely, thought-provoking, and a major contribution to the literature on correctional treatment."

Craig Hemmens, JD, PhD
*Chair and Professor, Department of Criminal Justice Administration
Boise State University*

More pre-publication
REVIEWS, COMMENTARIES, EVALUATIONS . . .

"A GREAT CHOICE FOR COURSES in evaluation research, criminal justice, and substance abuse. . . . Would also work nicely in seminar courses in social work, public administration, and public policy. BROAD, WELL INTEGRATED, READABLE, AND NEATLY PACKAGED, this anthology makes a significant contribution to the literature on boot camps."

David R. Rudy, PhD
*Professor of Sociology and Dean
Institute for Regional Analysis
and Public Policy
Morehead State University*

"For anyone involved in corrections, for any sheriff's office or private business that operates a boot camp, or for anyone considering starting a boot camp, THIS BOOK IS A MUST-HAVE! It is clear, well-written, and contains invaluable information for scholars and practitioners alike."

Wayman C. Mullins, PhD
Professor, Department of Criminal Justice, Texas State University

"ONE OF THE BEST EDITED BOOKS I'VE READ. . . . It is informative, well-written, and holds together as a book. The contributors are experts in their fields. As a former corrections officer who is old enough to have participated in the Scared Straight models of change and who has since studied rehabilitation, I found this book both refreshing and informative. Drs. Benda and Pallone obviously took great pains to make sure the various chapters are integrated in such a way that the reader is not left dangling. I enjoyed all the chapters, but found the one on the rise and fall of boot camps particularly noteworthy."

John R. Belcher, PhD, MDiv, LCSW-C
*Professor, School of Social Work
University of Maryland*

More pre-publication
REVIEWS, COMMENTARIES, EVALUATIONS...

"COVERS EVERY IMPORTANT ASPECT OF THE BOOT CAMP STORY.... Excellent reading for anyone who wants to know about the multiple realities of penal innovation.... A terrific short course in the ignominious story of boot camps in America."

Todd Clear, PhD
*Professor and Director
Program of Doctoral Studies
in Criminal Justice
The Graduate Center
John Jay College of Criminal Justice,
City University of New York*

"ONE OF THE FINEST CONTRIBUTIONS TO THE LITERATURE on the rehabilitative efforts of military style boot camps. ... A quick reading guide to see where we have been in regard to boot camps and the pitfalls of a quick-fix approach. Especially noteworthy were the insights on why women over men preferred to serve their sentences in them. The book challenges many of the basic premises behind boot camps and OFFERS USEFUL AND APPROPRIATE IMPROVEMENT SUGGESTIONS. I HIGHLY RECOMMEND THIS BOOK for those who care about improving rehabilitation efforts within the corrections field."

Joseph R. Carlson, PhD
*Professor of Criminal Justice
University of Nebraska at Kearney*

The Haworth Press, Inc.

Rehabilitation Issues, Problems, and Prospects in Boot Camp

Rehabilitation Issues, Problems, and Prospects in Boot Camp has been co-published simultaneously as *Journal of Offender Rehabilitation*, Volume 40, Numbers 3/4 2005.

Monographic Separates from the *Journal of Offender Rehabilitation*

For additional information on these and other Haworth Press titles, including descriptions, tables of contents, reviews, and prices, use the QuickSearch catalog at http://www.HaworthPress.com.

Rehabilitation Issues, Problems, and Prospects in Boot Camp, edited by Brent B. Benda, PhD, and Nathaniel J. Pallone, PhD (Vol. 40, No. 3/4, 2005). *"A well-researched, well-written, and well-presented collection of chapters by the leading experts on the subject. Required reading for policymakers and scholars interested in discovering what works (and what doesn't) in corrections. This book collects some of the best and most recent empirical research on boot camps, along with several excellent summaries of the extant research. It is timely, thought-provoking, and a major contribution to the literature on correctional treatment."* (Craig Hemmens, JD, PhD, Chair and Professor, Department of Criminal Justice Administration, Boise State University)

Treating Substance Abusers in Correctional Contexts: New Understandings, New Modalities, edited by Nathaniel J. Pallone, PhD (Vol. 37, No. 3/4, 2003). *"Intriguing and illuminating. . . . Includes qualitative and quantitative research on juvenile and adult-oriented programs in the United States, Britain, and Hong Kong. . . . Examines a multitude of issues relevant to substance abuse treatment in the criminal justice system. . . . Also includes several chapters examining the effectiveness of drug courts. . . . Provides some answers to the questions being asked about RSAT programs and highlights what may be the most intriguing and encouraging development in corrections in the past quarter-century. I highly recommend this book to anyone interested in substance abuse treatement programs."* (Craig Hemmens, JD, PhD, Chair and Associate Professor, Department of Criminal Justice Administration, Boise State University)

Transcendental Meditation® in Criminal Rehabilitation and Crime Prevention, edited by Charles N. Alexander, PhD, Kenneth G. Walton, PhD, David Orme-Johnson, PhD, Rachel S. Goodman, PhD, and Nathaniel J. Pallone, PhD (Vol. 36, No. 1/2/3/4, 2003). *"Makes a strong case that meditation can accelerate development in adult criminal populations, leading to reduced recidivism and other favorable outcomes. . . . Contains original research and reviews of over 25 studies that demonstrate the effectiveness of TM programs in criminal rehabilitation."* (Juan Pascual-Leone, MD, PhD, Professor of Psychology, York University)

Religion, the Community, and the Rehabilitation of Criminal Offenders, edited by Thomas P. O'Connor, BCL, BTheol, MS, and Nathaniel J. Pallone, PhD (Vol. 35, No. 3/4, 2002). *Examines the relationship between faith-based programs, religion, and offender rehabilitation.*

Drug Courts in Operation: Current Research, edited by James J. Hennessy, PhD, and Nathaniel J. Pallone, PhD (Vol. 33, No. 4, 2001). *"As one of the founders of the drug court movement, I can testify that Dr. Hennessy's book represents the highest level of sophistication in this field."* (Michael O. Smith, MD, Director, Lincoln Recovery Center, Bronx, New York; Assistant Clinical Professor of Psychiatry, Cornell University Medical School)

Family Empowerment as an Intervention Strategy in Juvenile Delinquency, edited by Richard Dembo, PhD, and Nathaniel J. Pallone, PhD (Vol. 33, No. 1, 2001). *"A hands-on book. . . . Provides detailed guidelines for counselors regarding implementation of the FEI curriculum . . . accurately describes the scope of counselor responsibilities and the nature of treatment interventions. Unique in its coverage of counselor competencies and training/supervision needs. Innovative and based on solid empirical evidence."* (Roger H. Peters, PhD, Professor, University of South Florida, Tampa)

Race, Ethnicity, Sexual Orientation, Violent Crime: The Realities and the Myths, edited by Nathaniel J. Pallone, PhD (Vol. 30, No. 1/2, 1999). *"A fascinating book which illuminates the complexity of race as it applies to the criminal justice system and the myths and political correctness that have shrouded the real truth. . . . I highly recommend this book for those who study causes of crime in minority populations."* (Joseph R. Carlson, PhD, Associate Professor, University of Nebraska at Kearney)

Sex Offender Treatment: Biological Dysfunction, Intrapsychic Conflict, Interpersonal Violence, edited by Eli Coleman, PhD, S. Margretta Dwyer, MA, and Nathaniel J. Pallone, PhD (Vol. 23, No. 3/4, 1996). *"Offers a review of current assessment and treatment theory while addressing critical issues such as standards of care, use of phallometry, and working with specialized populations such as exhibitionists and developmentally disabled clients. . . . A valuable addition to the reader's professional library." (Robert E. Freeman-Longo, MRC, LPC, Director, The Safer Society Press)*

The Psychobiology of Aggression: Engines, Measurement, Control, edited by Marc Hillbrand, PhD, and Nathaniel J. Pallone, PhD (Vol. 21, No. 3/4, 1995). *"A comprehensive sourcebook for the increasing dialogue between psychobiologists, neuropsychiatrists, and those interested in a full understanding of the dynamics and control of criminal aggression." (Criminal Justice Review)*

Young Victims, Young Offenders: Current Issues in Policy and Treatment, edited by Nathaniel J. Pallone, PhD (Vol. 21, No. 1/2, 1994). *"Extremely practical. . . . Aims to increase knowledge about the patterns of youthful offenders and give help in designing programs of prevention and rehabilitation." (S. Margretta Dwyer, Director of Sex Offender Treatment Program, Department of Family Practice, University of Minnesota)*

Sex Offender Treatment: Psychological and Medical Approaches, edited by Eli Coleman, PhD, S. Margretta Dwyer, and Nathaniel J. Pallone, PhD (Vol. 18, No. 3/4, 1992). *"Summarizes research worldwide on the various approaches to treating sex offenders for both researchers and clinicians." (SciTech Book News)*

The Clinical Treatment of the Criminal Offender in Outpatient Mental Health Settings: New and Emerging Perspectives, edited by Sol Chaneles, PhD, and Nathaniel J. Pallone, PhD (Vol. 15, No. 1, 1990). *"The clinical professional concerned with the outpatient treatment of the criminal offender will find this book informative and useful." (Criminal Justice Review)*

Older Offenders: Current Trends, edited by Sol Chaneles, PhD, and Cathleen Burnett, PhD (Vol. 13, No. 2, 1985). *"Broad in scope and should provide a fruitful beginning for future discussion and exploration." (Criminal Justice Review)*

Prisons and Prisoners: Historical Documents, edited by Sol Chaneles, PhD (Vol. 10, No. 1/2, 1985). *"May help all of us . . . to gain some understanding as to why prisons have resisted change for over 300 years. . . . Very challenging and very disturbing." (Public Offender Counseling Association)*

Gender Issues, Sex Offenses, and Criminal Justice: Current Trends, edited by Sol Chaneles, PhD (Vol. 9, No. 1/2, 1984). *"The contributions of the work will be readily apparent to any reader interested in an interdisciplinary approach to criminology and women's studies." (Criminal Justice Review)*

Current Trends in Correctional Education: Theory and Practice, edited by Sol Chaneles, PhD (Vol. 7, No. 3/4, 1983). *"A laudable presentation of educational issues in relation to corrections." (International Journal of Offender Therapy and Comparative Criminology)*

Counseling Juvenile Offenders in Institutional Settings, edited by Sol Chaneles, PhD (Vol. 6, No. 3, 1983). *"Covers a variety of settings and approaches, from juvenile awareness programs, day care, and vocational rehabilitation to actual incarceration in juvenile and adult institutions. . . . Good coverage of the subject." (Canada's Mental Health)*

Strategies of Intervention with Public Offenders, edited by Sol Chaneles, PhD (Vol. 6, No. 1/2, 1982). *"The information presented is well-organized and should prove useful to the practitioner, the student, or for use in in-service training." (The Police Chief)*

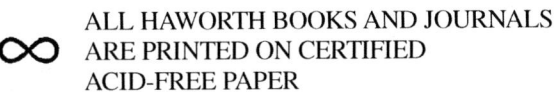

∞ ALL HAWORTH BOOKS AND JOURNALS
ARE PRINTED ON CERTIFIED
ACID-FREE PAPER

Rehabilitation Issues, Problems, and Prospects in Boot Camp

Brent B. Benda
Nathaniel J. Pallone
Editors

Rehabilitation Issues, Problems, and Prospects in Boot Camp has been co-published simultaneously as *Journal of Offender Rehabilitation*, Volume 40, Numbers 3/4 2005.

The Haworth Press, Inc.
New York • London • Victoria (AU)
www.HaworthPress.com

Rehabilitation Issues, Problems, and Prospects in Boot Camp has been co-published simultaneously as *Journal of Offender Rehabilitation*, Volume 40, Numbers 3/4 2005.

© 2005 by The Haworth Press, Inc. All rights reserved. No part of this work may be reproduced or utilized in any form or by any means, electronic or mechanical, including photocopying, microfilm and recording, or by any information storage and retrieval system, without permission in writing from the publisher. Printed in the United States of America.

The development, preparation, and publication of this work has been undertaken with great care. However, the publisher, employees, editors, and agents of The Haworth Press and all imprints of The Haworth Press, Inc., including The Haworth Medical Press® and Pharmaceutical Products Press®, are not responsible for any errors contained herein or for consequences that may ensue from use of materials or information contained in this work. Opinions expressed by the author(s) are not necessarily those of The Haworth Press, Inc. With regard to case studies, identities and circumstances of individuals discussed herein have been changed to protect confidentiality. Any resemblance to actual persons, living or dead, is entirely coincidental.

Cover design by Kerry E. Mack

Library of Congress Cataloging-in-Publication Data

Rehabilitation issues, problems, and prospects in boot camp / Brent B. Benda, Nathaniel J. Pallone, editors.
    p. cm.
    "Rehabilitation issues, problems, and prospects in boot camp has been co-published simultaneously as Journal of offender rehabilitation, Volume 40, Numbers 3/4 2005."
    Includes bibliographical references and index.
    ISBN 0-7890-2821-2 (hard cover : alk. paper) – ISBN 0-7890-2822-0 (soft cover : alk. paper)
    1. Shock incarceration–United States. 2. Correctional institutions–United States. 3. Criminals–Rehabilitation–United States. I. Benda, Brent B. II. Pallone, Nathaniel J. III. Journal of offender rehabilitation.

HV9278.5.R45 2005
365'.34–dc22

2004026937

Indexing, Abstracting & Website/Internet Coverage

This section provides you with a list of major indexing & abstracting services and other tools for bibliographic access. That is to say, each service began covering this periodical during the year noted in the right column. Most Websites which are listed below have indicated that they will either post, disseminate, compile, archive, cite or alert their own Website users with research-based content from this work. (This list is as current as the copyright date of this publication.)

Abstracting, Website/Indexing Coverage . . . . Year When Coverage Began

- *Business Source Corporate: coverage of nearly 3,350 quality magazines and journals; designed to meet the diverse information needs of corporations; EBSCO Publishing <http://www.epnet.com/corporate/bsourcecorp.asp>* 2003
- *Criminal Justice Abstracts* 1986
- *Criminal Justice Periodical Index <http://www.proquest.com>* 1980
- *e-psyche, LLC <http://www.e-psyche.net>* 1999
- *EBSCOhost Electronic Journals Service (EJS) <http://ejournals.ebsco.com>* 2001
- *ERIC Database (Education Resource Information Center) <http://www.eric.ed.gov>* 2004
- *Expanded Academic ASAP <http://www.galegroup.com>* 1999
- *Expanded Academic ASAP–International <http://www.galegroup.com>* 1999
- *Family Index Database <http://www.familyscholar.com>* 2004
- *Family & Society Studies Worldwide <http://www.nisc.com>* 1996
- *Family Violence & Sexual Assault Bulletin* 1992
- *Google <http://www.google.com>* 2004
- *Google Scholar <http://scholar.google.com>* 2004

(continued)

- *Haworth Document Delivery Center* 1990
- *IBZ International Bibliography of Periodical Literature*
  <http://www.saur.de> 1996
- *Index Guide to College Journals (core list compiled by integrating*
  48 indexes frequently used to support undergraduate programs
  in small to medium sized libraries) 1999
- *Index to Periodical Articles Related*
  to Law <http://www.law.utexas.edu> 1991
- *InfoTrac OneFile <http://www.galegroup.com>* 1999
- *Internationale Bibliographie der geistes- und*
  sozialwissenschaftlichen Zeitschriftenliteratur ... See IBZ
  <http://www.saur.de> 1996
- *Magazines for Libraries (Katz) ... (see 2003 edition)* 2003
- *National Clearinghouse on Child Abuse & Neglect Information*
  Documents Database <http://nccanch.acf.hhs.gov> 1990
- *National Criminal Justice Reference Service*
  <http://www.ncjrs.org> 1982
- *OCLC ArticleFirst <http://www.oclc.org/services/databases/>* 2002
- *OCLC ContentsFirst <http://www.oclc.org/services/databases/>* 2002
- *Psychological Abstracts (PsycINFO) <http://www.apa.org>* 1976
- *Referativnyi Zhurnal (Abstracts Journal of the All-Russian*
  Institute of Scientific and Technical Information–in Russian) ... 1986
- *Sage Urban Studies Abstracts (SUSA)* 1992
- *Sexual Diversity Studies: Gay, Lesbian, Bisexual & Transgender*
  Abstracts (formerly Gay & Lesbian Abstracts) provides comprehensive &
  in-depth coverage of the world's GLBT literature compiled by
  NISC & published on the Internet & CD-ROM
  <http://www.nisc.com> 2001
- *Social Sciences Abstracts indexes and abstracts more than 460*
  publications, specifically selected by librarians and
  library patrons. Wilson's databases comprise the peer-reviewed
  and peer-selected core journals in each field
  <http://www.hwwilson.com> 1999
- *Social Sciences Index (from Volume 1 and continuing)*
  <http://www.hwwilson.com> 1999
- *Social Sciences PlusText. Contents of this publication are indexed*
  and abstracted in the Social Sciences PlusText database (includes
  only abstracts ... not full-text) available on ProQuest
  Information & Learning <http://www.proquest.com> 1980
- *Social Services Abstracts <http://www.csa.com>* 1991

(continued)

- *Social Work Abstracts*
  <http://www.silverplatter.com/catalog/swab.htm>............ 1982
- *Sociological Abstracts (SA)* <http://www.csa.com> 1991
- *Special Educational Needs Abstracts* 1989
- *Studies on Women and Gender Abstracts*
  <http://www.tandf.co.uk/swa> 1998
- *SwetsWise* <http://www.swets.com> 2001
- *Violence and Abuse Abstracts: A Review of Current Literature on Interpersonal Violence (VAA)* 1994
- *Wilson OmniFile Full Text: Mega Edition (only available electronically)* <http://www.hwwilson.com> 1999
- *Women, Girls & Criminal Justice Newsletter. For subscriptions, write: Civic Research Institute, 4490 Rte. 27, Box 585, Kingston, NJ 08528* 2002
- *zetoc* <http://zetoc.mimas.ac.uk> 2004

Special Bibliographic Notes related to special journal issues (separates) and indexing/abstracting:

- indexing/abstracting services in this list will also cover material in any "separate" that is co-published simultaneously with Haworth's special thematic journal issue or DocuSerial. Indexing/abstracting usually covers material at the article/chapter level.
- monographic co-editions are intended for either non-subscribers or libraries which intend to purchase a second copy for their circulating collections.
- monographic co-editions are reported to all jobbers/wholesalers/approval plans. The source journal is listed as the "series" to assist the prevention of duplicate purchasing in the same manner utilized for books-in-series.
- to facilitate user/access services all indexing/abstracting services are encouraged to utilize the co-indexing entry note indicated at the bottom of the first page of each article/chapter/contribution.
- this is intended to assist a library user of any reference tool (whether print, electronic, online, or CD-ROM) to locate the monographic version if the library has purchased this version but not a subscription to the source journal.
- individual articles/chapters in any Haworth publication are also available through the Haworth Document Delivery Service (HDDS).

ABOUT THE EDITORS

Brent B. Benda, PhD, is Professor in the School of Social Work at the University of Arkansas at Little Rock. He has published articles on crime and delinquency, substance abuse, adolescent sexual behavior, and homelessness in journals such as *Youth & Society, Journal of Research in Crime and Delinquency, Criminal Justice and Behavior, Journal of Criminal Justice, Journal of Social Service Research, Social Work Research, Journal of Youth and Adolescence, Journal of Adolescence, Journal of Adolescent Research, Journal of Offender Rehabilitation, Journal of Drug Issues, Psychiatric Services, Suicide & Life-Threatening Behavior,* and *Psychiatric Rehabilitation Journal.*

Nathaniel J. Pallone, PhD, Editor of the *Journal of Offender Rehabilitation,* is University Distinguished Professor (Psychology), Center of Alcohol Studies, Rutgers University, where he previously served as dean and as academic vice president.

Rehabilitation Issues, Problems, and Prospects in Boot Camp

CONTENTS

Introduction: Boot Camps Revisited: Issues, Problems, Prospects   1
  BRENT B. BENDA
  University of Arkansas at Little Rock

From Optimistic Policies to Pessimistic Outcomes: Why Won't Boot Camps Either Succeed Pragmatically or Succumb Politically?   27
  JEANNE B. STINCHCOMB
  Florida Atlantic University

The Rise and Fall of Boot Camps: A Case Study in Common-Sense Corrections   53
  FRANCIS T. CULLEN
  University of Cincinnati
  KRISTIE R. BLEVINS
  University of Cincinnati
  JENNIFER S. TRAGER
  University of Cincinnati
  PAUL GENDREAU
  University of New Brunswick at Saint John

A Randomized Evaluation of the Maryland Correctional Boot Camp for Adults: Effects on Offender Antisocial Attitudes and Cognitions   71
  OJMARRH MITCHELL
  University of Nevada, Las Vegas
  DORIS L. MACKENZIE
  University of Maryland
  DEANNA M. PÉREZ
  Virginia Department of Corrections

Survival Analysis of Recidivism of Male and Female Boot Camp
Graduates Using Life-Course Theory   87
    BRENT B. BENDA
    University of Arkansas at Little Rock
    NANCY J. HARM
    University of Arkansas at Little Rock
    NANCY J. TOOMBS
    North Little Rock, Arkansas

Self-Control, Gender, and Age: A Survival Analysis of Recidivism
Among Boot Camp Graduates in a 5-Year Follow-Up   115
    BRENT B. BENDA
    University of Arkansas at Little Rock
    NANCY J. TOOMBS
    North Little Rock, Arkansas
    ROBERT FLYNN CORWYN
    University of Arkansas at Little Rock

Boot Camp Prisons as Masculine Organizations: Rethinking
Recidivism and Program Design   133
    FAITH E. LUTZE
    Washington State University
    CORTNEY A. BELL
    Washington State University

Gender Differences in the Perceived Severity of Boot Camp   153
    PETER B. WOOD
    Mississippi State University
    DAVID C. MAY
    Eastern Kentucky University
    HAROLD G. GRASMICK
    University of Oklahoma

Native American Ethnicity and Childhood Maltreatment as Variables
in Perceptions and Adjustments to Boot Camp vs. "Traditional"
Correctional Settings   177
    ANGELA R. GOVER
    University of Florida

Ruminating About Boot Camps: Panaceas, Paradoxes, and Ideology   199
    JAMES O. FINCKENAUER
    Rutgers University

Index   209

Introduction:
Boot Camps Revisited:
Issues, Problems, Prospects

BRENT B. BENDA

University of Arkansas at Little Rock

ABSTRACT This introduction discusses the purposes and goals of boot camps within the historical context of correctional reforms. A historical review of circumstances–such as the sharp rise in crime and overtaxed budgets–ideological concerns, and political climate offers an understanding of why these programs were adopted. Philosophical themes that arose in the '70s in reaction to high crime rates and disillusionment with rehabilitation efforts are recounted within this context. Existing evidence regarding the effectiveness of boot camp programs is presented, along with male and female inmates' perception of the benefits of these programs. A discriminant analysis of non-recidivists, felony recidivists, and parole violators is discussed in terms of potential value to practice. Deficits and problems in boot camp programs are examined, including abuses, with particular emphasis on gender differences. Finally, the salient methodological problems beleaguering research on boot camps are enumerated for consideration in future research. These problems are intricate and complex, requiring sophisticated understanding of statistical procedures and underlying assumptions, but seemingly not insurmountable. *[Article copies available for a fee from The Haworth Document Delivery Service: 1-800-HAWORTH. E-mail address:*

<docdelivery@haworthpress.com> Website: <http://www.HaworthPress.com>
© 2005 by The Haworth Press, Inc. All rights reserved.]

KEYWORDS Boot camps, philosophical tenets of corrections, history of boot camps, correctional reforms, problems in boot camp

The contemporary implementation of a militaristic program in the correctional system has elicited diverse opinions regarding ethics, purpose, rehabilitation, and impact on criminal recidivism. The manuscripts found in this tome address many of the hotly debated issues surrounding what are called "boot camps" or "shock incarceration." Although some writers use these terms interchangeably, "shock incarceration" is not used synonymously with "boot camps" because the former term refers to a broader category of intermediate sanctions–intermediate between probations and traditional prison, such as intensive probation or parole supervision, house arrest, day treatment centers, fines, and community service or restitution (Morris & Tonry, 1990). For convenience of discussion, the term "traditional prison" will be used to refer to secured facilities in the Department of Corrections that are used to incarcerate felons without military regimens that typify boot camps.

An operational definition of boot camp is problematic because of the vast diversity of programs found in different facilities. This diversity presents thorny challenges to researchers and evaluators in trying to make multisite comparisons and comparisons between different types of correctional interventions, such as traditional prison or probation. Because of the popularity of the concept of boot camp among legislators and other interested constituencies, proponents and planners have used the term to include a wide range of dissimilar programs (Cronin, 1994). More generically, researchers associated with the National Institute of Justice have identified the following characteristics of boot camp: (a) programs designed with military regimens and routines, (b) discipline and rules adopted from the armed services' model, and (c) secured facility intended to be a community alternative to traditional prison (Cronin, 1994; MacKenzie, 1990; Parent, 1989). Identifying these characteristics has provided some parameters, but researchers still struggle with the heterogeneity of programs in trying to make generalizations about boot camps.

CONCEPTION OF THE CONTEMPORARY BOOT CAMP PROGRAM

The idea of resurrecting a militaristic intervention in the justice system has been traced back to an internal memo circulated in the Georgia Department of Corrections–the assumption is that the idea arose from discussions between the Commissioner of Corrections and a local judge. The concept came to fruition with the designing of Dodge Correctional Institution in 1983. This institution was completed, however, after the opening of a boot camp facility in Oklahoma (Osler, 1991; Parent, 1989). By 1983, there were 36 states under court order or facing litigation because their prisons were overcrowded: Boot camps, in large measure, were constructed to house criminals in a cheaper secured facility for a shorter duration than traditional prison. Other interventions, such as electronic monitoring and house arrest, also were instituted to handle the volume of offenders being committed to Department of Correction because of "getting tough on crime" policies, including wholesale incarceration of drug offenders (Morris & Tonry, 1990).

As a result of noteworthy increases in drug offenses in the '80s, Congress imposed strict mandatory sentences on persons possessing and selling certain substances such as cocaine. These laws would reshape the social composition of state and federal prisons. The dramatic rise in admissions to Departments of Correction forced officials to create alternative interventions to expensive traditional prisons. The use of the military model in corrections certainly was not novel (Anderson, Dyson, & Burns, 1999). According to Anderson et al., Warden Zebulon Brockway at Elmira Reformatory, located in Elmira, New York, first instituted a militaristic approach in an American correctional facility in 1888. The military model was adopted to invoke discipline and keep inmates active to avert the boredom of prison life. As these authors note, military approaches to training and discipline have been used in a variety of correctional interventions since their introduction at Elmira.

To many decision-makers confronted with the ever-worsening problem of how to manage the overflow created by "get-tough on crime" policies, boot camps appeared to offer the ideal solution. Boot camps were marketed as serving multiple purposes–the impression created was that the boot camp intervention addressed a potpourri of ideological concerns. For conservatives, boot camp provided a secure facility where inmates were forced to deal with the harsh consequences of crime, and in addition to punishment, they would learn self-control through regimented military training and hard labor. The discipline of the military training would be assimilated in into inmates' thinking and behavior. Although boot camps do not appear to have been conceived with a systematic theory in mind, a loosely translated social learning framework would seem to apply, particularly the concepts of modeling and differential reinforcement (Akers, 1998; Akers & Sellers, 2004). Liberals believed the same programs would offer education and services that would ultimately alter attitudes and thinking to favor more conventional choices. Because of their wide appeal, boot camps proliferated in the late '80s and early '90s, and by 1995, there were 75 state-operated boot camps. Then, disillusionment with their performance led to a decline in the number of boot camps: By 2000, only 51 of these facilities remained–the average daily population in State boot camps also dropped more than 30 percent (Parent, 2003, p. 2).

Since their inception, the express purposes of boot camps have been to shock neophyte offenders out of a criminal lifestyle, to reduce prison overcrowding and rising costs of incarceration, and to offer an alternative intermediate sanction between probation and prison in a secured facility. The distinguishing feature of these programs is the emphasis on the military discipline of basic training, including standing at attention, speaking only when spoken to, marching, calisthenics, and attention-riveting confrontations by drill instructors. Many programs also include rehabilitative components such as problem-solving classes, individual and group counseling, education, and substance use information (Cronin, 1994; MacKenzie & Armstrong, 2004).

In a word, boot camps have been publicized as being "all things to all people" (Parent, 1989, p. 6). While this marketing claim is exaggerated, the multitask nature of boot camps has been the Achilles heel of these programs. A discussion ensues to articulate the characteristics of boot camp and of program participants that would seem at least to weaken the prospects of accomplishing the goals that have been identified.

PROGRAM GOALS AND OBJECTIVES

There seems to be a consensus among researchers that the primary goals of boot camp are: (a) deterrence, (b) rehabilitation, (c) punishment, (d) incapacitation, and (e) reduction of prison costs and crowding (Parent, 1989, pp. 11-12; Osler, 1991, pp. 35-36; Cronin, 1974, p. 6).

Deterrence

Deterrence typically is discussed in terms of specific and general deterrence. Specific deterrence refers to a sanction deterring the particular individual punished, whereas general deterrence refers to vicariously learning from seeing other people punished. The assumption underlying "shock incarceration" is that the unpleasant experience per se will be a potent disincentive to further commission of unlawful behavior. Many boot camps are even located in close geographical proximity to more traditional prisons to emphasize the potential for serving "hard time." Boot camps have been criticized for verbal abuses, such as drill instructors calling inmates "maggot," "scumbag," "boy," "a fool," and "sissies" (Sechrest, 1989), and for threatening boot camp participants that they will have to endure sexual assaults if they are returned to prison because of failure in the boot camp program (Lutze & Brody, 1999). Physical maltreatment includes inmates carrying heavy railroad ties on their back, crawling on hot sidewalks, and exercising until one is unconscious. Certainly, it is unreasonable to assume that these merciless practices are compatible with any rehabilitation efforts (Lutze & Brody, 1999). It is plausible to assume that these adverse experiences generate or enhance hostility, aggression, and opposition to any rehabilitation efforts.

Administrators, legislators, and the public assume the harsh realities of boot camp deter the general citizenry from crime. In theory at least, the media portrayal of wake-up calls at 5 a.m., long jogs before breakfast, screaming drill sergeants, and wearisome work (e.g., cleaning highways) will induce people to exercise self-control. Politicians endorse boot camps because of their supposed deterrent effect–empirical evidence of specific and of general deterrence clearly is needed. Recidivism studies done by the author (Benda, Toombs, & Peacock, 2002, 2003a, 2003b) and others (see review, MacKenzie & Armstrong, 2004) do not suggest that boot camps provide specific deterrence.

Rehabilitation

Many boot camps now offer rehabilitation services in addition to what some assume is the general "shock effect" of incarceration in a intensely demanding military program. A variety of educational classes and counseling groups are offered to discourage risky peer associations and drug use, and to promote healthier beliefs, such as self-esteem and self-efficacy. In the strongest study to date, MacKenzie, Brame, McDowall, and Souryal (1995) found that while boot camps in general did not reduce recidivism, programs incorporating greater levels of therapeutic activities (e.g., drug treatment, academic education, life skills education) and programs targeting prison-bound offenders did significantly reduce recidivism in comparison to traditional correctional institutions. Mitchell, MacKenzie and Pérez suggest in this tome that it is premature to conclude that boot camp programs are ineffective at crime reductions–they conjecture that it is possible that the integration of the boot camp model and therapeutic programming may produce a synergy capable of reducing criminal recidivism.

Cullen, Blevins, Trager, and Gendreau (in this tome) argue to the contrary that boot camps, based on common-sense ideas, have demonstrated failure in rehabilitating offenders, and are draining valuable resources from evidence-based programs. If recidivism is the criterion, boot camps do not seem to be successful: For example, Benda, Toombs, and Peacock (2003a) find that the rate of return to the Arkansas Department of Correction in a 5-year follow-up study is 61.5 percent for male graduates of the only boot camp for adults–20 percent are parole violators. However, studies are needed that examine subgroups and individual changes that may be directly related to specific services in boot camp. It is possible that boot camps are having some impact on recidivism for certain identifiable inmates. Too often the fate of intervention is decided on the bases of aggregate statistics without attempts to discriminate between subgroups that may have very different failure rates (Gottfredson & Tonry, 1987; Jones, 1996). Meanwhile, Benda, Toombs, and Peacock (2002) and Gover, MacKenzie, and Styve (2000) present preliminary data to show that positive perceptions of the boot camp environment are inversely related to recidivism.

Punishment

A major selling point in marketing boot camps is that they provide a cheaper means of punishing large numbers of criminals than prison. Boot camp programs are very strenuous and stressful, intimidating and humiliating, and overwhelmingly demanding–they are, uh, punishing. To my knowledge, the issue of how punishing inmates find boot camp has not been directly studied. Trying to investigate how inmates rate the level of punishment for boot camps is not straightforward and is complicated by personal characteristics and perspectives. For example, Wood, May, and Grasmick present valuable information showing that men are more likely than women to choose prison over any duration of boot camp, and men identify more strongly than women with reasons to avoid alternative sanctions. Women are willing to remain in boot camp longer than are men. Their results suggest that women may be more willing to enter boot camp because it provides a more expeditious way of getting home to children than traditional prison. While their study is concerned with hypothetical choices rather than a rating of the gravity of punishment, their findings suggest that personal perspectives and needs, such as being with children, likely confound assessment of punishment. And these confounding factors may differ by gender.

Incapacitation

Boot camp programs, being short in duration, are not intended to incapacitate offenders until the natural desires for risky behaviors have waned (Wilson, 1975). Rather, another marketing claim is that boot camps are able to handle a relatively larger volume of offenders in a shorter period of time than traditional prison. This is, of course, an artifact of design–boot camp programs typically last four to six months, whereas most incarcerations in prison are for at least one year (Cronin, 1994; Parent, 2003). A more skeptical perspective on boot camps is that they rapidly process a large amount of offenders, giving the appearance of "getting tough on crime," while releasing inmates as soon as public scrutiny has diminished. In a sense, boot camps are a "release valve" to reduce the public's clamor for punishing criminals and making their streets safer.

Reduce Overcrowding and Cut Costs

In a National Institute of Justice sponsored analysis of research conducted over the past 10 years, Parent (2003, p. 2) concludes:

> . . . researchers agree that correctional boot camps might achieve small relative reductions in prison populations. Boot camps could reduce the number of prison beds needed in a jurisdiction, which would lead to modest reductions in correctional costs. . . . However, restrictive entry criteria for boot camp participants often made it impossible to reduce prisons populations.

A confounding issue in discussing the impact of boot camps on overcrowding in prisons is that the factual bases are often derived from simulations and calculations based on projections instead of actual data. That is, data are hypothetical, and are based on assumptions, for example, that boot camp participants otherwise would have been imprisoned. However, it is just as plausible that many drug offenders and others would have received alternative sanctions because of prison overcrowding. Boot camps are more expensive than probation, for example, and if prison sentences are shortened, boot camps can be as expensive as prison (MacKenzie & Parent, 1992).

Parent (2003, p. 5) continues:

> Most studies that examined boot camps' cost impact multiplied the estimated charges attributed to the boot camp in person-days of confinement by the average operating costs for each person-day of confinement. However, this approach may overstate cost savings because staffing costs will not vary unless changes in confinement person-days are large enough to allow the actual closing of facilities. Small population reductions avert marginal costs only. Moreover, states vary in how they determine costs, making comparisons across states problematic.

BRIEF HISTORICAL CONTEXT

The best metaphor for characterizing the past 150 years of correctional policies is the proverbial pendulum that swings back and forth between liberal and conservative ideologies and practices (Harland, 1996). It seems fair to say the foci of policies have been on the extremities of the continuum between liberal and conservative philosophies of social control.

Finckenauer (1982) observed that the history of corrections in this country is awash with failed panaceas–that is, interventions that would dramatically reduce if not eradicate crime from the landscape of this country. For example, in the halcyon era of optimism of the 1950s and '60s, it seemed to many criminologists and criminal justice practitioners that they were on the throes of a social movement away from strictly punitive responses to interventions with treatment, rehabilitation, and reintegration motifs. The Great Society programs of the '60s ushered in a new Zeitgeist supporting programs that could prevent and favorably alter criminal patterns in early adulthood. A pivotal goal was to avert and to mitigate unlawful behavior before young persons became habituated to crime. Assumed to be more responsive and malleable than older career criminals, younger offenders were the primary targets of rehabilitative services. Under the rubric of treatment, a myriad of institutional and community-based rehabilitation programs were designed, implemented, and evaluated during the '60s and '70s (Tonry, 1996).

However, a crime boom occurred between about 1960 and 1975, and then reached a plateau marked by fluctuating but consistently high crime rates until about 1991. For example, the lowest reported murder rate since World War II occurred in 1957, and the lowest robbery rate was recorded in 1956. By contrast, murder rates nearly doubled and robbery more than tripled from about 1960 to 1975–the highest rates were recorded during the plateau period. The elevation of homicide rates endured for 12 years from 1963 to 1974. For example, there was a tripling of homicide-victimization rates for African Americans between the ages of 13 and 17 years, and nearly a 300 percent growth in youth homicide arrest rates from 1983 to 1994 (Snyder & Sickmund, 1999). Two companion schools of thought have been used to explain the spike in crime during these years: The illicit economy perspective states that the drug trade, particularly the crack market, escalated a host of crime-related activities, including gangs, illicit entrepreneurial enterprises, revenge slayings, and preemptive violence (Blumstein & Wallman, 2000). The street culture perspective locates the sources of crime in the cultural conditions associated with impoverished, inner-city neighborhoods, such as unemployment, fractured familial relations, dilapidated housing, rampant substance abuse, and lack of resources and services (Anderson, 1999; Wilson, 1996). However, the era of social experimentation of the Great Society aimed at the societal sources of crime was over by the early '80s–the accepted rhetoric had become lenient sanctions had encouraged more crime and so a tougher response to lawbreaking was required. Threats of severer punishment and increased surveillance were seen as requisite to effectively reducing the crime rate. Disillusionment with the social programs of the '60s and '70s was fueled by the rapidly rising rates of crime despite these programs. The failure of the Great Society programs was the result of an array of problems–ranging from lack of resources and training of staff to embezzlement of funds–that are documented elsewhere (Moynihan, 1969). However, the many commentators and citizens had decided that social experimentation was futile, and the correctional system needed to fulfill its original mandate–which was, uh, to correct or punish, and get criminals off the streets so the law-abiding citizenry could live in tranquility. After all, knowledge of what to do to truly alter life choices was too limited to guide services and treatment (Empey, Stafford, & Hay, 1999).

In reaction to the explosion of crime, Federal, state, and local legislators and correctional policy-makers declared "war" on a host of lawbreakers, including drug users and distributors, sex offenders, drunk drivers, violent lawbreakers, and an assortment of specialty offenders (e.g., hate crimes in

Massachusetts, car jackings in Washington, D.C.). People were arrested, prosecuted, convicted, and incarcerated in record numbers, resulting in dramatic increases in jail and prison populations and in the costs associated with running the justice system (Bureau of Justice Statistics, 1993). A new wave of "get tough" surveillance-focused correctional programs was created to provide control in the community, including boot camps, home detention, and day-reporting centers (Byrne, Lurigio, & Petersilia, 1992; DiIulio, 1991). The pendulum of correctional policy had swung from a focus on rehabilitation to one on punishment, deterrence, retribution, "just deserts," and incapacitation. The "get tough" theme had caught on and has continued into the present, with increasing reliance upon confinement strictly as a punitive measure (Cullen, Latessa, Burton, & Lombardo, 1993). Other manifestations of the "get tough" approach have included the "3-Strikes You're Out" and "Safe Streets" bills, as well as the President's "War on Crime" campaigns. The "Truth in Sentencing" laws required offenders to serve increasingly longer terms of confinement as well. Succinctly stated, correctional interventions became what have been characterized as the "penal harm movement" and the "imprisonment binge" (Clear, 1994). The ostensible shifts in policies prompted Albanese (1996, p. 558) to state, "We just can't seem to punish enough." These "get tough" initiatives culminated in an organized rejection of rehabilitation themes in favor of "reforms" buttressed by a flurry of thought-provoking treatises on the purposes of corrections (e.g., Fogel, 1975; Morris, 1974; Schur, 1973; van den Haag, 1975; Von Hirsch, 1976; Wilson, 1975). A unifying theme underlying those philosophical discourses was the bankruptcy of rehabilitation.

Protagonists argued that knowledge of the full range of sources of crime was lacking, and the "causes" that had been identified lay beyond the pale of viable or acceptable intervention (e.g., most people would oppose a unilateral redistribution of wealth). Instead of rehabilitation, the utilitarian philosophers argued that the purpose of the justice system should be to ensure that legal punishment is certain, swift, and severe–chronic offenders should be incapacitated until the impulse to commit crimes had "naturally" subsided with bio-psychological development (e.g., van den Haag, 1975; Wilson, 1975). The "just deserts" philosophers argued that since rehabilitation had failed, the only defensible policy was one that ensures that justice is administered uniformly and according to gravity of offenses. In contradistinction to utilitarian philosophers, "just deserts" proponents argued that social policy should be more concerned with the justice of administration than with administration of justice (Fogel, 1975).

The "bankruptcy of rehabilitation" theme was elevated to a new level of acceptance by the oft-cited book authored by Lipton, Martinson, and Wilks (1975). In a sequel, Martinson (1974, p. 25) concluded: "With few and isolated exceptions, the rehabilitative efforts that have been reported so far have had no appreciable effect on rehabilitation." Martinson entitled his article "What Works?: Questions and Answers About Prison Reform," but this critique of 231 existing studies of correctional treatments quickly became known as the "nothing works" report. Parenthetically, although attributed to Martinson, the infamous adage "nothing works" appeared to be a contrivance of the popular press, which was adopted in more scholarly work (Farabee, 2002). Contrary to many chronicles, Lipton et al. did not make a sweeping claim that "nothing works." Instead, they actually cited positive outcomes in 48 percent of the programs evaluated.

In a different sociopolitical climate, the "nothing works" indictment may have faded into obscurity–along with a plethora of other gloomy evaluations. However, the crime boom of the '60s and '70s, in tandem with the allure of seminal philosophical deliberations about the true mandate of corrections (a la van den Haag and Wilson), caused many policy-makers to view Martinson's indictment–or at least how it was characterized–as the *finis coronat opus* on the futility of rehabilitation. Martinson's article became the autopsy that officially documented the "cause of death" of rehabilitation–it was the "other shoe" that observers had feared would drop.

Putative evidence and cogent arguments notwithstanding, some scholars thought the foreclosure on rehabilitation was premature–even Martinson (1979) recanted his earlier testimony. A panel of experts from diverse disciplines was convened by the National Academy of Sciences to examine the report issued by Lipton et al. This panel concluded that the report was reasonably accurate in appraising the effectiveness of treatment programs; however, Lipton et al. had been too lenient in their assessment of the quality of existing research (Sechrest, White, & Brown, 1979). The panel concluded that research on the effects of treatment programs was so weak it did not offer reliable information about the viability of rehabilitation (Martin, Sechrest, & Redner, 1981). Panelists also noted that there may be limited evidence that some treatments are effective for subgroups of offenders–nevertheless, the most accurate conclusion would be that the effectiveness of treatment had not been confirmed or disconfirmed (Sechrest et al., 1979, p. 6). Moreover, the meager evidence for the benefits of treatment was largely the responsibility of investigators:

> In general, techniques have been tested as isolated treatments rather than as complex combinations, which would seem more suitable to the task. And even when techniques have been tested in good designs, insufficient attention has been paid to maintaining their integrity, so that often the treatment to be tested was delivered in a substantially weakened form. It is also not clear that all the theoretical power and the individual imagination that could be invoked in the planning of rehabilitation efforts have ever been capitalized on. Thus, the recommendation in this report that has the strongest support is that more and better thinking and research should be invested in efforts to devise programs for offender rehabilitation. (Sechrest et al., 1979, pp. 3-4)

Introduction

Despite the less than stellar evaluations of rehabilitation, the panel (Martin et al., 1981) unequivocally affirmed the potential benefits of treatment:

> The currently fashionable suggestion that society abandon efforts to find more effective programs to rehabilitate offenders is, we believe, irresponsible and premature. . . . The promise of the "rehabilitation ideal" . . . is so compelling a goal that the strongest possible efforts should be made to determine whether it can be realized and to seek to realize it. (Martin et al., 1981, pp. 17, 22)

In the grand scheme of decision-making, however, this affirmation of the potential of rehabilitation was largely ignored. Instead, we essentially observed a two-decade long experiment of using incarceration to stem the torrential tide of crime in this country. In essence, the correctional system in America went on an "imprisonment binge"; yet the expected reductions in crime did not occur (Clear, 1994; Irwin & Austin, 1994). The "get tough" policies and elevated crime rates led to overcrowding of prisons and eventually to fiscal constraints. These converging conditions kindled ideas about community control and intermediate sanctions, including but not limited to intensive probation, house arrest, and boot camps. The choice of intermediate sanctions, such as boot camps, was not ipso facto the right one to make: Rather, these options seemed to resonate with the widespread "get tough" frame of reference–when confronted with the exigencies of limited fiscal resources (Clear, 1994; Petersilia & Turner, 1993). After all, the prevailing public discourse was permeated with philosophical ideas that rehabilitation was not achievable and was not the *raison d'être* of corrections anyway (e.g., van den Haag, 1975; Wilson, 1975). An intermingling of dissonant ideas–deterrence, punishment, incapacitation, and retribution–characterized discourse during the '70s and '80s and into the '90s–to be sure, there were staunch supporters who stoked the embers of rehabilitation (Andrews, Zinger, Hoge, Bonta, Gendreau, & Cullen, 1990; Cullen, Cullen, & Wozniak, 1988; Gendreau & Ross, 1987; Greenwood & Zimring, 1985; Halleck & Witte, 1977; Palmer, 1983, 1992, 1994; Van Voorhis, 1987).

It was this maelstrom of correctional ideas that provided the allure of boot camps. Boot camps were marketed to appeal to decision-makers with disparate mindsets concerning the proper purpose of corrections. For example, Tonry (1996, p. 110) notes, "images of offenders participating in military drill and hard physical labor make boot camps look demanding and unpleasant, characteristics that crime-conscious officials and voters find satisfying." In addition to incarceration and punishment, boot camps also were peddled as a deterrent to criminal careers. The all-encompassing and daunting experience of boot camp would instill a primal dread of society's unpleasant response to lawbreaking–this memory would serve as a deterrent to further crime. "Through these attention-riveting measures, staff work at instilling order, respect, and rational decision-making into lifestyles that have often been characterized more by disorder, disrespect, and self-absorbed instinctive behavior" (Stinchcomb & Terry, 2001, p. 222).

In sum, boot camps held a promise of "something for everyone" (Parent, 1989). But, as Jeanne Stinchcomb observes in this volume, even the best-intentioned public policies are simply untested assumptions about what will be accomplished. Without well-conceived and controlled implementation, the potential of something-for-everyone can turn into the pitfall of nothing-for-anyone (Stinchcomb, 1999).

CONCLUSIONS AND OBSERVATIONS ABOUT BOOT CAMP

As Cullen et al. and Stinchcomb cogently argue in this volume, boot camps resonated with many people because of popular conception that the military is where young people learn discipline, responsibility, and self-initiative. "Many Americans," observes Tonry (1996, p. 110), "have experienced life in military boot camps and remember the experience as not necessarily pleasant but as an effective way to learn self-discipline and to learn to work as part of a team." The ubiquitous cultural image is that the military is where many young persons "straighten out their lives" and become stakeholders in adulthood. However, this common-sense basis for embracing boot camps as a correction intervention has diverted attention from the lack of empirical support for their effectiveness (see Cullen et al. and Stinchcomb in this volume). In some respects, boot camps might be labeled "Teflon programs" because they seemingly are resistant to damaging evidence–empirical criticism simply does not stick.

The preponderance of evidence does not support the effectiveness of boot camps in altering behavior or antisocial attitudes (see Mitchell et al. in this tome). A recent meta-analysis of 44 independent comparison-group contrasts did not find significant differences in reduction of criminal recidivism between boot camp and traditional interventions (e.g., probation, prison) (MacKenzie, Wilson, & Kider, 2001). Certainly, the recidivism rates of 61.5 percent and 41.7 percent for men and women graduates, respectively, of the Arkansas boot camp suggest that the program does not deter people from unlawful acts (Benda, Harm, & Toombs; Benda, Toombs, & Corwyn in this volume).

Correctional officials generally are loath to discuss recidivism rates unless they favor a desired intervention, which is understandable from an organizational culture perspective–albeit it is not an ethical justification. However, when pressed by the media and legislators, administrators report recidivism rates that are based on faulty methods that need to be discussed because they communicate an unwarranted optimism about the impact of boot camp. That is, administrators typically report recidivism rates based on all releases, irrespective of date of release. Such wholesale calculation of recidivism yields a much lower rate than one that allows everyone an equal amount of time in which to become a recidivist. The wholesale method includes people who were released from incarceration last week with those who actually have had time to be a recidivist–obviously, it usually takes longer than a week for crime to be detected and for people to be arrested and returned to the Department of Corrections. Wholesale rates are artificial and distort the reality of the effect of boot camp on recidivism–yet, too often these figures are the ones reported to the general public and legislators. In fairness, a caveat should be inserted to point out that these artificial rates are not always the result of selective calculation–the author has found that many correctional officials simply had not realized that calculating wholesale recidivism rates is problematic.

There are a variety of methods and criteria used to derive recidivism rates, so I am uncertain how these rates were obtained: However, at the time of the drafting of this manuscript, there is a Website that states "The Arkansas Boot Camp reports a 16.7 percent recidivism rate for its graduates as compared with the institutional rate of 38 percent" (National Institute of Justice, 1996, no pp.). Another Website, retrieved on the same date, indicates that the regular spokesperson for the Arkansas Department of Correction reports there is a 50 percent recidivism rate to a local newspaper (Smith, 2003). The data for the two Benda et al. studies reported in this volume were gathered in 1996 from the same boot camp as featured on these Websites. Our findings indicate that the recidivism rates in a 5-year follow-up are 61.5 percent for men, and 41.7 percent for women, graduates of the only Arkansas boot camp for adults. Individual follow-ups were conducted so everyone had the same time frame in which to become a recidivist. While we believe our rates are more accurate, unquestionably these rates do not reflect all recidivism. There is undetected crime and there are offenders who leave the state without permission–an unknown percentage of these migratory graduates commit crime after graduation from boot camp. (Migration, however, did not appear to be a serious problem, and was likely less than 5 percent.) The criteria for recidivism were not presented on the two Websites. Our criteria were arrest for felonies, which resulted in return to the Department of Correction, and parole violation. Twenty percent of the men and fifteen percent of the women were returned to the Department of Correction for parole violations.

We conducted another study of 572 male graduates of the Arkansas boot camp to determine what factors discriminated between (a) non-recidivists, (b) recidivists with felonies, (c) technical parole violators, and (d) parole violators due to drugs (Benda, Toombs, & Peacock, 2003b). The discriminators between non-recidivists and various types of recidivists in the study were indicators of informal social controls (Sampson & Laub, 1993) such as marriage, employment, children, and religiosity. Discriminators of felony recidivists were early sexual and physical abuse, gang membership, peer association with criminals, carrying a weapon, and early onset of crime. Discriminators associated with technical parole violation were attachment to female caregivers, self-esteem and self-efficacy, and perception that boot camp stimulated thinking about choices in life.

The distinct profiles of characteristics yielded by the discriminate analyses (Klecka, 1980) are plausible and confirm experiential observations. Indeed, felony recidivists typically are precocious offenders, who are affiliated with gangs and carry weapons for protection and preemptive strikes against competitors in the drug market. Frequently, these younger offenders report a history of abuse. It is plausible that persons who are victimized in childhood are likely to rebel by entering a life trajectory (Sampson & Laub, 1993) of crime and analogous behaviors (Gottfredson & Hirschi, 1990)–they are the life-course offenders described by Moffitt (1993). Early abuse has been associated with a variety of problems in adulthood, including crime (Benda, 2002a, 2002b, 2002c, 2003a, 2004a, 2004b, 2005, in press; Benda & Corwyn, 2002; Weeks & Widom, 1998; Widom, 2001).

The characteristics selected by discriminant analysis to identify non-recidivists are in accord with the life-course theory of Sampson and Laub (1993). That is, the assumption of adult responsibilities–such as marriage, children, and employment–often represents a "turning point" in people's lives when they adopt more conventional thoughts and behavior (e.g., Giordano, Cernkovich, & Rudolph, 2002; Griffin & Armstrong, 2003; MacKenzie, Wilson, Armstrong, & Gover, 2001; Piquero, Brame, Mazerolle, & Haapanen, 2002; Simons, Stewart, Gordon, Conger, & Elder, 2002 Uggen, 2000). They strengthen their social bonds to society. While the social bonds of religiosity and spirituality are less often studied, there are theological and empirical bases for believing that these are important bonds to deterring unlawful behavior (Baier & Wright, 2001; Belcher & Benda, in press; Benda, 2002a; Clear & Sumter, 2002). Religiosity, or commitment to and practices of religion, can deter unlawful behavior through moral prescriptions, whereas a relationship to God, or spirituality, encourages conformity to the Ten Commandments (Benda & Toombs, 2002).

The final discriminant function may be less convincing than those already discussed; however, it seems plausible that it may be personal assets and perceptions of benefits of boot camp that insulate people from crime and parole violations (Gover et al., 2000). Self-efficacy and self-esteem could be personal resources or assets that motivate or allow people to remain free of infractions (Benda, 2003b; Cullen, Wright, Chamlin, 1999). Whether these individuals, and persons who maintained tenure in the community without violating parole or being arrested for crime, are "shocked out of a criminal lifestyle" by exposure to boot camp needs investigation. Existing studies indicate that boot camps do not significantly reduce recidivism in comparison to alternative interventions, such as prison and parole supervision (MacKenzie & Armstrong, 2004). Mitchell et al. in this volume report that boot camp does not reduce antisocial attitudes, which are associated with crime. Studies do show an association between perceptions of benefits of boot camp and recidivism (Benda et al., 2002, 2003a; Gover et al., 2000). However, perceptions of boot camp are not objective measures of the effects of programs, and are influenced by many extraneous factors (Hemmens & Marquart, 2000).

Boot camps need more rigorous evaluation to determine what if any effects they have on participants–effects on criminal recidivism, thinking, self-perceptions, and so on. If the correctional system continues to use this intermediate sanction, we must have a greater understanding of exactly what is being accomplished–whether positive or negative–in these programs. Cullen et al. raise legitimate concerns about the siphoning off of scarce resources by ineffectual programs that actually are designed to teach people to fight in combat (Morash & Rucker, 1990; Welch, 1997). Lutze also offers a compelling argument that boot camp programs are permeated with a hypermasculine culture that likely undermines any treatment efforts and may encourage and reinforce aggression and criminal inclinations. More than a decade ago, Morash and Rucker (1990) expressed concerns that boot camps would instill the very attitudes that encourage or facilitate crime. Lutze and Murphy (1999) found–in a study including both boot camp and traditional prisons–that those who defined the prison environment as more masculine reported "greater levels of assertiveness, isolation, helplessness, stress, and conflict with other inmates and with the staff" (p. 725).

It is questionable whether rehabilitative efforts can be effective in an environment that is otherwise pervaded with attention-riveting confrontations, verbal humiliation and abuse, aggression, exhausting physical demands, and maltreatment. The literature is replete with descriptions of humiliation and abuses of inmates in boot camps that cannot continue to be ignored (Lutze & Brody, 1999; cf. MacKenzie et al., 2001; McCorkle, 1995). Inmates are routinely called humiliating names such as "scumbag," "sissy," and "loser," and are subjected to physical abuses (Lutze & Brody, 1999).

Especially heinous are the reports of sexual abuse of women in boot camps by male inmates and staff (MacKenzie & Armstrong, 2004)–anecdotal accounts suggest that sexual abuses of women are not isolated occurrences. These accounts come from multiple sources, and in tandem with similar reports in the literature, appear creditable. Women inmates in boot camp are particularly vulnerable to sexual and other abuses because of the near-absolute power staff have over incarcerated persons, and the subjugation to which they are acculturated in the militaristic training. To challenge a male drill instructor is to invite harsh consequences! Actually, the same is true of women staff and male inmates: But, while there are accounts of women staff humiliating male inmates and ordering them to perform punishing physical feats, I have not heard of men being sexually abused by women staff members. Sexual harassment, on the other hand, seems to be initiated and received by both genders. These acts are emasculating to men and demeaning to women, and can be sadistic–certainly, they run counter to rehabilitative goals.

Clinical observations by staff in boot camps indicate that maltreatment of inmates provokes aggression and hostility, and for inmates who lack self-control and the ability to play the "prison game," it incites undesirable behavior that leads to harsh sanctions–recycling and dropping out of the programs, and being sent back to traditional prison to serve the full sentence. (The "prison game" is a charade where inmates pretend to progress through the program–some inmates have defense mechanisms that allow them to basically remain–at least overtly–unaffected by degrading demands). Experience suggests that the inmates who are best equipped to play the "prison game" are the more sociopathic persons, who have high recidivism rates. More psychologically vulnerable persons are often set up to fail by being singled out for unrelenting harassment by staff–then, when inmates react in frustration, they are harshly reprimanded and maltreated. It is imperative that systematic research be done to verify these more experiential observations and anecdotal accounts, for they represent deplorable treatment of inmates and jeopardize any rehabilitative potential.

SOME CONCLUDING OBSERVATIONS AND RECOMMENDATIONS

It is very likely that abused persons are further traumatized by these harsh experiences in boot camp. The rampant humiliation and abuses raise serious questions about the viability of boot camps as an alternative sanction, especially for persons who have a history of sexual molestation and physical maltreatment. After two decades, it is time to systematically determine if boot camps have any beneficial effects for offenders. If boot camps do benefit anyone, experience suggests that benefits accrue only to certain offenders.

Research is desperately needed that establishes which offenders benefit in what specific ways in boot camp. For example, a very preliminary study, which needs to be verified in other research, suggests persons with the following profile may not be deterred from crime by boot camp: a history of sexual and physical abuse, gang membership, peer association with criminals, carrying a weapon, and early onset of crime (Benda, Toombs, & Peacock, 2003b). In contrast, experience suggests that the offenders who may be "shocked out of a crime lifestyle" are older persons who have commitments to conventional partners, children, employment, and religion. These social bonding factors (Sampson & Laub, 1993) are prominent predictors of tenure in the community without further crime or parole violations in this 5-year follow-up study (Benda et al., 2003b). If confirmed by other researchers, these predictors would provide valuable clues for intervention: For example, they should raise serious questions about the wisdom of restricting visitation during the boot camp program. Rather than disrupting familial relationships, it may be wiser to reinforce social bonding processes that may insulate people from crime.

The point is investigations are needed that identify and examine the effects of different policies and practices of boot camps on a range of outcomes for different offenders, including criminal recidivism and parole violation.

The lacuna in knowledge about the effects of boot camp need to be addressed because–as Cullen et al. observe in this volume–common sense can be wrong. For example, the harsh realities of boot camp are not prima facie evidence that women find these programs completely undesirable. To the contrary, Wood, May, and Grasmick report in this tome that men are more likely than women to choose traditional prison over any duration of boot camp. Their analyses for the total sample, and by gender, reveal that prior experience serving boot camp increases the likelihood that offenders will enroll in boot camp to avoid one year of imprisonment, as well as the amount of boot camp that offenders are willing to serve. Being a parent has a significant, positive impact on the amount of boot camp that women (but not men) are willing to endure to avoid one year of prison.

Wood et al.'s findings are very informative and should stimulate more detailed research to learn exactly why women are more receptive than men to participation in a boot camp. As they indicate, women may choose boot camp to expedite their return home to be with children–typically, boot camp reduces the duration of incarceration in comparison to time they would serve in prison. Research is needed, for instance, to determine if women who are choosing boot camp generally have a history of abuse because it is possible that some women are enduring considerable trauma in order to hasten their release to be at home with children. Measures of change in depression, stress, suicidal ideation, and the like during boot camp are needed to assess the psychological toll boot camp practices may have on women, especially those who have a history of victimization. This level of detail is needed in the next generation of research to have a better understanding of the range of effects of boot camp programs. These programs must be more thoroughly researched because it is possible they are having detrimental consequences. Omissions can be as problematic as commissions: For example, boot camp policies often deny visitation for much if not all of the program, which can cause emotional turmoil for parents, the majority of whom are women. Women also are more likely to need job training (Parent, 2003), and yet boot camps offer limited if any preparation for employment. Many of these observations may apply to men as well, especially to those who have been abused.

Boot camps have been designed for men and do not offer specialized services for women. For example, drug counseling groups comprised of both genders present risks of harassment and sexual assault for women, and add potential dynamics to interactions and to the environment that are reminiscent of perpetrator-victim relationships. Moreover, there is evidence that victimized women respond better to female therapists, and they are more comfortable in groups comprised only of women. Women need to be in therapeutic milieus conducive to sharing feelings and beliefs that they often find shameful, guilt inducing, and self-recriminating, without the additional concerns of rejection and labeling by men (Bride & Real, 2003; Zilberman, Tavares, Blume, & el-Guebaly, 2003). There also are reports of women being assaulted after revealing vulnerabilities in such groups.

The undesirable conditions and lack of resources per se should be sufficient grounds for revisiting the judiciousness of placing women in boot camps. While this concern is valid for men as well, existing boot camps do not offer equality of services if "equality" is defined as meeting the specific needs of women and men instead of defining it as meaning the same treatment irrespective of gender and needs. The issue of "equality" obviously is an ideologically sensitive one; however, meeting needs should not be sacrificed at the altar of a "political correct" definition of equality–people should not have to forego having their needs met to satisfy some political definition. It could be argued that equality means building boot camps specifically designed for women. Currently, there are boot camps where women are housed in a separate facility from men, and a few programs that are exclusively for women–other programs are integrated with men and women. However, before embarking on a building campaign and proliferating untested programs, based on ideological claims, we should invest time and resources to thoroughly examine existing programs to be sure there are verifiable benefits–that is, if boot camps are continued.

If programs need to be augmented to offer viable rehabilitation, this should be done on a limited scale to allow empirical validation before committing to building more boot camps. At the very least, existing policies and practices should be evaluated to ensure that they promote, rather than impede, rehabilitation of women (Hemmens, Stohr, Schoeler, & Miller, 2002).

More generally, it is difficult to imagine how serious rehabilitation can be accomplished in four to six months in a therapeutic setting where most participants have committed felonies. In a militaristic setting, with virtually no freedom and a plethora of indignities, it is inconceivable that interventions can bring about desired changes for inmates. This is not to say I am confident that there are no benefits associated with the boot camp experience. Certainly, studies I have conducted show that men and women perceive benefits from boot camp. However, it is time to directly assess the benefits and liabilities of boot camp to determine, on balance, if these programs should be retained, and if so, for whom. If boot camps are retained because of a reasonable balance of benefits, the professionalism of staff needs to be seriously upgraded. Persons, who have psychological needs to humiliate and abuse people, should not be placed in a position of such power over others. As seen at Abu Ghraib prison in Iraq (Silove, 2004), unfettered control over detainees can result in horrific abuses by staff in an environment characterized by aggression and dehumanization. A healthy respect for the dignity and worth of other human beings, and a restraint fashioned by a realization that "but for the grace of God, there go I," are requisite to having almost absolute power over others.

Despite the brevity and "low-dosage" of boot camp programs, and the harsh realities of the environment, it is still possible that some persons benefit from these programs. In this tome, for example, Gover finds that adolescents in boot camp report more benefits than do youth who served in traditional incarceration. A huge impediment in making decisions about boot camps is that evaluation of these programs is fraught with complex problems. Some of the most bewildering problems are presented for consideration: As stated earlier, the heterogeneity of programs and participants makes multisite comparisons exceedingly difficult to implement and interpret. There is considerable variance across boot camps in terms of admission criteria, staffing, length and composition of programs, and aftercare. Many programs, for example, last for 4 to 6 months, and only admit neophyte offenders who have a relatively limited sentence and no history of violence. Other programs allow considerable diversity in age, types of offenses, and length of sentence. Some states have separate boot camps and programs for men and for women, whereas other states have separate facilities but the same program for male and female inmates. Many boot camps have services aimed at rehabilitation, while others are focused on military training (MacKenzie & Armstrong, 2004).

Experimental designs are essential to definitive evaluation of program effectiveness, and yet random assignment is not acceptable to most decision-makers. Even with random sampling, and random assignment to groups, admission criteria and regional peculiarities constrain generalization. The more common quasi-experimental designs are problematical because the types of offenders in boot camps typically differ from lawbreakers in comparison groups selected from prison or probation. Often offenders sent to boot camp programs would not have been incarcerated if these programs had not existed–this raises the question, then, of whether boot camp participants should be compared to inmates in traditional prisons or those on probation. Outcome rates can be an artifact of how much supervision graduates of boot camp receive upon release, as well as the quality of aftercare. Randomness and frequency of drug screening, for example, can significantly affect recidivism rates. Maintaining employment or social supports that tend to lessen recidivism may depend, in some cases, on encouragement of parole officers. The immense disparities in aftercare services across systems make comparisons and generalizations exceedingly complex.

The differences in intensity of adverse experiences from one boot camp to another very likely influence some outcomes, and these are very difficult to measure because of their clandestine nature and participants' reticence to report this information. Program components, of necessity, are short-term and often are ill conceived and implemented. As noted by Stinchcomb in this volume, even well conceived services are frequently poorly administered. Routinely, administrators and practitioners are unable to articulate the goals, objectives, activities, and desired outcomes of services or the program as a whole. Program evaluation too often is a low priority for those in charge of boot camps, and so barriers to obtaining high-value data are commonplace. It is especially difficult to administer scales that measure personality and relationships that might prove to be valuable targets for interventions. Administering these scales during aftercare is exceedingly difficult without atypical cooperation from officials in different segments of the justice system and in many satellite offices.

In conclusion, these methodological problems and others make evaluation of boot camps very challenging. However, efforts to evaluate these programs are preferred over relying on common sense, practitioners' observations, or political preferences. Evidence-based interventions are proving to be more cost effective and beneficial for individuals and systems (Andrews & Bonta, 2003; Cullen & Gendreau, 2001; MacKenzie, 2000; Sherman, Farrington, Welsh, & MacKenzie, 2002). Quantitative evidence is more systematic and verifiable than these other approaches to knowledge claims.

REFERENCES

Akers, R. L. (1998). *Social learning and social structure: A general theory of crime and deviance*. Boston: Northeastern University Press.

Akers, R. L., & Sellers, C. S. (2004). *Criminological theories: Introduction and evaluation* (4th ed). Los Angeles, CA: Roxbury.

Albanese, J. (1996). Five fundamental mistakes of criminal justice. *Justice Quarterly, 13*, 551-565.

Anderson, E. (1999). *Code of the streets: Decency, violence, and the moral life of the inner city*. New York: Norton.

Anderson, J. F., Dyson, L., & Burns, J. C. (1999). *Boot camps: An intermediate sanction*. New York: University Press of America.

Andrews, D. A., & Bonta, J. (2003). *The psychology of criminal conduct* (3rd. ed.). Cincinnati: Anderson.

Andrews, D. A., Zinger, I., Hoge, R. D., Bonta, J., Gendreau, P., & Cullen, F. T. (1990). Does correctional treatment work? A clinically relevant and psychologically informed meta-analysis. *Criminology, 28*, 369-404.

Baier, C. J., & Wright, B. R. E. (2001). If you love me, keep my commandments: A meta-analysis of the effect of religion on crime. *Journal of Research in Crime and Delinquency, 38*, 3-21.

Belcher, J. R., & Benda, B. B. (in press). Issues of divine healing in psychotherapy: Opening a dialog. *Social Thought*.

Benda, B. B. (2002a). Religion and violent offenses among youth entering boot camp: Structural equation model. *Journal of Research in Crime and Delinquency, 39*, 92-101.

Benda, B. B. (2002b). Test of a structural equation model of comorbidity among homeless and domiciled military veterans. *Journal of Social Service Research, 29*, 1-35.

Benda, B. B. (2002c). Factors associated with rehospitalization among veterans in a substance abuse treatment program. *Psychiatric Services, 53*, 1176-1178.

Benda, B. B. (2003a). Discriminators of suicide thoughts and attempts among homeless veterans who abuse substances. *Suicide & Life-Threatening Behavior, 33*, 430-442.

Benda, B. B. (2003b). Survival analysis of criminal recidivism of boot camp graduates using elements from general and developmental explanatory models. *International Journal of Offender Therapy and Comparative Criminology, 47*(1), 89-101.

Benda, B. B. (2004a). Gender differences in the rehospitalization of substance abusers among homeless military veterans. *Journal of Drug Issues, 34*, 723-750.

Benda, B. B. (2004b). Life-course theory of readmission for substance abuse among homeless veterans. *Psychiatric Services, 55*, 1308-1310.

Benda, B. B. (2005). Gender differences in predictors of suicidal thoughts and attempts among homeless veterans that abuse substances. *Suicide & Life-Threatening Behavior, 35*, 106-116.

Benda, B. B. (in press). The robustness of self-control in relation to form of delinquency. *Youth & Society*.

Benda, B. B., & Corwyn, R. F. (2002). The effect of abuse in childhood and adolescence on violence among adolescents. *Youth & Society, 33*, 339-365.

Benda, B. B., & Toombs, N. J. (2002). The effects of religiosity on drug use among inmates in boot camp: Testing a theoretical model with reciprocal relationships. *Journal of Offender Rehabilitation, 35*, 161-183.

Benda, B. B., Toombs, N. J., & Peacock, M. (2002). Ecological factors in recidivism: A survival analysis of boot camp graduates after three years. *Journal of Offender Rehabilitation, 35*, 63-85.

Benda, B. B., Toombs, N. J., & Peacock, M. (2003a). An examination of competing theories in predicting recidivism of adult offenders five years after graduation from boot camp. *Journal of Offender Rehabilitation, 37*, 43-75.

Benda, B. B., Toombs, N. J., & Peacock, M. (2003b). Discriminators of types of recidivism among boot camp graduates in a 5-year follow-up study. *Journal of Criminal Justice, 31*, 539-559.

Blumstein, A., & Wallman, J. (2000). *The crime drop in America*. New York: Cambridge University Press.

Bride, B. E., & Real, E. (2003). Project assist: A modified therapeutic community for homeless women living with HIV/AIDS and chemical dependency. *Health & Social Work, 28*, 166-177.

Byrne, J. M., Lurigio, A. J., & Petersilia, J. (Eds.) (1992). *Smart sentencing: The emergence of intermediate sanctions*. Newbury Park: CA: Sage.

Clear, T. R. (1994). *Harm in American penology: Offenders, victims, and their communities*. Albany, NY: State University of New York Press.

Clear, T. R., & Sumter, M. T. (2002). Prisoners, prison, and religion: Religion and adjustment to prison. In T. P. O'Connor and N. J. Pallone (Eds.) *Religion, the community, and the rehabilitation of criminal offenders* (pp. 127-159). New York: The Haworth Press.

Cronin, R. (1994). *Boot camps for adult and juvenile offenders: Overview and update*. Washington, DC: U.S. Department of Justice.

Cullen, F. T., Cullen, J. B., & Wozniak, J. F. (1988). Is rehabilitation dead?: The myth of the punitive public. *Journal of Criminal Justice, 16*, 303-317.

Cullen, F. T., & Gendreau, P. (2001). From nothing works to what works: Changing professional ideology in the 21st century. *The Prison Journal, 81*, 313-338.

Cullen, F. T., Latessa, E., Burton, V., & Lombardo, L. (1993). Prison wardens: Is the rehabilitative ideal supported. *Criminology, 31*, 69-87.

Cullen, F. T., Wright, J. P., & Chamlin, M. B. (1999). Social support and social reform: A progressive crime control agenda. *Crime and Delinquency, 45*, 188-207.

DiIulio, J. J., Jr. (1991). *No escape: The future of American corrections.* New York: Basic Books.

Empey, L. T., Stafford, M. C., & Hay, C. H. (1999). *American delinquency: Its meaning and construction* (4th ed.). Belmont, CA: Wadsworth.

Farabee, D. (2002). Reexamining Martinson's critique: A cautionary note for evaluators. *Crime and Delinquency, 48*, 189-192.

Finckenauer, J. (1982). *Scared straight and the panacea phenomenon.* Englewood Cliffs, NJ: Prentice-Hall.

Fogel, D. (1975). *We are the living proof: The justice model for corrections.* Cincinnati, OH: Anderson.

Gendreau, P., & Ross, R. R. (1987). Revivification of rehabilitation: Evidence from the 1980s. *Justice Quarterly, 4*, 349-408.

Giordano, P. C., Cernkovich, S. A., & Rudolph, J. L. (2002). Gender, crime, and desistance: Toward a theory of cognitive transformation. *The American Journal of Sociology, 107*, 990-1064.

Gottfredson, D. M., & Tonry, M. (Eds.) (1987). *Prediction and classification: Criminal justice decision making.* Chicago: University of Chicago Press.

Gottfredson, M., & Hirschi, T. (1990). *A general theory of crime.* Palo Alto, CA: Stanford University Press.

Gover, A. R., MacKenzie, D. L., & Styve, G. J. (2000). Boot camps and traditional correctional facilities for juveniles: A comparison of the participants, daily activities, and environments. *Journal of Criminal Justice, 28*, 53-68.

Greenwood, P. W., & Zimring, F. E. (1985). *One more chance: The pursuit of promising intervention strategies for chronic juvenile offenders.* Santa Monica, CA: RAND.

Griffin, M. L., & Armstrong, G. S. (2003). The effect of local life circumstances on female probationers' offending. *Justice Quarterly, 29*, 213-225.

Halleck, S. L., & Witte, A. D. (1977). Is rehabilitation dead? *Crime and Delinquency, 23*, 372-382.

Harland, A. T. (Ed.) (1996). *Choosing correctional options that work.* Thousand Oaks, CA: Sage.

Hemmens, C., & Marquart, J. W. (2000). Friend or foe? Race, age, and inmate perceptions of inmate-staff relations. *Journal of Criminal Justice, 28*, 197-213.

Hemmens, C., Stohr, M. K., Schoeler, M., & Miller, B. (2002). One step up, two steps back: The progression of perceptions of women's work in prisons and jails. *Journal of Criminal Justice, 30*, 473-490.

Irwin, J., & Austin, J. (1994). *It's about time: America's imprisonment binge.* Belmont, CA: Wadsworth.

Jones, J. (1996). Risk prediction in criminal justice. In A. T. Harland (Ed.) *Choosing correctional options that work* (pp. 33-68) Thousand Oaks, CA: Sage.

Klecka, W. R. (1980). *Discriminant analysis.* Beverly Hills, CA: Sage.
Lipton, D., Martinson, R., & Wilks, J. (1975). *The effectiveness of correctional treatment: A survey of treatment evaluation studies.* New York: Praeger.
Lutze, F. E., & Brody, D. (1999). Mental abuse and unusual punishment: Do boot camp prisons violate the Eighth Amendment? *Crime and Delinquency, 45,* 242-255.
Lutze, F., & Murphy, D. (1999). Ultramasculine prison environments and inmates' adjustment: It's time to move beyond the 'Boys will be Boys' paradigm. *Justice Quarterly, 16,* 709-733.
MacKenzie, D. (1990). Boot camp prisons: Components, evaluations, and empirical issues. *Federal Probation, 54,* 44-52.
MacKenzie, D. L. (2000). Evidence-based corrections: Identifying what works. *Crime and Delinquency, 46,* 457-471.
MacKenzie, D. L., & Armstrong, G. S. (2004). *Correctional boot camps: Studies examining military basic training as a model for corrections.* Thousand Oaks, CA: Sage.
MacKenzie, D. L., Brame, R., McDowall, D., & Souryal, C. (1995). Boot camp prisons and recidivism in eight states. *Criminology, 33,* 327-357.
MacKenzie, D. L., & Parent, D. (1992). Boot camps and prisons for young offenders. In J. M. Byrne, A. J. Lurigio, & J. Petersilia (Eds.) *Smart sentencing: The emergence of intermediate sanctions* (pp. 103-119). Newbury Park: CA: Sage.
MacKenzie, D. L., Wilson, B. D., Armstrong, G. S., & Gover, A. R. (2001) The impact of boot camps and traditional institutions on juvenile residents: Perceptions, adjustment, and change. *Journal of Research in Crime and Delinquency, 38,* 279-313.
MacKenzie, D. L., Wilson, D. B., & Kider, S. B. (2001). Effects of correctional boot camps on offending. *The Annals of the American Academy of Political and Social Sciences, 578,* 126-143.
Martin, S. E., Sechrest, L. B., & Redner, R. (1981). *New directions in the rehabilitation of offenders.* Washington, DC: National Academy of Sciences.
Martinson, R. M. (1974). "What works" questions and answers about prison reform. *Public Interest, 35,* 22-54.
Martinson, R. (1979). New findings, new views: A note of caution regarding sentencing reform. *Hofstra Law Review, 7,* 243-258.
McCorkle, R. C. (1995). Correctional boot camps and change in attitude: Is all this shouting necessary? A research note. *Justice Quarterly, 12,* 365-375.
Moffitt, T. E. (1993). Adolescence-limited and life-course persistent antisocial behavior: A developmental taxonomy. *Psychological Review, 100,* 674-701.
Morash, M., & Rucker. L. (1990). A critical look at the idea of boot camp as a correctional reform. *Crime & Delinquency, 36,* 204-222.
Morris, N. (1974). The future of imprisonment. Chicago: University of Chicago Press.
Morris, N., & Tonry, M. (1990). *Between prison and probation: Intermediate punishment in a rational sanctioning system.* New York: Oxford University Press.
Moynihan, D. P. (1969). *Maximum feasible misunderstanding: Community action in the war on poverty.* New York: Free Press.
National Institute of Justice (1996). *Inventory of aftercare provisions for 52 boot camp programs.* Retrieved June 14, 2004, www.ncjrs.org/txtfiles/invafter.txt

Osler, M. (1991). Shock incarceration: Hard realities and real possibilities. *Federal Probation, 55,* 34-42.

Palmer, T. (1983). The "effectiveness" issue today: An overview. *Federal Probation, 46,* 3-10.

Palmer, T. (1992). *The re-emergence of correctional intervention.* Newbury Park, CA: Sage.

Palmer, T. (1994). *A profile of correctional effectiveness and new directions for research.* Albany: State University of New York Press.

Parent, D. (1989). Shock incarceration: An overview of existing programs. *Issues and Practices.* Washington, DC: U.S. Department of Justice, National Institute of Justice.

Parent, D. (2003). *Correctional boot camps: Lessons from a decade of research.* Washington, DC: National Institute of Justice, U.S. Department of Justice.

Petersilia, J., & Turner, S. (1993) Intensive probation and Parole. In M. Tonry (Ed.) *Crime and justice: A review of research* (Vol. 17, pp. 281-335). Chicago: University of Chicago Press.

Piquero, A. R., Brame, R., Mazerolle, P., & Haapanen, R. (2002). Crime in emerging adulthood, *Criminology, 40,* 137-169.

Sampson, R. J., & Laub, J. H. (1993). *Crime in the making: Pathways and turning points through life.* Cambridge, MA: Harvard University Press.

Schur, E. M. (1973). *Radical nonintervention: Rethinking the delinquency problem.* Englewood, NJ: Prentice-Hall.

Sechrest, D. (1989). Prison boot camps do not measure up. *Federal Probation, 53,* 15-20.

Sechrest, L., White, S. O., & Brown, E. D. (1979). *The rehabilitation of criminal offenders.* Washington, DC: National Academy Press.

Sherman, L. W., Farrington, D. P., Welsh, B. C., & MacKenzie, D. L. (Eds.). (2002). *Evidence-based crime prevention.* New York: Routledge.

Silove, D. (2004). Challenges in fighting torture: From September 11 to Abu Ghraib. *Lancet, 363,* 1915-1917.

Simons, R. L., Stewart, E., Gordon, L. C., Conger, R. D., & Elder, G. H. (2002). A test of life-course explanations for stability and change in antisocial behavior from adolescence to young adulthood. *Criminology, 40,* 401-434.

Smith, D. (2003). Shaping up in prison boot camp. Retrieved June 14, 2004, www.arktimes.com/031031coverstorya.html

Snyder, H. N., & Sickmund, M. (1999). *Juvenile offenders and victims: 1999 national report* (NCJ 178257), Washington, DC: U.S. Department of Justice, Office of Juvenile Justice Programs, Office of Juvenile Justice and Delinquency Prevention.

Stinchcomb, J. B. (1999). Recovering from the shocking reality of shock incarceration: What correctional administrators can learn from boot camp failures. *Corrections Management Quarterly, 3,* 43-52.

Stinchcomb, J. B., & Terry, W. C., III. (2001). Predicting the likelihood of rearrest among shock incarceration graduates: Moving beyond another nail in the boot camp coffin. *Crime and Delinquency, 47,* 221-242.

Tonry, M. (1996). *Sentencing matters.* New York: Oxford University Press.

Uggen, C. (2000). Work as a turning point in the life course of criminals: A duration model of age, employment, and recidivism. *American Sociological Review, 65,* 529-546.
van den Haag, E. (1975). *Punishing criminals: Concerning a very old and painful question.* New York: Basic Books.
Van Voorhis, P. (1987). Correctional effectiveness: The high cost of ignoring success. *Federal Probation, 51,* 56-62.
Von Hirsch (1976). *Doing justice: the choice of punishments.* New York: Hill & Wang.
Weeks, R., & Widom, C. S. (1998). Self-reports of early childhood victimization among incarcerated adult male felons. *Journal of Interpersonal Violence, 13,* 346-356.
Welch, M. (1997). A critical interpretation of correctional boot camps as normalizing institutions. *Journal of Contemporary Criminal Justice, 13,* 184-205.
Widom, C. S. (2001). Alcohol abuse as risk factor for and consequence of child abuse. *Alcohol Research and Health, 25,* 52-58.
Wilson, J. Q. (1975). *Thinking about crime.* New York: Basic Books.
Wilson, W. J. (1996). *When work disappears: The world of the new urban poor.* New York: Knopf.
Zilberman, M. L., Tavares, H., Blume, S. B., & el-Guebaly, N. (2003). Substance use disorders: Sex differences and psychiatric comorbidities. *Canadian Journal of Psychiatry, 48,* 5-14.

AUTHOR'S NOTE

Dr. Brent B. Benda is a professor in the School of Social Work at the University of Arkansas at Little Rock. He has published articles on crime and delinquency, substance abuse, adolescent sexual behavior, and homelessness in journals such as *Youth & Society, Journal of Research in Crime and Delinquency, Criminal Justice and Behavior, Journal of Criminal Justice, Journal of Social Service Research, Social Work Research, Journal of Youth and Adolescence, Journal of Adolescence, Journal of Adolescent Research, Journal of Offender Rehabilitation, Journal of Drug Issues, Psychiatric Services, Suicide & Life-Threatening Behavior,* and *Psychiatric Rehabilitation Journal.*

The author acknowledges a debt of gratitude to Dr. Nathaniel J. Pallone for his gracious encouragement and patience throughout a challenging period in the Bendas' lives–his words of support made the task of writing in a tumultuous time much less onerous; to Dr. Nancy Toombs, who spent time making sure the project stayed true to the realities of the correctional system; and, above all, to Shirley Benda for her immense patience and understanding at a time when she had to grapple with trepidation in her own life, and whose stellar performance provides a model for emulation.

Address correspondence to Dr. Brent B. Benda, School of Social Work, University of Arkansas at Little Rock, Little Rock, AR 72204 (E-mail: BBBENDA@UALR.EDU).

Rehabilitation Issues, Problems, and Prospects in Boot Camp. Pp. 27-52.
http://www.haworthpress.com/web/JOR
© 2005 by The Haworth Press, Inc. All rights reserved.
Digital Object Identifier: 10.1300/J076v40n03_02

From Optimistic Policies to Pessimistic Outcomes: Why Won't Boot Camps Either Succeed Pragmatically or Succumb Politically?

JEANNE B. STINCHCOMB

Florida Atlantic University

ABSTRACT Although much of the evaluation research conducted to date on correctional boot camps has produced less-than-favorable results, unimpressive outcomes do not appear to have had a significant impact on their steadfast endurance. To some extent, this may be a reflection of the basic reality that correctional practices have not traditionally been strongly influenced by empirical research. Yet, in this era of public accountability, fiscal constraints, and demands to identify "what works," similarly consistent findings might well have sounded the death knell for less notable correctional interventions. Why have boot camps been spared? Addressing this question calls for an analysis of the policy-making process itself, since the untimely endurance of a popular initiative may have more to do with the conditions promoting its acceptance than the conclusions discouraging its continuance. Probing boot camps from the perspective of the public policy process–ranging from conceptualization to formulation, implementation, and ultimately, evaluation–offers valuable insights into where breakdowns may have occurred between initial intentions and ultimate outcomes. Moreover, if correctional boot camps are not ready to succumb politically, perhaps such insights can provide guidance toward undertaking the modifications necessary to enhance their chances of succeeding pragmatically. *[Article copies available for a fee from The Haworth Document Delivery Service: 1-800-HAWORTH. E-mail address: <docdelivery@haworthpress.com> Website: <http://www.HaworthPress.com> © 2005 by The Haworth Press, Inc. All rights reserved.]*

KEYWORDS Boot camps, correctional policies, public policy, outcomes and prospects

In recent years, boot camps have shattered the mediocrity of correctional programming to ignite public imagination, political imagery, and popular support. While boot camps are hardly the only–or even the most prevalent–alternative for dealing with youthful offenders, they are undoubtedly the most widely publicized. Although the public is unlikely to be widely cognizant of such prevailing juvenile justice initiatives as anger management, conflict resolution, or family group conferencing, the same level of obscurity does not protect boot camps. To the contrary, boot camps emerged under the bright spotlight of instant celebrity status and have since continued to remain in the public's eye. But as all celebrities know, there is a price to be paid for such high-profile attention. As a result of their grassroots popularity, boot camps were never able to take advantage of the mantle of disinterest that has shielded more traditional or less notable correctional programming from closer scrutiny. Thus, they have been the focus of more intense empirical attention than perhaps any other contemporary correctional initiative.

Moreover, boot camps entered the correctional arena with immense acclaim. Rarely has a public policy initiative been ushered into practice with such exalted fanfare, widespread support, and hopeful anticipation. Boot camps are conceptually appealing to an impressively broad-based variety of stakeholders (Parent, 1989), ranging across the political spectrum from liberals to conservatives; from veterans to civilians; from judges to public defenders.

In large part, this expansive advocacy is a byproduct of the promise of boot camps to fulfill a wide variety of agendas. Law-and-order champions like the command-and-control military setting. Former veterans nostalgically recall the "shaping up" process of military discipline. Taxpayers applaud the Spartan, no-frills conditions. Save-the-children advocates embrace any alternative to juveniles serving hard time. Judges appreciate the availability of another intermediate sanction. And even offenders themselves may welcome "one more chance" to avoid a traditional prison term. Thus, boot camps appeared on the public policy horizon with a promise of "something for everyone" (Parent, 1989). But even the best-intentioned public policies are simply untested conceptions of what might or might not work in practice. Without careful nurturing during the implementation process, the potential of something-for-everyone can turn into the pitfall of nothing-for-anyone (Stinchcomb, 1999).

Nevertheless, at least in part as a result of their cross-sectional appeal, correctional boot camps have captured both public support and political endorsement over the past two decades. Demonstrating the potential for addressing concerns of virtually everyone on the ideological continuum, the military orientation of boot camps satisfies conservative demands for a punitive response to law violations, while at the same time providing a less coercive and more meaningful option to prison confinement for those with a more liberal political outlook. Since the first modern correctional boot camps were established for adults in 1983 in Georgia and Oklahoma and for juveniles in 1985 in Louisiana (Tyler, Darville, & Stalnaker, 2001), the popularity of this initiative has multiplied throughout the country–prompted by motives ranging from the disillusionment of crime-weary voters to the no-nonsense agendas of frustrated policy-makers, the nostalgic reflections of service veterans, and the never-ending search for innovative correctional alternatives.

COMPATIBILITY WITH THE JUSTICE MODEL

Convinced that military principles can be applied to civilian life–and fueled by $21 million in funding from the U.S. Department of Justice (Special Insert, 1995: 1)–boot camps have proliferated throughout the correctional landscape. Although there is no uniform definition of exactly what a boot camp entails (Colledge & Gerber, 1998), it has been noted that because they are so popular with legislators, many program developers have found it in their interest to stretch the term to include as broad a range of programs as possible (Cronin, 1994: 1). A 1994 survey identified 59 programs operating in 29 states (Cronin, 1994: 13), but a few years later, their numbers began declining, as boot camps were terminated in states ranging from California to New Hampshire (Allen, 1997). By 2000, "nearly one-third of state prison boot camps had closed," and the average daily population in those remaining had dropped by more than 30 percent (Parent, 2003: 2).[1]

In part, the appeal of boot camps can also be traced to their compatibility with the principles of the justice model that have dominated correctional policymaking since the late 1970s (Stinchcomb & Fox, 1999: 31). The justice model's "get-tough" philosophy is grounded in the rationality, respect for authority, personal accountability, obedience, and self-discipline that are characteristic of the values upon which boot camp programming is typically based. In that regard, boot camps have always been popular for their punitive image–which, in fact, is what initially inspired their identity as "shock incarceration" programs. Operating in a quasi-military environment, the shock element of these programs is designed to stop young offenders in their tracks–literally and figuratively (Stinchcomb & Terry, 2001). From the moment they enter the barracks, new recruits are confronted with the "in-your-face" trademarks of boot camp–strict rules, stern discipline, rigorous physical demands, and regimented living. "Through these attention-riveting measures, staff work at instilling order, respect, and rational decision-making into lifestyles that have often been characterized more by disorder, disrespect, and self-absorbed instinctive behavior" (Stinchcomb & Terry, 2001: 222).

When boot camps first hit the political scene in the mid-1980s, there was considerable optimism that the highly regimented training techniques used so effectively to achieve cohesive unity in the military could be applied equally successfully to develop structure and discipline among youthful offenders whose lack of such attributes often brought them into contact with the justice system. Use of the military model to attain such transformations has been justified on the basis that the offenders targeted for boot camp participation:

- Are still young enough, (or insufficiently committed to criminal lifestyles), to change.
- Have few basic skills, are in poor physical condition, and have not experienced success or pride in conventional pursuits like employment and education.
- Lack self-esteem, or their self-esteem is based on criminal exploits and the approval of criminal peer groups.
- Lack self-discipline, respect for authority, and the ability or motivation to take responsibility and be accountable for their actions (Hengesh, 1991).

Boot camps attempt to address these deficits through a relatively short, intensive experience based on military structure and discipline. Average program duration is only 90 to 120 days (Cronin, 1994: 29). Like new recruits in the military, the idea is to teach offenders self-discipline, responsibility, and teamwork in an effort to enhance self-esteem and guide them along a pathway directed toward new lifestyles (Hengesh, 1991). Certainly, the concept made intuitive sense–if widely divergent, rough-around-the-edges military recruits could be transformed into the fine-tuned precision of obedient soldiers, surely the untamed products of urban wilderness could benefit from a similar immersion.

REALITIES OF EMPIRICAL EVIDENCE

But in large measure, the glow of intuitive reasoning has, over the years, been replaced by the glare of empirical reality. At first, boot camps appeared to achieve positive results. Some of the early reports cited lower recidivism (Boot Camps, 1991: 3), improved self-control, and greater likelihood of seeking, obtaining, and maintaining employment upon release (Parent, 1989: 33).

The promise of these initial results, however, was not fulfilled as more in-depth findings were subsequently reported across multiple sites. More recently, evidence that boot camps may not be reducing recidivism has been rapidly accumulating:

- One multisite evaluation of eight programs concluded that their impact on recidivism was "at best negligible" (MacKenzie & Souryal, 1994: 28).
- A U.S. General Accounting Office review of research findings similarly reported that graduates had only marginally lower recidivism rates, and any differences tended to diminish over time (U.S. General Accounting Office, 1993).
- Another multisite assessment found that, despite short-term success in the residential phase, reoffending youth from the boot camps actually committed new offenses more quickly than comparison groups (Peters et al., 1997: 23).
- A study of several sites in one state prompted a U.S. Department of Justice official to note that they were not only ineffective, but also potentially harmful to some youths (Associated Press, 1998).
- Overall, one comprehensive analysis of the boot camp literature concluded that the weight of empirical research evidence has been either negative or inconclusive (Burns, 1996: 43), and another stated that "there is no compelling evidence that boot camp participants recidivate less than groups with which evaluators have compared them" (Cronin, 1994: 43).[2]

In one respect, perhaps none of these findings should be surprising. After all, how realistic is it to expect that a lifetime of social deficits could be overcome in 90 to 120 days? How much potential is there for offsetting significant educational deficiencies within less time than it takes to complete a semester of coursework? How likely is it that clients without secure bonds to family, school, and/or conventional society could firmly establish commitments and relationships within less time than the probationary period for new employees in most agencies? How plausible is it to anticipate that a client overwhelmed by personal failure could build a foundation of positive self-esteem within the time parameters of a single football season? Especially in the absence of aftercare follow-up, how feasible is it that any changes that might occur would survive the subsequent "test of the streets" upon release? . . . in the reality of a world "where drill instructors are replaced by drug dealers; . . . where secure confinement is replaced by self-control; . . . where marching in straight lines is replaced by hanging on street corners" (Stinchcomb & Terry, 2001: 240).

Yet, these were not questions that policy-makers were asking when boot camps accelerated to the pinnacle of the public policy agenda. To the contrary, it was political overtures rather than pragmatic outcomes that were of greater concern to policy-making boot camp advocates. In the political realm, boot camps became the attractive answer for everyone from justice model advocates seeking to hold offenders accountable for their actions to medical model adherents holding out hope for behavioral change. But in the ensuing years, it has become apparent that reality intervened somewhere between exalted intentions and unimpressive evaluations.

PUBLIC POLICY DISILLUSIONMENTS

Boot camps are hardly alone among public policies that have started with great fanfare, raised high expectations, and resulted in disappointment. In that regard, they join a public policy wasteland scattered with the remains of intuitively appealing concepts that either did not survive empirical scrutiny, or resulted in so many unexpected complications and/or costly consequences that original objectives were significantly undermined. For example, the deinstitutionalization of mental health services was designed to provide community-based treatment alternatives to replace the warehousing of patients in large, secluded "insane asylums." But decades later, it has largely been responsible for the mentally ill becoming disproportionately represented among the homeless (see Ditton, 1999; The Sentencing Project, 2002), and has virtually turned local jails into second-rate mental health institutions (Torrey et al., 1992). Wandering the streets, vulnerable to arrest, there are now, in fact, more people with mental illnesses confined in local jails than in mental health facilities (Cox et al., 2001; DiMascio, 1997: 22).

More recently, the primary intent of politically popular presumptive sentencing guidelines such as "three strikes" was to rid the streets of serious, violent criminal predators. Yet evidence is accumulating that such legislation has been responsible for disproportionately filling our prisons with those convicted of relatively petty, nonviolent property or drug-related crimes, at an annual cost of over $94 billion (Irwin & Austin, 1997: 32, 14; Auerhahn, 2002; Luna, 1998). Likewise, mandatory minimum sentencing for use of a firearm in conjunction with the commission of a crime was hailed as a measure that would prompt criminals to "think twice" before packing a gun. Widely publicized through such catchy slogans as "One with a gun gets you two," (referring to a two-year mandatory prison sentence), the strategy was based on the justice model's rational-choice presumption that potential criminals would be deterred from carrying a firearm on the basis of certainty and severity of punishment.

But again, reality indicates that rather than being a deterrent, such provisions have become a plea-bargaining tool and have encouraged the use of discretion earlier in the justice process in order to "avoid having to impose overly harsh sanctions" (Mauer, 1999: 58). Even eliminating plea-bargaining for certain types of offenses has apparently "only served to push discretion further back in the system" (Walker, 1991: 187). These operational adjustments to public policy have been described as the self-adjusting "thermodynamics" of criminal justice–i.e., as pressure is experienced at one point in the system (e.g., getting tougher on crime through mandatory minimum sentencing), it is diffused at some other point (e.g., early release) (Walker, 1989). As critics of presumptive sentencing have complained, "politicians could act irresponsibly in raising statutory penalties to appease public passion without affecting actual time served" (Martin, 1983: 267), thereby enabling them to convey a *"sense* of seriousness rather than actually *being* serious" (Wallace, 1993: 12, emphasis added).

To some extent, such disappointments are perhaps a natural result of translating the ambiguity of theory into the utility of practice. Just as linguistic translators might interpret words literally but fail to capture the essence of what was said, social policy "loses something in translation" as it moves from theoretical concept to practical application. Thus, the outcomes and byproducts of major social change do not always materialize in the manner or the direction that might have been expected. For if it is true that some of the consequences of social action are unanticipated (Merton, 1976: 145-55), it is equally true that some of its *anticipated* effects do not necessarily materialize as originally envisioned. To determine why, it is necessary to more closely analyze the policy development process.

THE POLICY-MAKING PROCESS

Social policy does not simply "emerge" without prior forewarning, like the sudden sprouting of spring flowers or the appearance of fall leaves. Nor does it occur with the certainty of seasonal changes or the precision of physical sciences. To the contrary, policy-making falls within the muddled realm of social sciences. Thus, it is the ambiguous outcome of a lengthy and cumbersome process of bargaining, negotiating, and coalition building (Anderson, 1994; Fabelo, 1994). Unlike the predictable precision of the "hard" sciences, social policy "revolves around needs, emotions, unanticipated events, and a good deal of irrationality" (Gerston, 1997: 7). As such, it is subject to the perpetual ebb and flow of political tides.

But while the product of public policy may be unpredictable, the *modus operandi* of policy-making is a relatively definitive process that can be sequentially analyzed as it meanders through consecutive stages of evolution–from initial conceptualization to legislative formulation, strategic development, organizational implementation, and outcome evaluation (see Figure 1).[3] Moreover, if empirical assessment ultimately indicates that original intentions have not been achieved, the policy itself may be reconceptualized and can reemerge in modified form, thus renewing the cycle. In some respects, this process can be compared to the ferris wheel at an amusement park (Gerston, 1997: 8). Like the fundamental pattern of our policy-making process, the ferris

Figure 1: The policy formulation, development, and implementation process.

- PROBLEM CONCEPTUALIZED
- LEGISLATIVE ACTION
- STRATEGIC DEVELOPMENT
- POLICY IMPLEMENTATION
- OUTCOME EVALUATION

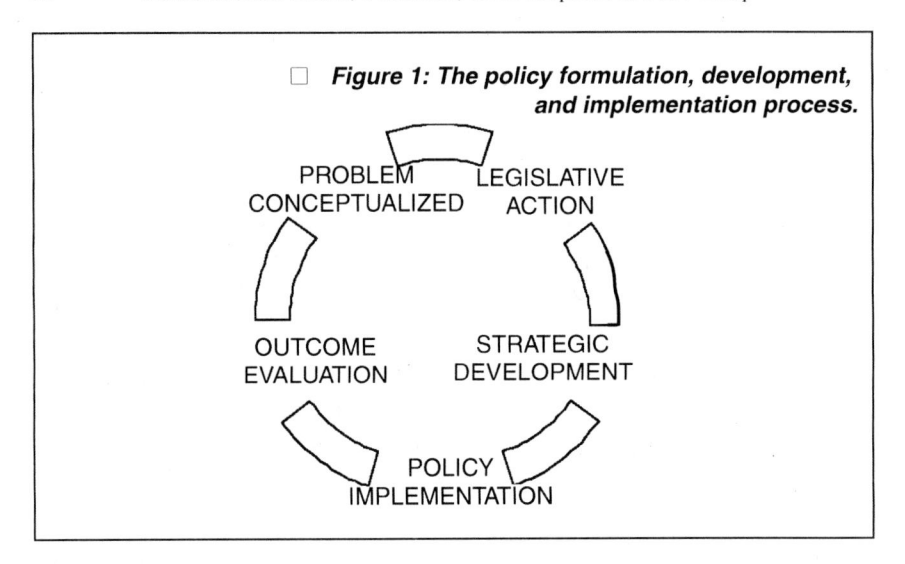

wheel's movement in a continuous, circular motion is ongoing and predictable. But the entries, departures, and combinations of the passengers that it accommodates are not as predetermined–any more than the intensity, longevity, or outcome of public policy debates.

By examining the progression of policy-making through each of these developmental phases, it is possible–with the twenty-twenty vision of hindsight–to make plausible estimates of where an unsuccessful policy went astray. The importance of doing so is self-evident. For the critical issue is not simply establishing *that* a policy failed to live up to expectations, but rather, ascertaining, *why*–or more precisely, where it was in the process that things did not materialize as anticipated. Without that piece of the puzzle, future policy-making efforts are inevitability consigned to randomly throwing darts with the unsubstantiated hope that some may fortuitously hit the target. With the long-term relevance of such a policy-analytic context in mind, the remainder of this article explores the question of just where it was in the policy-making process that boot camps missed the mark.

POLICY CONCEPTUALIZATION

Long before policy is enacted, it is envisioned. Envisioning is the conceptualization of a future state of affairs that would in some way be an improvement over the existing status quo. But first, it is necessary to determine that something about the status quo is inadequate, ineffective, or insufficient–and therefore deserving of attention. Inasmuch as policy-making takes place within the political arena, this means that an issue must first capture public attention. The initial conceptualization of policy, then, begins at the point at which a problem advances to the forefront of social concern.

In that regard, there is little doubt that the challenge of crime, disorder, and troublesome behavior among juveniles and young adults has been at or near the top of the social policy agenda for several decades. The increasing number and escalating seriousness of criminal involvement by this population has been documented in official statistics (Snyder, 2002: 6), fueled by prevalence of a crime-prone age cohort (Blumstein, 2002: 3), and fanned by the flames of a crime-obsessed media (Lehman & Labecki, 1998: 45-47). As a result, juvenile crime has generated personal fear, public outrage, and policy-making attention.

With every indicator pointing toward apparent "failure" of the rehabilitative intent upon which the juvenile justice system was founded nearly a century before, a renewed search for more productive alternatives was launched by the 1980s. Inasmuch as public policy in the adult system had by then shifted toward the justice model, it was not surprising that efforts to address juvenile law violations concomitantly embraced greater accountability and more punitive approaches. To a considerable extent, this has often translated into the juvenile court waiving its jurisdiction and transferring more of its clients into adult criminal courts–what has been termed the "adultification" of the juvenile justice system (Lederman, 1999: 24). While such policies were certainly in alignment with the free choice and just deserts philosophy of the justice model, research indicates that they have not notably increased the severity of sanctions for any but the most serious offenders, and more significantly, that transferred youth were actually more likely to re-offend (and to re-offend earlier) than those who were retained in the juvenile system (Altschuler, 1999). Moreover, there was nothing particularly innovatively eye-catching about policies directed toward holding juveniles accountable as adults that either excited reformers or ignited public interest.[4] Boot camps, however, were another story.

For youthful offenders, boot camps made considerable intuitive sense. They were not, however, conceptually well-grounded in theory. In fact, it has been noted that correctional policy in general has suffered from a "vision vacuum" (Harris & Smith, 1996), and that it has largely developed in a reactionary manner exclusive of either practice-based insights or research-based outcomes (Stinchcomb, 2000). Moreover, juvenile justice policy in particular has been criticized as lacking either an overall mission or a theoretical foundation (Bazemore & Washington, 1995). Nevertheless, it could potentially be argued that boot camps may be embraced within the theoretical structure of specific deterrence or rational choice (Anderson, Dyson, & Burns, 1999: 34). Additionally, their punishment-oriented aspects could be conceived as reflective of retributive theory, and to the extent that they incorporate treatment programming, there may be an argument for their relevance to behavior modification or other forms of rehabilitative programming.[5]

But all of this is post-hoc speculation. It is retroactively attempting to justify the theoretical grounding of boot camps in the absence of actual evidence that criminological, psychological, or social justice theory played a pivotal role in their conceptualization as a response to juvenile crime. To the contrary, much of the literature points to the emergence of boot camps on the basis of political grandstanding, public sentiment, military infatuation, and perhaps most importantly, the cost-consciousness concerns of taxpayers already overburdened with overflowing prisons and jails (Colledge & Gerger, 1998; Peters et al., 1997; Zaehringer, 1998).[6]

In other words, the introduction of boot camps as a policy choice for responding to youthful offending appears to have emerged from more emotional, political, and economic considerations than theory-driven deliberations. While that is not necessarily to say that boot camps were destined to be doomed from the onset because they lacked roots in a theoretical foundation, it has been documented that "opportunistic" public policies based on self-serving interests are considerably more likely to fail than those based more on analytical problem-solving (Scheirer, 1981). After all, if there is no underlying theoretical perspective offering a potential explanation for why boot camps could be expected to succeed where other alternatives have failed, there is no conceptual basis upon which to build faith in their capacity to accomplish what public policy is essentially designed to achieve–i.e., improve existing conditions by creating increased "public value" (Moore, 1995). Without theory-driven parameters to serve as directional guideposts, correctional policy has been drifting through the shifting sands of public opinion and politically charged minefields–hardly fertile soil in which to plant productive policy paradigms (Stinchcomb, 2000).

LEGISLATIVE ACTION

Whether emerging from theoretical, political, or simply pragmatic considerations, when the conceptualized response to a social problem rises to the forefront of public attention, it captures the attention of key decision-makers. As it makes its way onto the social action agenda, the problem begins to achieve legislative recognition at this point. Given the power-based realities of the political process in a democratic government, issues that are "consistent with the prevailing political climate, that are favored by the incumbent administration and legislative majority, and that have interest group support" are more likely to reach the pinnacle of the policy-making agenda (Denhardt, 1991: 47). What more accurate delineations could be applied to boot camps? Consistent with the prevailing justice-oriented paradigm, in concert with the predominance of political conservativism at the time, and championed by interest groups ranging from reform advocates to military devotees, it was virtually inevitable that this concept would be propelled to the forefront of legislative agendas.

In a broader sense, of course, it was actually the unrelenting problem of juvenile crime that captivated so much intense publicity, personal outrage, and public outcry that any legislator or public official remotely interested in reelection or reappointment could hardly ignore it (and more specifically, its political consequences). Conveniently, boot camps fortuitously appeared on the political radar screen with just the right formula to presumably address the problem in a manner that appeared to offer everything to gain and little or nothing to lose.

Combined with broad-based constituent support, the necessity to take bold (but not risky) action, and the premise of cost reductions for a justice system that was straining under the weight of escalating client populations in the absence of commensurate resources, the legislative attraction to boot camps was like a moth to light. Here was the potential "holy grail" for addressing the "anxiety barometer" of increasing crime (Benekos, 1992), appeasing constituents, saving taxpayer dollars, and relieving crowded correctional facilities. Moreover, the military metaphor supplied the additional enhancement of affiliation with a time-tested symbol of success, status, and prestige.

Boot camps thus emerged as the "poster child" for resolving the ills of a dysfunctional justice system, (at least for youthful offenders or young adults who were presumably still somewhat salvageable). In that regard, it has been observed that such a "quick fix" can serve a pragmatic goal by removing an irritating problem from the public agenda (Gerston, 1997: 9)–which is precisely what occurred. Cheaper, shorter, and more symbolically appealing than existing alternatives, boot camps met "quick fix" criteria. But what became lost in legislative endearment with boot camps was the fact that posters are more capable of advertising problems than advancing solutions, and quick fixes are themselves oxymoronic. In the real world, few miracles occur in the 90 to 120 days of typical boot camp residence (Stinchcomb, 1999: 50).

STRATEGIC DEVELOPMENT

In terms of describing the manner in which boot camps emerged on the public policy agenda, an ancient proverb comes to mind–i.e., "If you don't know where you're going, any road will get you there." In other words, if goals–and the means of achieving them–are not clearly prescribed legislatively, it should be no surprise if the result becomes aimless meandering along a path filled with admirable intentions but lacking unambiguous directions. As shown in Figure 1, strategic development is the link between legislative enactment and policy implementation. Without well-focused guidance at the policy-making level, there is no strategic foundation upon which to build as the policy is launched into the "real world." Lacking a theory-driven foundation, fueled by the demands of frustrated constituents, and propelled onto the legislative stage by diverse political motives, boot camps were never the beneficiaries of a solid strategic infrastructure.

Strategy essentially represents the manner through which the broad outlines of legislative policy design are executively translated into the specific parameters of policy implementation. In that regard, policy has been described as generally containing both goals and the means for achieving them (Pressman & Wildavsky, 1973: xiii). Yet public policy goals can be as overly ambitious as "reducing youth crime" and the associated means as open-ended as "boot camps." In fact, to a considerable extent, such ambiguity is purposive, for "by its very nature, legislation is general and lacking in detail" (Denhardt, 1991: 48). At least in part, this is because legislative action occurs within a macro-oriented arena that encompasses a comprehensive perspective devoid of operational details. Additionally, the more prescriptive a public policy becomes, the less likely it is to equally fit the needs of all affected jurisdictions, and therefore, the less political support it is likely to gain. Because the support of varied coalitions is needed to enact public policy, it becomes necessary to appeal to groups with "differing interests and diverse values" (Anderson, 1994: 244). This politically charged compromise and negotiation process almost inevitably produces weakly defined strategies for translating policy into practice. For example, the criterion outlined by federal policy for boot camp aftercare simply indicates that states shall submit a plan describing "the provisions that the state will make for the continued supervision of juveniles following release" (Zaehringer, 1998: 2, citing U.S. Code 42, Sec. 5667[f]-3).

This is not meant to imply that the prescriptive strategies promulgated for boot camps are more open-ended than those accompanying any number of other legislative initiatives. To the contrary, such ambiguity is completely in concert with the very definition of public policy as general principles that guide the development of strategies designed to address concerns associated with broad issues (Houston & Parsons, 1998). Without more detailed attention to strategy, however, agencies are left to their own devices to "fill in the details." On the one hand, such flexibility entails beneficial aspects, since it is desirable to build some degree of autonomy into the subsequent implementation process in order to accommodate local needs. Moreover, legislators could not possibly envision all of the issues that might arise in the policy implementation process, and therefore do not want to "tie the hands" of program administrators by being too restrictive (Denhardt, 1991: 48). To do otherwise could result in the unsavory situation of legislative micro-management.

But on the other hand, the prevailing process can leave so much open to individualized interpretation that the consistency and even integrity of the policy itself can be jeopardized. For example, returning to the issue of aftercare following boot camp, the strategy that a state employs to provide for the "continued supervision of juveniles following release" could range anywhere from the type of intensive counseling, training, education, or mentoring designed to promote post-release reintegration to the type of intensive probation supervision designed primarily to "trail 'em, nail 'em, jail 'em."[7] To some extent, such diversity reflects a laudable attempt to "customize programs" to fit the specific needs of individual offenders, but it may also be indicative of the less praiseworthy reality that "we still don't know what works best" (Tyler et al., 2001). In part, that is because nothing works equally well with everyone. In any event, the subsequent success of boot camp graduates released into such divergent aftercare environments is likely to be equally diverse–which means that empirical findings are not truly capable of making definitive determinations about actual effectiveness. When strategies are more specifically described, policy analysts are subsequently provided with a stronger basis upon which to determine whether a policy's less-than-desirable outcome can be traced to strategic failure. In that regard, another provision of the boot camp criteria outlined in federal policy is that "a person shall be eligible for assignment to a boot camp if he or she is considered to be a juvenile under the laws of the state . . . and has been adjudicated to be delinquent . . . or upon approval of the court, voluntarily agrees to the boot camp assignment without a delinquency adjudication" (Zaehringer, 1998: 1). Apparently, the intent here is to target youthful offenders whose transgressions are not yet so great that they are waived from the jurisdiction of juvenile court. If, however, an agency ignored that guideline and instead opened boot camp eligibility to serious habitual offenders adjudicated in adult court, a serious question could be raised as to whether, in fact, unfavorable outcomes reflect a strategic failure. It therefore becomes apparent that, even to the extent that policies may be well-designed strategically, their ultimate efficacy is irrevocably intertwined with the realities of implementation details.

POLICY IMPLEMENTATION

The excitement surrounding public policy occurs almost exclusively within the political arena–where the issue is brought to legislative attention, emotionally debated, discreetly negotiated, and excitedly enacted. But long after the legislative session ends and the political grandstanding is over, the most important aspect of the policy cycle begins. In contrast to policy enactment, its implementation takes place quietly in the unobtrusive halls of low-visibility bureaucracies that have little direct accountability to the public. Assuming that the policy does not suffer from inadequate conceptualization or inappropriate strategic development, implementation becomes the true test of its success. In fact, it may even be possible to salvage policies suffering from some of these fundamental deficiencies with creative implementation techniques.

That is because during the implementation process, policy-related goals are subject to being changed, redefined, and reshaped (Levine, Musheno, & Palumbo, 1980: 118). To some extent, a policy may therefore be reconceptualized and/or restrategized during the implementation process, although doing so to an extensive degree would obviously sacrifice its inherent integrity. In that respect, it has been observed that when application is inconsistent with intent, "policy has neither substance nor significance" (Gerston, 1997: 97).

Policies are, after all, merely plans. It is in the implementation process where "the rubber meets the road" and these plans are converted into reality. But actually, there are no standardized procedures for doing so (Gerston, 1997: 95, 98). During implementation, policies become subject to diverse interpretations, discretionary judgments, and differential translations. Such adaptations are essential to accommodate local exigencies. But the more policies are modified to meet community needs, the less congruence there is likely to be between original intentions and local adaptations. Essentially, implementation represents a series of trade-offs that ultimately attempt to strike a balance between the autonomy of local control and the authority of legislative intent.

This means that discretionary decision-making inevitably becomes a key feature of the policy implementation process. Putting policy into practice is therefore not simply a routine "mechanical act." To the contrary, agencies are actually formulating policy as they implement it (Levine, Musheno, & Palumbo, 1980: 133, 140). This helps to explain why there is no universal definition of what a boot camp actually is (Colledge & Gerber, 1998: 54) or what operational components it must, by definition, include. As a result, boot camps throughout the country vary by size, requirements, and program structure (Zaehringer, 1998: 1). In fact, perhaps the only ubiquitous commonalities that boot camps appear to have in common are an abbreviated time commitment and a military-style structure.

Even the operational definition of "abbreviated" appears to range considerably, inasmuch as the length of state-operated boot camp programs varies extensively from a low of 30 to a high of 240 days (U.S. General Accounting Office, 1993; Cronin, 1994). Since the policy-making process that spawned national predisposition toward boot camps was not accompanied by definitive operational guidelines, agencies have largely been left to their own initiative to develop goals and related procedures for achieving them–both of which may be quite different from what was intended by the initial legislative action (Levine, Musheno, & Palumbo, 1980: 132). In that regard, it is relevant to recall that boot camps first emerged under the designation of "shock incarceration" programs–whose immediate intent was to vividly capture the attention of young, criminogenically immature offenders who were presumably more salvageable than their older, hard-core counterparts. But as boot camps were operationalized, they became an attractive intermediate option for judges desperately searching for an alternative to prison for somewhat more sophisticated–yet still youthful–offenders (Stinchcomb & Terry, 2001). While boot camps may provide an expanded range of sentencing options–thereby serving as an "escape valve" for those who would otherwise be facing the harsh realities of confinement in an adult prison–utilizing them in this manner entails the potential for both compromising their initial intent and diminishing their empirical assessment.

Likewise, as boot camps have meandered through the transition from public policy to practical reality, they have often been encumbered by contradictory goals. For example, these facilities are at the same time expected to both reform their clients and reduce the time they serve. But the array of behavioral challenges, educational deficits, alienated lifestyles, and dysfunctional relationships that tend to characterize entering recruits are unlikely to be effectively addressed within such a short time span. Particularly for the multidimensional needs and recurrent relapses that can be expected of substance abusers, it should not be surprising when the "quick fix" promised by boot camps translates into a meagerly insufficient intervention.

Another illustration of the manner in which the establishment of contradictory goals can provoke the potential for boot camp failure relates to the manner in which aftercare is implemented. "Aftercare" is a concept that long predates boot camps in the juvenile justice system, having been considered the general equivalent of adult parole for much of the past century. With the public policy paradigm shift from the medical model to the justice model, the nature of adult parole has undergone a substantial transition, both in terms of the manner in which release decisions are made and the nature of post-release supervision (Stinchcomb & Fox, 1999: 423; 439). In almost parallel fashion, aftercare has likewise experienced a similar transformation in the juvenile justice system. Just as hospitals phase-out the release of seriously injured patients through a planned program of gradually diminishing therapeutic follow-up, the very terminology "aftercare" conjures an image of benevolent post-release caretaking– in the traditional casework or brokerage models of social work (Abadinsky, 2000: 320-21). That is not, however, typically descriptive of the nature of post-boot camp aftercare. Beyond the fact that aftercare is not an integral component of most boot camps (Parent, 2003: 4), when it is provided, post-release efforts tend to be focused more on monitoring and surveillance than providing services (Anderson, Dyson, & Burns, 1999; Bourque et al., 1996; Altschuler & Armstrong, 1996). Just as the nature of adult parole has shifted toward a sanction orientation, "aftercare" following boot camp often takes the form of intensive supervision probation rather than intensive service provision. In that regard, it has long been recognized that closely supervised probation is virtually destined to escalate recidivism rates (Petersilia & Turner, 1993), and it would appear that implementing an analogous post-release model for youthful offenders likewise intensifies boot camp failure rates. Perhaps even more significantly from the taxpayer's point of view, to the extent that it is responsible for creating higher levels of revocation and subsequent institutional commitment, increasing the scrutiny of follow-up supervision unintentionally but inevitably increases costs as well as prison crowding (Colledge & Gerber, 1998: 60).[8]

Whether the deficiency relates to inadequate aftercare provision, inappropriate time remission, or insufficient remedial programming, it is evident that the manner in which boot camp-related policy has been implemented entails significant implications when its effectiveness is ultimately subjected to empirical assessment. Inasmuch as the public policy process is only as strong as its weakest link, the interactive relationship between implementation and prior stages in the policy development cycle (see Figure 1) can perhaps best be viewed in the context of outcome evaluations–particularly when the results are unfavorable, unanticipated, or counterintuitive.

OUTCOME EVALUATION

Assessing the impact of public policy is not a straightforward matter conducted in a pristine environment unencumbered by real-world realities. To the contrary, any number of pragmatic constraints imposes obstacles to the valid evaluation of public policy, ranging from uncertainty about the policy's actual goals to the difficulty of establishing causality and the diffuse nature of the policy's impact (Anderson, 1994: 244). Especially when the independent variable represents an intervention that has purposely been acclaimed for its ability to offer "something for everyone," it is not difficult to envision how these constraints might complicate boot camp assessments.

In that respect, it has been noted that, unlike the basic sciences, evaluations in the social sciences do not aim for "truth" or "certainty," but rather, are directed toward identifying how to improve future programming and policy-making (Weiss, 1997: 516). That is because the evaluation component does not function in isolation from the remainder of the policy-development cycle. While such an interactive perspective reflects a desire to pragmatically apply evaluative findings, that is a lofty aspiration. This phase of the process is expected not only to produce an assessment of results, but also–if the outcome is unfavorable–to identify where in the policy cycle things went awry. Policy evaluation therefore represents the "last major opportunity to bring the policy back into the decision-making arena if it has been mismanaged, or if it has had undesirable impacts or unintentional consequences" (Gerston, 1997: 120). Such expectations do not, however, assure that evaluative findings will necessarily be utilized pragmatically to make appropriate adjustments in the policy development cycle. For this is also the point in the process where political agendas come head-to-head with programmatic deficiencies.

Unlike laboratory-controlled discoveries in the physical sciences, social science research results do not tend to establish the same foundation of unfettered confidence that serves as a definitive springboard from which incremental knowledge-building can emerge. In contrast, particularly with regard to boot camps, it has been observed that we often allow "superficial short-term results, the needs of political power, and public demand for increased vigilance against delinquency color our perspective of a program's effectiveness" (Tyler et al., 2001). To some extent, this inclination can be viewed as a "don't-confuse-me-with-facts" outlook of those committed to a publicly popular, politically prescribed policy agenda. But even when the pressure of mounting empirical evidence can no longer be ignored, legitimate questions can be raised concerning the generalizability of outcome findings (Colledge & Gerber, 1998: 54). In fact, given the lack of a standardized implementation model and the resulting diversity of operational practices among boot camps, the validity of inter-agency evaluation comparisons has been cited as "at least questionable if not highly problematic" (Mack, 1992: 145).

If utilized in a manner consistent with its penultimate position in the public policy cycle, outcome evaluation can be a powerful tool because of its potential for casting doubt upon initial assumptions and "reframing" an issue that was once presumed to be resolved by policy-makers (Gerston, 1997: 120). Yet unlike the tangible products of basic science research, the somewhat more intangible results of social science findings must be accommodated within the constraining parameters of organizational structures and political agendas. In that regard, it is common knowledge that an inherent tendency to resist change characterizes much of the public domain. Thus, to the extent that empirical results suggest the need for altering existing practices, both politics and organizational inertia become serious obstacles to implementing evaluation findings in the realm of public policy (Anderson, 1994: 249).

In addition to such implicit, passive resistance is the active impediment of organizational preservation–which, by promoting the protection of parochial self-interests, results in greater concern with projecting a positive image than with discovering the "objective truth" about ongoing programs (Levine, Musheno, & Palumbo, 1980: 55). To some extent, that is because there is an inverse relationship between the rigor of a study's methodological standards (i.e., what will withstand academic scrutiny) and the likelihood of its utility by policy-makers (i.e., what will shape operational practices). To become applicable to the policy-making process, the uncontaminated "ivory tower" research product must be converted into a "street-wise" functional context (Levine et al., 1980: 551). Not unlike many other public policy assessments, boot camp evaluations are not always developed and delivered in a manner that is readily interpreted by and relevant to the interests, needs, and concerns of key stakeholders and decision-makers.

But even if evaluation results could be compiled and communicated in a user-friendly fashion, both organizational and legislative cultures would require substantial change in order for research findings to be accepted as a natural component of decision-making (Fabelo, 1994: 2). Since such change is not abundantly forthcoming, the impact of social research on policy revisions and organizational practices is hardly commensurate with the momentum that rigorous evaluations should be able to sustain (Petersilia, 1991: 4). Thus, practitioners may be tempted to either ignore or overreact to the findings of boot camp evaluations–i.e., by blindly continuing with "business as usual" or completely abolishing the program. Yet these irrational reactions overlook the potential that research provides for obtaining operational insights that can enable administrators to take advantage of the potential to make necessary functional modifications that would capitalize on the public support which maintains political advocacy for boot camps (Stinchcomb, 1999: 44).

The overall issue here is not simply whether or not initially envisioned expectations were achieved. Even in those cases where outcome assessments report positive results, it is essential to be able to identify what key component/s evoked the commendable findings (Zaehringer, 1998: 2). But especially if they were not, it is critical to examine the "extent of congruity" throughout the policy cycle (Gerston, 1997: 98) in order to determine where original expectations broke down. In that respect, it has been observed that many programs that seem to have the benefit of logic on their side nevertheless fail to fulfill their original potential (Weiss, 1997: 520). Correctional boot camps clearly fit within that descriptive parameter–at least in part because a seemingly logical intuitive assumption is not the same as a sound theoretical foundation.

Of course, the fundamental purpose of evaluation research in the social sciences is not merely to determine whether change in the desired direction occurred, but if so, why–and if not, why not. With theory-driven programming, the researcher can progress beyond the basics of merely identifying the elements associated with change and begin to actually specify the causal process by which change can most effectively be accomplished (Weiss, 1997: 511; Stinchcomb, 2001). Moreover, inasmuch as public policy and related evaluations do not exist in a vacuum, action research must take into consideration the impact of outside influences–which, in the case of boot camps, can range from client selection by the judiciary to funding decisions by the legislature. Examining these external influences can likewise help to explain any observed dysfunctions between articulated goals and achieved outcomes (Bondi, 1991: 121).

But although these attributes of policy-related research are designed with the ultimate intent of improving operational practices, which does not necessarily mean that practitioners will employ the results in such a pragmatic fashion. Those with a vested interest in the program are unlikely to curtail their support for it merely on the basis of negative evaluative findings. In fact, one close observer of the political scene and its relationship to program evaluation and policy-making has observed that: "I am unable to think of a governmental program that has been terminated solely as a consequence of an unfavorable systematic evaluation" (Anderson, 1994: 250). Since there are so many with confidence and/or vested interests in boot camps, it is not surprising to find that their support has not significantly dwindled with the evidence forthcoming from less-than-favorable outcome assessments.

SUMMARY AND CONCLUSIONS

Boot camps have been vigorously promoted politically and enthusiastically embraced operationally. But at the same time, they have been inadequately conceptualized, inappropriately strategized, and inconsistently implemented. Certainly, the diversity of boot camp programs underscores the importance of not considering them as one generic model cut from the same cloth. Nevertheless, from the perspective of public policy analysis, it may be possible to draw some general lessons from the experience of boot camps as viewed through a policy development lens.

From the very beginning of the policy-making process, an inherent distinction can be identified between the philosophical framework of those responsible for conceptualizing policy and those who are eventually empowered to implement it. For example, the lens through which policy-makers view their role is politically pragmatic, highly consensual, and pointedly symbolic–as illustrated by the liberal use of metaphors associated with such popular pro-American concepts as baseball ("three strikes"), military might ("war on crime"), and righteousness indignation ("zero tolerance"). In that regard, boot camps found a secure niche within prevailing political ideology and patriotic symbolism. But in contrast to the intuitive, emotional nature of politically driven, symbolic frames of reference, the perspective of those charged with policy implementation is shaped by a more rationally objective, structural lens (Bolman & Deal, 1984) that gives priority to the reality of operational considerations.

As a result, it is not surprising to find not only that the nature of each of their contributions to the policy process differs significantly, but also, that each has differing outcome-oriented expectations–from holding offenders accountable for their actions to having access to a sentencing option that maintains community integration and holds out greater potential for long-term success. Such varying objectives and constituencies obviously generate equally divergent assessment approaches. Methodologies for determining a policy's impact "may therefore be directed toward many different audiences and serve many different purposes" (Denhardt, 1991: 257).

Moreover, it is not only inconsistent evaluation methodologies that prevent us from deciding whether or not public policies are "successful" (by whatever criteria success is measured). To the extent that attention to implementation realities and accompanying resource allocation is overlooked, it is simply not feasible to accurately gauge a policy's effectiveness. In light of such shortcomings, for example, the efficacy of neither the justice model nor its medical model predecessor has actually been able to be determined. Operationally, the widespread availability of treatment programs and therapeutic personnel necessary to accomplish the medical model's rehabilitative mandate was never forthcoming (Stinchcomb & Fox, 1999: 334-35); nor was the prolific prison bed space needed to fulfill the punitive mandate of the justice model. Yet to determine whether a policy has merit, we must know whether the enacted product is the same as the conceptualized design (Harris & Smith, 1996). Without the proper alignment of implementation details, fiscal resources, and policy intentions, even the most sophisticated evaluations cannot determine whether failure to achieve objectives resulted from conceptual or operational shortcomings.

Boot camps have potentially suffered from both. Conceptually, legitimate questions can be raised in terms of the nonexistent theoretical rationale for expecting a short-term, military-based immersion to counteract the multifaceted behavioral problems of offenders typically targeted for this intervention. With regard to potential implementation shortcomings, it can similarly be debated whether boot camps have been selecting appropriate clientele, sufficiently emphasizing education and treatment while they are in custody, and providing satisfactory aftercare upon their release.

One thing is certain–few evaluations have unconditionally affirmed their success. So why do they prevail? In part, the answer relates to their political appeal, along with the desperation of judges seeking alternatives to meaningless, unproductive time behind bars. But more fundamentally, the answer may relate to both the nature of evaluation research and its practical utility. Regarding the former, empirical assessments in the social sciences are not designed to make clear-cut, dichotomous, "thumbs-up/thumbs-down" choices. Unlike their counterparts in the physical sciences, public policy evaluations are not designed to definitively determine whether an intervention does or does not "work." Rather, the most effective policy analyses provide input, feedback, and guidance to improve the ultimate product (Cordner, 1985). But to the limited extent that boot camp assessments have done so, their message has had little impact on administrators–whose response has tended to be either underreaction (i.e., ignoring the findings) or overreaction (i.e., destroying the program) (Stinchcomb, 1999: 44).[9] At least in part, this is additionally a reflection of the reality that criminal justice policy-makers, evaluators, and practitioners are functionally fragmented, thus diminishing the interdependent, multidimensional utility of research results.

While this deficit of interactive partnerships and the loss of their mutually beneficial potential have not been addressed in practice, it has not been unheeded in the literature. In recent years, demands for research-driven correctional policy-making have been mounting (e.g., Perrone & Pratt, 2003; Stinchcomb, 2001; MacKenzie, 2000; Sherman et al., 1997). But while empirical studies would significantly enhance their utility by contributing to policy and practice, that is not to argue for research becoming the exclusive basis for policy decisions (Petersilia, 1996).[10] Nevertheless, utilizing the best available empirical evidence to inform decision-making would seem to make inherent common sense. But the unlikelihood of doing so is not confined to the criminal justice system. The aversion of researchers, practitioners, and policy-makers to collectively collaborate actually reflects a deep-seated conflict that pervades policy-making within a democratic form of government; i.e.:

> On the one hand, people want policy to be informed and well analyzed. On the other hand, they want policy-making to be democratic, hence necessarily political. In slightly different words, on the one hand they want policy-making to be more scientific; on the other, they want it to remain in the world of politics. (Lindblom, 1980: 12)

Regardless of the reasons, the consequences have undoubtedly been less-than-satisfactory in the boot camp arena of public policy-making. Analyzing the intricacies of the policy development cycle reveals many possible reasons for such disappointing results (Houston & Parsons, 1998). As described herein, these could encompass any number of possibilities occurring at any point in the policy development process, including:

- An overall perspective focused more on disobedient kids than dysfunctional families–i.e., *inadequate conceptualization*;
- Legislation that is intentionally vague or ambiguous–i.e., *inappropriate legislative action*;
- Goals that are nebulous or even contradictory–i.e., *strategic failure*;
- Insufficient–or nonexistent–education, training, treatment, and/or aftercare programming–i.e., *implementation failure*;
- Limited concern for measurement, methodologically unsound assessments, and/or lack of operational impact on the part of valid outcome findings–i.e., *evaluation failure*.

Of course, boot camps hardly stand alone in terms of public policy initiatives that have not succeeded empirically but, nevertheless, will not succumb politically. To say that their lofty aspirations remain unfulfilled is to say nothing more than what is equally true of other similarly ambitious endeavors ranging from the deinstitutionalization of mental health to the implementation of sentencing guidelines. But as was noted some four decades ago with regard to another policy reform focused on youth–i.e., the juvenile court movement: "failure is most striking when hopes are highest" (President's Commission, 1967: 7).

NOTES

1. It should be noted, however, that data from multiple sources may not be comparable. For example, some statistics may include only juvenile boot camps, while others incorporate both juvenile and adult; some may count only those operated by state correctional agencies, whereas others may also encompass those administered by county jails or private companies; and some may simply use a differing definition of boot

camps than others. (For a description of significant differences in program characteristics, see Peters et al., 1997.)

2. As with data reporting the number of boot camps throughout the country, a cautionary note is in order here. Given the considerable diversity among boot camps themselves, along with differing criteria for measuring recidivism, evaluation results of one program cannot necessarily be generalized to others (Colledge & Gerber, 1998: 54; Tyler, Darville, & Stalnaker, 2001).

3. With modification and revision, Figure 1 is based roughly on Anderson, 1994: 37, which in turn, was adapted from Anderson, Brady, & Bullock, 1984.

4. In fact, it could legitimately be argued that such "adultification" trends represent nothing more imaginative than a return to the widely accepted practice of treating children like miniature adults that was prevalent prior to the advent of the juvenile court at the turn of the 20th century.

5. For example, Anderson et al. (1999: 34) maintain that Alabama's boot camp program stems from Yochelson and Samenow's (1977) work on the criminal personality, and an intensive aftercare program for high-risk juvenile offenders has been developed that incorporates strain theory, social learning theory, and social control theory (Altschuler & Armstrong, 1996).

6. However, it has been noted that one ironic and unintended effect is that boot camps may actually end up costing taxpayers more if their recidivists are recommitted to a prison sentence that is as long or longer than the sentence they would originally have received if not for the boot camp alternative (see Anderson et al., 1999: 59).

7. In that regard, it has been acknowledged that intensively-supervised probation is often synonymous with the concept of aftercare following release from juvenile boot camps (Tyler et al., 2001).

8. This happens because recidivating graduates will likely face a regular prison sentence, thereby costing taxpayers for both boot camp confinement and subsequent imprisonment (Anderson, Dyson, & Burns, 1999: 59).

9. As has been noted in this regard concerning drug-related policy, "the failure continues as government officials cannot learn enough from their initial failures to overcome the unsuccessful implementation" (Reed, 2000: 76).

10. For example, regardless of whether they reduce recidivism, some initiatives may be justified on the basis of achieving other noteworthy goals, such as reducing costs or sentencing inequities (Petersilia, 1996), or because benefits outweigh costs or inconveniences (Harris & Smith, 1996).

REFERENCES

Abadinsky, H. (2000). *Probation and parole.* Upper Saddle River, NJ: Prentice Hall.

Allen, M. (November 1997). Boot camps fail to pass muster. *Governing, 11* (2): 40-41.

Altschuler, D.M. (1999). Trends and issues in the adultification of juvenile justice. In P. Harris (Ed.). *Research to results: Effective community correction.* Lanham, MD: American Correctional Association.

Altschuler, D.M., & Armstrong, T.L. (December 1996). Aftercare not afterthought: Testing the IAP model. *Juvenile Justice, III,* 15-27.

Anderson, J.E. (1994). *Public policymaking: An introduction.* Geneva, IL: Houghton Mifflin.

Anderson, J.E., Brady, D.W., & Bullock, C. (1984). *Public policy and politics in the United States.* Monterey, CA: Brooks/Cole Publishing.

Anderson, J.F., Dyson, L., & Burns, J.C. (1999). *Boot camps: An intermediate sanction.* New York: University Press of America.

Associated Press. (June 1, 1998). U.S. Justice Department says boot camps do more harm than good. Available online at *http://silcon.com/ptave/usjd.htm.*

Auerhahn, K. (July 2002). Selective incapacitation, three strikes, and the problem of aging prison populations: Using simulation modeling to see the future. *Criminology and Public Policy, 1,* 353-388.

Bazemore, G., & Washington, C. (Spring 1995). Charting the future of the juvenile justice system: Reinventing mission and management. *Spectrum,* 51-66.

Benekos, P. (March 1992). Public policy and sentencing reform: The politics of corrections, *Federal Probation,* 4-10.

Blumstein, A. (March 2002). Why is crime falling–Or is it? *Perspectives on Crime and Justice: 2000-2001 Lecture Series.* NCJ document 187100. Washington, DC: National Institute of Justice.

Bolman, L.G., & Deal, T.E. (1984). *Modern approaches to understanding and managing organizations.* San Francisco: Jossey-Bass.

Bondi, C.B. (1991). When policies conflict: Can retributive state policy goals be met effectively by rehabilitative alternative sentencing strategies? *Criminal Justice Policy Review, 5,* 121-132.

Boot camps seen lowering recidivism. (May 31, 1991). *Law Enforcement News,* 3-4.

Bourque, B.B., Han, M., & Hill, S.M. (1996). A national survey of aftercare provision for boot camp graduates. *National Institute of Justice: Research in Brief.* Washington, DC: U.S. Department of Justice.

Burns, R. (July-August 1996). Boot camps: The empirical record. *American Jails,* 42-49.

Cooledge, D., & Gerber, J. (June 1998). Rethinking the assumptions about boot camps. *Federal Probation, 62,* 54-61.

Cordner, G. (1985). Police research and police policy: Some propositions about the production and use of knowledge. In W.A. Geller (Ed.). *Police leadership in America: Crisis and opportunity* (pp. 383-396). New York: Praeger/American Bar Foundation.

Cox, J.F., Morschauser, P.C., & Banks, S. (May 2001). A five-year population study of persons involved in mental health and local corrections systems. *Journal of Behavioral Health Services and Research, 28,* 177-87.

Cronin, R.C. (1994). Boot camps for adult and juvenile offenders: Overview and update. *National Institute of Justice: Research in Brief.* Washington, DC: U.S. Department of Justice.

Denhardt, R.B. (1991). *Public administration: An action orientation.* Pacific Grove, CA: Brooks/Cole Publishing.

DiMascio, W.M. (1997). *Seeking justice: Crime and punishment in America.* New York: Edna McConnell Clark Foundation.

Ditton, P.M. (July 1999). *Mental health and treatment of inmates and probationers.* BJS document #174463. Washington, DC: U.S. Department of Justice, Bureau of Justice Statistics.

Fabelo, T. (1994). Sentencing reform in Texas: Can criminal justice research inform public policy? *Crime and Delinquency, 40*, 282-293.

Gerston, L.N. (1997). *Public policy making: Process and principles.* Armonk, NY: ME Sharpe.

Harris, P., & Smith, S. (1996). Developing community corrections: An implementation perspective. In A.T. Harland (Ed.). *Choosing correctional options that work: Defining the demand and evaluating the supply* (pp. 183-222). Thousand Oaks, CA: Sage.

Hengesh, D.J. (October 1991). Think of boot camps as a foundation for change, not an instant cure. *Corrections Today*, 106-108.

Houston, J., & Parsons, W.W. (1998). *Criminal justice and the policy process.* Chicago: Nelson Hall.

Irwin, J., & Austin, J. (1997). *It's about time: America's imprisonment binge.* Belmont, CA: Wadsworth Publishing.

Lederman, C.S. (December 1999). The juvenile court: Putting research to work for prevention. *Juvenile Justice, VI*, 22-30.

Lehman, J.D., & Labecki, L.S. (1998). Myth versus reality: The politics of crime and punishment and its impact on correctional administration in the 1990's. In T. Alleman & R.L. Gido, *Turnstile justice: Issues in American corrections.* Upper Saddle River, NJ: Prentice Hall, 1998, 42-70.

Levine, J.P., Musheno, M.C., & Palumbo, D.J. (1980). *Criminal justice: A public policy approach.* New York: Harcourt Brace Jovanovich.

Lindblom, C.E. (1980). *The policy-making process.* Englewood Cliffs, NJ: Prentice Hall.

Luna, E.G. (1998). Three strikes in a nutshell. *Thomas Jefferson Law Review, 20*:1; viewed online at didspoo@psc1862.lexis-nexis.com.

Mack, D. (1992). Combining shock incarceration and remedial education. *Journal of Correctional Education, 43*, 144-150.

MacKenzie, D. (2000). Evidence-based corrections: Identifying what works. *Crime and Delinquency, 46*, 457-476.

MacKenzie, D., & Souryal, C. (1994). Multisite evaluation of shock incarceration. *National Institute of Justice: Research Report.* Washington, DC: U.S. Department of Justice.

Martin, S.E. (1983). The politics of sentencing reform: Sentencing guidelines in Pennsylvania and Minnesota. In A. Blumstein, J. Cohen, S.E. Martin & M.H. Tonry (Eds.). *Research on sentencing: The search for reform*, Vol. II. Washington, DC: National Academy Press.

Mauer, M. (1999). *Race to incarcerate.* Washington, DC: The Sentencing Project.

Merton, R.K. (1976). The unanticipated consequences of social action. In R.K. Merton, *Sociological ambivalence and other essays.* New York: Free Press.

Moore, M.H. (1995). *Creating public value: Strategic value in government.* Cambridge, MA: Harvard University Press.

Parent, D. (1989). Shock incarceration: An overview of existing programs. *Issues and Practices.* Washington, DC: U.S. Department of Justice, National Institute of Justice.

Parent, D. (2003). *Correctional boot camps: Lessons from a decade of research. Research for Practice.* Washington, DC: National Institute of Justice.

Perrone, D., & Pratt, T.C. (September 2003). Comparing the quality of confinement and cost-effectiveness of public versus private prisons: What we know, why we do not know more, and where to go from here. *The Prison Journal, 83*, 301-322.

Peters, M., Thomas, D., & Zamberlan, C. (1997). *Boot camps for juvenile offenders: Program summary.* Washington, DC: Office of Juvenile Justice and Delinquency Prevention.

Petersilia, J. (1991). Policy relevance and the future of criminology. *Criminology, 29*, 1-15.

Petersilia, J. (1996). Improving corrections policy: The importance of researchers and practitioners working together. In A.T. Harland (Ed.). *Choosing correctional options that work: Defining the demand and evaluating the supply* (pp. 223-231). Thousand Oaks, CA: Sage Publications.

Petersilia, J., & Turner, S. (1993). Evaluating intensive supervision probation/parole: Results of a nationwide experiment. *National Institute of Justice: Research in Brief.* Washington, DC: U.S. Department of Justice.

President's Commission on Law Enforcement and Administration of Justice. (1967). *Task force report: Juvenile delinquency and youth crime.* Washington, DC: U.S. Government Printing Office.

Pressman, J.L., & Wildavsky, A. (1973). *Implementation.* Berkeley, CA: University of California Press.

Reed, R. (2000). Marching after folly: An analysis of the drug war policy. *Corrections Management Quarterly, 4*, 76-85.

Scheirer, M.A. (1981). *Program implementation: The organizational context.* Beverly Hills, CA: Sage Publications.

Sherman, L.W., Gottfredson, D., MacKenzie, D., Eck, J., Reuter, P., & Bushway, S. (1997). Preventing crime: What works, what doesn't, and what is promising. *National Institute of Justice: Research in Brief.* Washington, DC: U.S. Department of Justice.

Snyder, H. (2002). *Juvenile Arrests 2000.* (NCJ document 191729). Washington, DC: U.S. Department of Justice, Office of Juvenile Justice and Delinquency Prevention.

Special insert: How does your boot camp rate? (September 5, 1995). *Corrections Alert, 2*, 1-2.

Stinchcomb, J.B. (1999). Recovering from the shocking reality of shock incarceration: What correctional administrators can learn from boot camp failures. *Corrections Management Quarterly, 3*, 43-52.

Stinchcomb, J.B. (2000). Corrections and public policy: Where we've been, where we're going. *Corrections Management Quarterly, 4*, vi-viii.

Stinchcomb, J.B. (2001). Using logic modeling to focus evaluation efforts: Translating operational theories into practical measures, *Journal of Offender Rehabilitation, 33*, 47-65.

Stinchcomb, J.B., & Fox, V.B. (1999). *Introduction to corrections.* (5th ed.) Englewood Cliffs, NJ: Prentice Hall.

Stinchcomb, J.B., & Terry, W.C. (2001). Predicting the likelihood of rearrest among shock incarceration graduates: Moving beyond another nail in the boot camp coffin. *Crime and Delinquency, 47*, 221-242.

The Sentencing Project (January, 2002). *Mentally ill offenders in the criminal justice system: An analysis and prescription.* Washington, DC: The Sentencing Project.

Torrey, F.E., Stieber, J., Ezckiel, J., Wolfe, S.M., Sharfstein, J., Noble, J.H., & Flynn, L.M. (1992). *Criminalizing the seriously mentally ill–The abuse of jails as mental hospitals.* Washington, DC: Joint Report of the National Alliance for the Mentally Ill and Public Citizen's Health Research Group.

Tyler, J., Darville, R., & Stalnaker, K. (2001). Juvenile boot camps: A descriptive analysis of program diversity and effectiveness. *The Social Science Journal, 38,* 445-60.

U.S. General Accounting Office. (1993). *Prison boot camps: Short-term prison costs reduced, but long-term impact uncertain.* Washington, DC: U.S. General Accounting Office.

Walker, S. (1989). *Sense and nonsense about crime: A policy guide.* Pacific Grove, CA: Brooks/Cole.

Walker, S. (1991). Should plea bargaining continue to be an accepted practice? In R.C. Mond (Ed.). *Taking sides: Clashing views on controversial issues in crime and criminology.* Guilford, CT: Dushkin Publishing.

Wallace, H.S. (September 1993). Mandatory minimums and the betrayal of sentencing reform: A legislative Dr. Jekyll and Mr. Hyde. *Federal Probation, 54,* 9-19.

Weiss, C.H. (1997). How can theory-based evaluation make greater headway? *Evaluation Review, 21,* 501-524.

Yochelson, S., & Samenow, S.E. (1977). *The criminal personality: The change process.* New York: Jason Aronson.

Zaehringer, B. (July 1998). *Juvenile boot camps: Cost and effectiveness vs. residential facilities.* Koch Crime Institute White Paper Report, available at http://www.kci.org/publication/white_paper/boot_camp/index.htm.

AUTHOR'S NOTE

Dr. Jeanne B. Stinchcomb is an associate professor in the Department of Criminology and Criminal Justice at Florida Atlantic University. She has evaluated local and national criminal justice programs, serves as a consultant to the National Institute of Corrections and the American Correctional Association, and in 2002 received the Peter P. Lejins Research Award for research that has contributed significantly to the field of corrections. The author of *Introduction to Corrections,* she is currently writing a book on correctional leadership. She has contributed to *Crime and Delinquency, Justice Quarterly, Criminal Justice Policy Review, American Journal of Criminal Justice,* and *Journal of Criminal Justice Education* in addition to *JOR.*

Address correspondence to Dr. Jeanne B. Stinchcomb, Department of Criminology and Criminal Justice, Florida Atlantic University, 111 E. Las Olas Blvd., HEC 1009, Ft. Lauderdale, FL 33301 (E-mail: stinchco@fau.edu).

Rehabilitation Issues, Problems, and Prospects in Boot Camp. Pp. 53-70.
http://www.haworthpress.com/web/JOR
© 2005 by The Haworth Press, Inc. All rights reserved.
Digital Object Identifier: 10.1300/J076v40n03_03

The Rise and Fall of Boot Camps: A Case Study in Common-Sense Corrections

FRANCIS T. CULLEN
University of Cincinnati

KRISTIE R. BLEVINS
University of Cincinnati

JENNIFER S. TRAGER
University of Cincinnati

PAUL GENDREAU
University of New Brunswick at Saint John

ABSTRACT "Common sense" is often used as a powerful rationale for implementing correctional programs that have no basis in criminology and virtually no hope of reducing recidivism. Within this context, we undertake a case study in "common-sense" corrections by showing how the rise of boot camps, although having multiple causes, was ultimately legitimized by appeals to common sense. We also reveal, however, how sustained, rigorous research attenuated this legitimacy and contributed to the diminished appeal of boot camps. The "fall" of this sanction suggests that evidence-based corrections may, at times, compete successfully with common-sense corrections. The policy and practice implications of this observation are explored. *[Article copies available for a fee from The Haworth Document Delivery Service: 1-800-HAWORTH. E-mail address: <docdelivery@haworthpress.com> Website: <http://www.HaworthPress.com> © 2005 by The Haworth Press, Inc. All rights reserved.]*

KEYWORDS Boot camps, correctional rehabilitation, common sense

The most enduring, seemingly intractable reality facing American corrections–a reality from which there has, for some time, appeared to be "no escape" (DiIulio, 1991)–is the steady replenishment of large numbers of offenders in prison and under state legal supervision. The statistics, of course, are familiar: On any given day, in excess of 1.4 million offenders are housed in state and federal prisons, a count that climbs to over 2 million when jail inmates are indexed; approximately 4 million people are on probation and another 750,000 are on parole; and, when all the figures are added up, more than 6.5 million offenders are supervised daily by the correctional system (Glaze, 2003; Harrison & Beck, 2003; Salant, 2002). Although there are some signs that the growth in prison populations may be slowing (Butterfield, 2001, 2003; Harrison & Beck, 2003), few commentaries on the status of U.S. corrections can avoid discussing the sheer number of offenders that must be managed day in and day out.

By contrast, an equally remarkable reality–but one that less frequently captures media headlines or scholarly notice–is the persistent commitment by correctional leaders and among the public to the goal of changing the criminally wayward for the better (Cullen, Fisher, & Applegate, 2000; Cullen, Pealer, Fisher, Applegate, & Santana, 2002). Good intentions have permeated the often dark history of corrections (McKelvey, 1977) and have surfaced even in recent years when corrections has been characterized as being in the grips of the "penal harm movement" and the "imprisonment binge" (Clear, 1994; Irwin & Austin, 1994). To be sure, this hope that offenders might be saved usually does not extend to the most heinous criminals and does not ensure the allocation of resources needed for the task of reforming criminals. Nonetheless, Americans believe that the correctional system should do more than warehouse and control; the system should, as its name implies, also "correct."

But realizing this goal of correcting offenders is hardly uncomplicated. Beyond incapacitation or the mere infliction of pain, the daunting puzzle confronted by corrections is *how to intervene* in such a way as to transform the lawless into the law-abiding. One answer increasingly being proposed is to base interventions "on the evidence"–that is, on what works to reduce recidivism. This approach, which is becoming known as "evidence-based corrections," draws its rationale from a similar movement within medicine (Cullen & Gendreau, 2000; Gendreau, 2000; MacKenzie, 2000; more generally, see Glenn, 2003; Sherman, Farrington, Welsh, & MacKenzie, 2002). In both cases, the logic is persuasive: Not to use scientific evidence to direct interventions is to risk subjecting people to procedures that are either harmful or ineffective. Of course, an evidence-based approach is not without its own demands. Thus, to have a salutary effect, knowledge on "what works" must be accumulated, transferred, and then implemented in the "real world." Still, the alternative to taking on these challenges is to engage in interventions that can rightly be called "quackery" (Latessa, Cullen, & Gendreau, 2002; see also, Salant, 2003).

Unfortunately, corrections is a field in which quackery is pervasive (Latessa et al., 2002). Undoubtedly, the reasons why so many ineffective interventions are invented, implemented, defended, and sustained are complex. Criminologists, for example, must share part of the blame for not generating, until recently, a body of research-based knowledge that could direct the selection of effective treatment modalities (Cullen & Gendreau, 2001). Correctional employees similarly have failed to define their work as a profession organized, like other professions, around expertise rooted in science and training (Latessa et al., 2002). It is safe to suggest that the current state of affairs also can be traced to a lack of resources, bureaucratic inertia, and politics. Nonetheless, another factor that richly deserves to be cited is the willingness of policy-makers, practitioners, and the public to embrace interventions on the basis of *common sense* (Gendreau, Goggin, Cullen, & Paparozzi, 2002).

Let us hasten to say that common sense is not inherently a recipe for failure in corrections. At times, the collective wisdom in a field can be just that: wisdom well worth consulting. The difficulty, however, is that common sense is often accorded a privileged status in which, as a basis of knowledge, it is allowed to trump science and more systematic ways of determining a course of intervention. In this scenario, common sense can be boldly cited both to preclude undertaking evaluation research "which will only prove what everyone already knows" or to reject contrary empirical evidence because "the study must be wrong since statistics can show anything you want them to show." Common sense thus becomes a socially constructed reality that is resistant to falsification. It is true virtually by definition.

In the current analysis, we propose that common sense was a key ingredient that facilitated the growth of "boot camps" as a correctional intervention. Boot camps were not rooted in empirical research and showed considerable resilience even when unfavorable research results mounted. Even so, the boot camp saga has had an ending that, for the positivists among us, has been happier rather than disappointing. Although boot camps persist as an intervention (Camp & Camp, 1999), the reputation of this intervention has been significantly tarnished. In this case, it appears that scientific research may be winning the battle with common sense.

THE APPEAL OF BOOT CAMPS

Although their origins can be traced back to at least 1971 in Idaho (Camp & Camp, 1999), correctional boot camps emerged as a significant initiative in the 1980s, with Oklahoma and Georgia developing such camps in 1983 (MacKenzie & Hebert, 1996). In the decade following the inception of these initial programs, over 40 boot camps were implemented, with camps found in over half the states (MacKenzie, Shaw, & Gowdy, 1993; see also, Tonry, 1996, p. 110). The sudden emergence and spread of boot camps thus raised the question of why the 1980s and the 1990s provided a receptive context for this particular correctional intervention. Why were boot camps appealing at this historical juncture?

"Getting Tough" Through Intermediate Sanctions

The answer to this query starts with the observation that boot camps were not an isolated venture but rather part of a broader movement called "intermediate sanctions" or "intermediate punishments." The term "intermediate" refers to a place somewhere in between "prison" and "probation" (Morris & Tonry, 1990). Commentators often decried that, when sentencing offenders, judges had only two main options: life-altering placement behind bars versus a mere "slap on the wrist" with probation. This would be tantamount to a doctor having to choose between hospitalizing patients or prescribing "two aspirins in the morning." For liberals, these disparate options inevitably prevented judges from allocating sentences that were more finely calibrated to the seriousness of the offense. Injustice thus was always on the horizon because, in their view, many offenders were sent to prison who did not truly deserve to be there–or did not deserve to be there more than others released into the community. If only judges had more options–something less stringent than prison but harsher than probation–then many of these individuals might well escape incarceration. In short, intermediate sanctions might allow for more justice in sentencing.

In the end, however, "justice" was only a subsidiary reason–one mostly trumpeted by progressives–why intermediate sanctions captured the imagination of policymakers. As DiIulio (1991) pointed out, officials were concerned that there was no escape from rising prison populations and the concomitant institutional crowding. Many conservatives were searching for a solution to the financial costs associated with housing burgeoning numbers of inmates. One option might have been the greater use of community "corrections," justified by the rationale that prisons were harmful places and the community was a location where rehabilitation services could be delivered more efficaciously. But in the context of the Reagan era and the movement of the United States toward the political right, such talk would have been–indeed was–dismissed as the empty rhetoric of bleeding hearts clinging to the therapeutic logic of the now-discredited welfare state. Instead, crime must be confronted with the iron fist, not the velvet glove, of the state, and criminals must be disciplined and scared into submission.

The genius of intermediate *sanctions* or *punishments* was that they ostensibly rejected the tradition of earlier community sanctions, which were assembled under the label of *corrections*. Instead, they pushed thinking in a dramatically different direction: What if interventions could be created that, though administered largely in the community, were oriented not toward social welfare for undeserving criminals but toward the control of, and the infliction of discomfort on, offenders? What if it were possible to "get tough" in the community? If so, then it would be feasible to lessen the prison crowding problem in a way that was both fiscally prudent and politically defensible.

Intermediate sanctions/punishments, of course, offered this seemingly perfect solution (Cullen, Wright, & Applegate, 1996). Offenders would no longer be "reintegrated" and counseled by probation and parole officers schooled in social work. Instead, community supervision would be transformed mainly into a policing function–what one observer called a "pee 'em and see 'em" style of corrections. In this new paradigm, offenders placed in the community would now be *controlled*; they would be subjected to random drug tests, intensive supervision, home incarceration, and/or electronic monitoring. They would experience these sanctions as unpleasant and would fear that stepping out of line would be quickly detected, with the threat of imprisonment looming for the uncooperative. It was assumed that only the irrational–the undeterrable–would dare trifle with such a newly vigilant state (Cullen, Pratt, Miceli, & Moon, 2002; Cullen et al., 1996).

Boot camps had some unique features, but largely "fit" with this intermediate sanctions movement and the larger "get tough" context in which they were enmeshed. Unlike the other sanctions, boot camps involved a stay in behind bars–albeit one that lasted only a few months (typically three to six months). Boot camps also promised not just to watch offenders but also to change them for the better–albeit through means (military discipline) that would not be mistaken for lenient, bleeding-heart corrections.

This last point is crucial. Although offering to exchange long prison stays for short prison stays–harshness for leniency–boot camps were acceptable precisely because they promised to be, well, boot camps! That is, they were prepared to subject offenders to a Spartan lifestyle, to exhausting physical demands, to planned and repeated humiliation, and to authoritarian (if secretly well-intentioned) drill sergeants who would be unrelenting in their discipline. As Tonry (1996, p. 110) notes, "images of offenders participating in military drill and hard physical labor make boot camps look demanding and unpleasant, characteristics that crime-conscious officials and voters find satisfying." Underneath it all, offenders might be "loved," but it was a love that would always be tough. Indeed, it is instructive that boot camps were sold not just as an intermediate sanction but as a "tough" intermediate sanction (MacKenzie &

Hebert, 1996). Equally illuminating, they were often given the alias of "shock incarceration."

In short, boot camps–like other intermediate sanctions–used a language and promised a toughness that resonated with the prevailing political climate. The task now was to randomly test, intensively supervise, electronically monitor, and discipline the wayward. With such an array of weapons, it would be safe–and much cheaper than paying for their prolonged imprisonment–to control offenders in the community, especially after the shock of life in a boot camp. The logic was certainly persuasive. However, for specific interventions to be enthusiastically accepted, something more than toughness and promised costs savings had to be present. One other ingredient would seal their popularity: There had to be some reason to believe that these intermediate sanctions actually would "work."

Consult the Evidence or Consult Common Sense?

One option might have been to review the extant empirical evidence and to develop the case that criminological scholarship, however limited, was on the side of the proposed intervention. Such an evidence-based approach would have required a professional orientation, a belief that libraries contain valuable information, and a willingness to expend the effort to sit and read for a bit. But if this approach had been embraced, it would have revealed troubling facts. For example, there has never been any consistent evidence that smaller probation caseloads that allow for more intensive supervision reduce recidivism (Gendreau, Cullen, & Bonta, 1994). We will return shortly to this point as it relates to boot camps.

There was no need, however, for boot-camp advocates to worry about the data. Another standard could be applied to justify the allocation of millions of dollars and untested interventions into the lives of thousands of offenders: common sense! Again, part of what made intermediate sanctions–including boot camps–sensible was that they rejected doing something *for* the offender and promised to do something *to* the offender. But "get tough" rhetoric aside, the common sense underlying most intermediate sanctions was the "parable of the hot stove." This means, of course, that we all grow up and learn–either firsthand or through cringing observation–that touching a hot stove immediately yields the pain of a burn. In the same way, intermediate sanctions were portrayed as making the state into a hot stove: As soon as the offender did something wrong, the drug test, the electronic monitor, and the intensively supervising probation officer would zap them with a the burn of a sanction. How could it not work?

Boot camps, however, were different, but the influence of common sense was, if anything, far more powerful. There was a widespread belief that the discipline of military experience would transform the immature and wayward into mature and contributing citizens. We can ask once again for the basis of this view. An evidence-based approach would have urged caution. If advocates of boot camps had taken the time to inspect research on military service, they would have discovered that the impact of such service is complex and often contradictory, and that the special effects of boot camps have not been disentangled from those of other experiences related to the military (e.g., job training and guaranteed employment while in the service, educational benefits after release, time spent in combat) (Rand, 1987; Sampson & Laub, 1996; Wright, Carter, & Cullen, in press).

Sampson and Laub's (1993) reanalysis of the Glueck and Glueck's (1950) longitudinal data set is instructive. The Gluecks' study was initiated in 1939 with boys ages 10 to 17; two-thirds of the sample would eventually enter the military, including many who had histories of delinquency. Sampson and Laub (1993, p. 223) recognize that being in the service might benefit some men and even help to "surmount childhood disadvantage." But they also note that "it is not inconsistent that the military can serve to turn some men's lives around, even as it disrupts other men's lives . . . or provides yet another setting for some men to continue their deviant behavior" (p. 222). Indeed, in their empirical analysis, they report that length of military service had an insignificant effect on later criminal behavior during adulthood (pp. 163-164). Equally salient, they show that, *despite the experience of being in a boot camp*, the military was not particularly successful in blunting the criminal predispositions of those with a past history of delinquency. For example, when compared with a matched sample of non-delinquents, individuals with an official record of delinquency (i.e., a prior placement in a juvenile correctional school) were three times more likely to commit crime in the military (64% versus 20%), and seven times more likely to be a frequent offender, to be a serious offender, and to be dishonorably discharged. Similar results were found for men who scored high on prior measures of unofficial or reported delinquency (Sampson & Laub, 1993, pp. 129-131; see also, Gottfredson & Hirschi, 1990, pp. 164-165). Not surprisingly, the United States military no longer recruits men or women with criminal records.

Although more positive in her assessment, Bouffard's (in press) examination of two longitudinal data sets of individuals in the Vietnam War era (born in 1945 and 1949, respectively) also shows the complexities of asserting that boot camps are panaceas for crime. In one data set drawn from Racine, Wisconsin, military service reduced offending. However, in the other data set drawn from Philadelphia, military service limited the likelihood of criminal involvement for those with no past record of delinquency, but had no effect on those with a delinquent record–precisely the group held to benefit from correctional boot camps. In neither study, we should note, did military service affect future violent offending (see also, Wright et al., in press).

Findings such as these, however, never surfaced in the rush to establish boot camps. As Tonry (1996) points out, correctional boot camps garnered instant legitimacy from the supposedly *transforming personal experiences* that many citizens believed they had had in the military. "Many Americans," observes Tonry (1996, p. 110), "have experienced life in military boot camps and remember the experience as not necessarily pleasant but as an effective way to learn self-discipline and to learn to work as part of a team." Thus, if they had been changed for the better by boot camps, it was only common sense that camps could save other wayward souls. Moreover, this common-sense commitment to boot camps could insulate its holders–at least for a time–from countervailing critical analysis and empirical data. Thus, when state officials in Georgia were presented with evaluation research revealing the ineffectiveness of boot camps, they responded in this illuminating way:

> Reacting to the study, a spokesman for Governor Zell Miller said that "we don't care what the study thinks"–Georgia will continue to use its boot camps. Governor Miller is an ex-Marine, and says that the Marine boot camps he attended changed his life for the better; he believes that the boot camp experience can do the same for wayward Georgia youth. . . . "Georgia's Commissioner of Corrections" . . . also joined the chorus of condemnation, saying that academics were too quick to ignore the experiential knowledge of people "working in the system" and rely on research findings. (Vaughn, 1994)

The common-sense appeal of correctional boot camps drew strength from another factor: the unchallenged, almost hegemonic cultural belief that military boot camps "break a person down" and then "build 'em back up." When probed, most people have no specific idea what this means–that is, they cannot articulate what is being broken down and what is being built back up. Rather, they harbor only some vague notion that boot camps strip away a recruit's youthful immaturity, slovenliness, and general disrespect for authority and "turn them into a man." This break-'em-down/build-'em-up theory comes to life in uplifting, if not heartwarming, television shows and movies, such as *An Officer and a Gentleman*. A familiar and comforting theme is repeated: We see the slightly delinquent, confused, perhaps self-centered, youthful rebel saved from personal and social failure by the demanding but ultimately caring drill sergeant who pulls the recruit back from the brink of going AWOL. The ending of these films is particularly revealing. They invariably show the group that had survived boot camp proudly marching out in their pristine dress uniforms just as a new group of recruits sporting long hair and ill-fitting clothes staggers off the bus to the inhospitable greetings of the drill sergeant. We all know what awaits them!

In a dialectical way, these images both reflect and reinforce the notion that boot camps are imbued with special, transforming powers. It thus becomes merely a matter of common sense to make the leap in logic–or, perhaps more accurately, the leap in faith–that *correctional* boot camps can break offenders down and build them back up. These notions obscure the dual reality that the causes of crime are complex and that the effects of military service are complex. Where caution should reign, common sense rushes us to the judgement that boot camps are a cure for crime that should be implemented without delay.

THE DANGERS OF COMMON-SENSE THINKING: LESSONS FROM MONEYBALL

We are in an era in which common sense is frequently trumpeted as the basis for prudent governmental policy (Gendreau et al., 2002). This celebration of common sense is typically pregnant with a disquieting anti-intellectualism. There is hostility to the notions that the social world is complex and that science might be used, step by step, to unravel these mysteries. Instead, common sense is portrayed as sweeping away needless obfuscation to provide simple answers that then allow for vigorous action.

As we have noted, common sense is not inherently wrong, as a challenge to "go touch a hot stove" quickly illuminates. But as issues become complex and solutions involve the careful balancing of multiple factors, common sense can result in gross miscalculations (Gendreau et al., 2002). Indeed, there is now a large body of social psychological research on cognitive processes that documents how common sense can promote "profound, systematic, and fundamental errors in judgment" (Nisbet & Ross, 1980, p. 6).

Within corrections, we can cite two that are likely to be likely to be troubling. First, there is what might be called the "N of 1" phenomenon. This is the assumption that one's own experiences and perceptions about "what works" generalize accurately to other people and contexts. There is the collateral tendency to overestimate the popularity or accuracy of one's views and to assume that other people with different "common sense" are incorrect. Second, there is the problem of "selective perception." Here, instances that confirm a person's opinions or examples of success are remembered, whereas countervailing evidence and examples of failure are suppressed. This allows correctional workers to cite vivid, even persuasive anecdotes buttressing their viewpoint. Unlike in the scientific method, potentially falsifying information is not recalled or counted systematically; such information is set aside as more comforting memories are trumpeted.

We should emphasize, however, that common sense is not unique to corrections. It permeates our everyday lives and virtually every sector of society. Its costs can be unrecognized and profound. An example from the game–or business–of professional baseball is revealing.

Going Against "The Book"

Michael Lewis's (2003) recent book, *Moneyball: The Art of Winning an Unfair Game*, is a poignant analysis of the costs of using common sense in professional baseball (see also, Thaler & Sunstein, 2003). This book ostensibly is an attempt to explain a peculiar pattern in baseball: How is it possible for the Oakland Athletics (the "A's") to regularly win almost as many games each season as the New York Yankees when their salary payroll, which ranks near the bottom of major league teams, is one-third that of the Yankees? For the 2003 season, for example, the Yankees won 101 games with a payroll of over $164 million, whereas the $50 million payroll of the A's yielded 96 wins. So-called "small market" teams with low payroll might occasionally have a great year and win a World Series (such as the Florida Marlins), but few are able to sustain this level of success. Following a championship, players are lured away by the prospect of huge salaries offered by more affluent teams, and the success is not be repeated. The Oakland A's, however, are not one-season wonders. Even though they lose star players (e.g., Jason Giambi to the Yankees), they win over 90 games and are in the playoffs just about every year.

Lewis's provocative answer to this dilemma holds broad significance: The A's win because their General Manager, Billy Beane, rejects common sense in favor of a statistics-based–or in our terms, an evidence-based–approach to player development and to game strategy. By using evidence, Beane is able to secure a competitive advantage that allows his team to outperform other clubs. His competitive advantage is possible only because those running other baseball franchises eschew statistics in favor of common sense rooted in the extant culture of baseball. The neglect of an evidence-based approach is ironic given that few areas in society collect and publish more statistics than baseball. Nonetheless, the baseball men have consistently ignored a statistical approach to their business–something called "sabermetrics"–despite a quarter century of publications by writers such as Bill James showing that much baseball "wisdom" is hogwash. Instead, as Lewis notes (2003, p. 64), they prefer to conduct their business in a "field of ignorance."

This culture–a set of beliefs often said to be compiled in an unwritten volume called "The Book" (as in "one goes by The Book")–is an expression of the accumulated wisdom of "baseball men" over the years (Thaler & Sunstein, 2003). Expertise thus is rooted in personal experience–that is, in what baseball insiders "know to be true" from having played, coached, or otherwise worked in the sport for years.

Take, for example, this scenario. Let's assume that a game is tied in the ninth inning, and the first batter of the inning gets a single. What would "The Book" say should come next? Without reflection, any shrewd follower of baseball would reply: The next batter should bunt the ball so as to advance the runner to second base; the runner would now be in "scoring position" where a single would likely win the game. As it turns out, however, statistical analysis reveals that this common-sense strategy actually *decreases* the likelihood that the winning run will be scored in the inning. The exchange of an out for a base reduces the team's scoring chances.

Or, let's take this scenario: It is draft day and the team is about make its first-round selection. A scout with twenty years of experience in baseball argues that the team should draft an 18-year-old high-school "phenom." From his personal observations, he excitedly notes that this boy is a strapping, six-foot-five "physical specimen"–a pitcher who "brings heat" at 95 mph! An actuarial approach would show, however, that high school pitchers have a very low probability of making it to the major leagues (e.g., they may suffer arm problems; they may not have the control and deception in their pitches to get out high-level hitters). The money for a first-round draft selection is thus more wisely invested on a college-age player who, regardless of the velocity of his pitches, has produced evidence over several years in competition against more advanced players that he has the ability to "get hitters out" (such as Barry Zito).

It is instructive that when developing his administrative staff, Beane hired Paul DePodesta, who had no baseball experience. Rather he was educated at Harvard and had the ability to "crunch numbers"–numbers that could be used to inform Beane of which personnel decisions would make the Oakland A's most successful in getting outs and in scoring runs. In *Moneyball*, Lewis notes how DePodesta sought to capitalize on the irrationality inherent in common sense:

> He was fascinated by irrationality, and the opportunities it created in human affairs for anyone who resisted it. He was just the sort of person who might have made an easy fortune in finance, but the market for baseball players, in Paul's view, was far more interesting than anything Wall Street offered. There was, for starters, the tendency for everyone who actually played the game to generalize wildly from his own experience. People always thought their own experience was typical when it wasn't. There was also a tendency to be overly influenced by a guy's most recent performance: what he did last was not necessarily what he would do next. Thirdly–but not lastly–there was the bias toward what people saw with their own eyes, or thought they had seen. The human mind played tricks on itself when it relied exclusively on what it saw, and every trick it played as a financial opportunity for someone who saw through the illusion to the reality. There was a lot you couldn't see when you watched a baseball game.

The Cost of Common-Sense Thinking

Common sense does not ineluctably lead to failure in baseball. The New York Yankees, for example, are able to compensate for mistakes in judgment by using their enormous resources to trade for high-priced players, win the competition for free agents, and sign foreign stars. But for baseball franchises without this financial luxury, the failure to use an evidence-based approach can consign them to episodic success at best and to years of futility at worse. Importantly, their ability to rise above the looming prospect of failure is restricted by their unwillingness to change what they do–to stubbornly rely on common sense and "The Book" rather than on the evidence on "what works" in baseball.

In this context, Lewis's *Moneyball* has three salient lessons for corrections. First, within state government, correctional budgets allotted to treatment interventions are more like that of the Oakland A's than of the Yankees. There are few luxuries and few resources left over to compensate for errors. Money spent on ineffective programs is not balanced with money spent on effective programs. We cannot buy our way to success. Worse still, much as baseball teams are "stuck" with players signed to large contracts who then perform poorly, once in existence, programs that do not work are likely to persist. Second, whereas research evidence is not a panacea for correctional failure–or to winning the World Series–it does provide a basis for a competitive advantage in deciding which programs to select from the universe of potential interventions. Programs can have a higher or lower "winning percentage." As in baseball, evidence-based interventions will outperform those rooted in common sense. They are our "best bets" (Rhine, 1998). Third, the cost of ignoring the evidence can be substantial (Van Voorhis, 1987). In baseball, teams fail, players are traded, managers and coaches are fired, and fans are disillusioned. In corrections, offenders in ineffective programs continue in criminal careers that invariably lead to years of imprisonment and that, along the way, potentially harm scores of victims.

The punch line in this section, of course, is that the choice of boot camps was not inconsequential. Disdaining research and constructing a conventional intervention based solely on unproven common sense opened up the possibility–indeed, the likelihood–of failure. At first, none of this mattered. Enthusiasm reigned and boot camps had their heyday. Over time, however, the appeal of boot camps has been tarnished. This is one case in which research evidence eventually proved too ominous to ignore.

THE FALL OF BOOT CAMPS

Two decades after the inception of the correctional boot camp movement, the bloom is off the rose: Boot camps no longer are seen as unproblematic and certain to work. To be sure, they continue to exist and have not lost all their popularity. But critics have succeeded in making them "controversial" (MacKenzie, Wilson, Armstrong, & Gover, 2001). Common sense, which was an important fuel to the movement, is no longer able to insulate boot camps against scrutiny and serious doubts.

Part of the decline in boot camps' appeal is due to the efforts of critics to deconstruct the image of boot camps as providing tough love that would instill much-needed character in wayward adolescents and younger adults. Instead they offer a different construction of reality: "Camp Fear" (Selcraig, 2000). Thus, boot camps are portrayed as places where youths are humiliated and potentially abused; as places where adult bullies are given unfettered power over vulnerable charges; and as places where aggression is celebrated and likely modeled. These characterizations have taken on meaning when investigations have uncovered instances in which youths experienced psychological deterioration, physical abuse, and callous neglect of illnesses and injuries that resulted in deaths (Selcraig, 2000; see also, Lutze & Brody, 1999; cf. MacKenzie, Wilson, Armstrong, & Gover, 2001; McCorkle, 1995).

But the most devastating blow to the boot camp movement has come from another source: evidence-based corrections. Over time, studies from diverse sources have accumulated that have reached the same discouraging conclusion: Contrary to optimistic claims rooted in common sense, boot camps have not proven effective in reducing recidivism (see, e.g., Cullen et al., 1996; Gendreau, Goggin, Cullen, & Andrews, 2000; Howell, 2003; Jones & Ross, 1997; MacKenzie, 2002; MacKenzie, Wilson, & Kider, 2001; Parent, 2003; Stinchcomb & Terry, 2001). These findings do not mean that some bright spots might not be detected. Thus, boot camps likely are no worse than traditional sanctions and correctional settings; some offenders do better in these camps than do others; they tend to induce short-term positive attitude change; when coupled with treatment and aftercare, they may provide a vehicle to provide effective treatment in a politically palatable way; a program here and there may modestly reduce recidivism; and so on (see, e.g., Benda, Toombs, & Peacock, 2002; Burton, Marquart, Cuvelier, Alarid, & Hunter, 1993; Cullen et al., 1996; Lutze, 1998; MacKenzie, Wilson, Armstrong, & Gover, 2001; Parent, 2003; Tonry, 1996; Trulson, Triplett, & Snell, 2001). Even so, the consensus in the criminological community is that the evidence is persuasive that boot camps are largely a failed enterprise. They have not lived up to expectations, and there is little reason to expose offenders to "shock incarceration" when more effective alternative interventions are available (Gendreau et al., 2000; Latessa et al., 2002).

Again, contrary evidence does not mean that a correctional intervention–in this case, boot camps–will vanish or lose all of their supporters (Stinchcomb & Terry, 2001; see also, Petrosino, Turpin-Petrosino, & Buehler, 2003). But advocates of boot camps now face the daunting prospect of facing critics equipped not simply with their dislike of "camp fear" but also with negative evaluation studies. In the battle against common sense, they are no longer defenseless.

CONCLUSION:
BEYOND COMMON-SENSE CORRECTIONS

Correctional officials and their agencies will be confronted repeatedly with the challenge of how best to invest public monies in the pursuit of public safety. In the past, they have too often made choices based on common sense–on what resonated with their understandings of the world and thus what struck them as most likely to reduce offender recidivism. To a degree, their choices in earlier days were excusable. More often than not, criminologists had provided only the vague admonition that "nothing works" in corrections (Cullen & Gendreau, 2001). Left to their own devices, officials had little direction on what might be the "best bets" in reforming the offenders under their charge.

Fortunately, criminologists no longer are silent regarding what works, what might be promising, and what is irresponsible, if not harmful, to attempt (Cullen & Gendreau, 2001; Lipsey, 1999; MacKenzie, 2000; Rhine, 1998; Sherman et al., 2002; Welsh & Farrington, 2001). We are now entering an era of "evidence-based corrections" in which research is accumulating that can guide programmatic choices (Cullen & Gendreau, 2000; MacKenzie, 2000). Scholars have developed principles of effective intervention that, if followed, produce meaningful reduction in re-offending (Andrews & Bonta, 2003; Cullen, 2002; Cullen & Gendreau, 2000). The decision not to consult this research and allow it to help inform which interventions are initiated is to remain–as those in major league baseball have long done–in a "field of ignorance" (Latessa et al., 2002; Lewis, 2003).

In fact, all of us should continue be wary of common sense. It is dangerous precisely because it seems so correct, leaves our biases unchallenged, and requires virtually no effort to activate. As we have seen, boot camps are a case study in what can occur when common sense is celebrated and allowed to shape our policy decisions. Countless offenders–many of them youths–have been subjected to military-style corrections. Should it not disturb us that these individuals have likely lost an important opportunity to turn their lives around? Should it not bother us that scarce agency funds have been ill spent when more effective interventions might have been employed? Should it not bother us that citizens have subsequently been victimized and public safety sacrificed because common sense blinded us to the inherent criminological defects in boot camps?

The temptation, of course, will be to find value in boot camps–to see how they might be tweaked and used to do some good, such as by grafting on treatment modalities and offering aftercare. We see this strategy as "throwing good money after bad," of ignoring the mounting evidence that boot camps are limited in their effectiveness and are not the best that we can do. Instead, we suggest an alternative vision: We urge officials to start over–to enter the marketplace of interventions, to survey the available correctional options, and then to select for implementation programs for which the research evidence is the most convincing. This approach requires a professional perspective and does not guarantee success. But it does offer the prospect of moving beyond common sense to a point where the most scientifically valid evidence at our disposal guides our correctional future. We have done–and could do–worse.

REFERENCES

Andrews, D. A., & Bonta, J. (2003). *The psychology of criminal conduct* (3rd. ed.). Cincinnati: Anderson.

Benda, B. B., Toombs, N. J., & Peacock, M. (2002). Ecological factors in recidivism: A survival analysis in boot camp graduates after three years. *Journal of Offender Rehabilitation, 35*, 63-85.

Bouffard, L. A. (in press). Examining the relationship between military service and criminal behavior during the Vietnam-era: A research note. *Criminology*.

Burton, V. S., Jr., Marquart, J. W., Cuvelier, S. W., Alarid, L. F., & Hunter, R. J. (1993). A study of attitudinal change among boot camp participants. *Federal Probation, 57* (September), 46-52.

Butterfield, F. (2001, August 10). Prisons grow at lower rate. *The Cincinnati Enquirer*, p. A2.

Butterfield, F. (2003, November 10). States rethink laws on crime. *The Cincinnati Enquirer*, p. A4.

Camp, C. G., & Camp, G. M. (1999). *The corrections yearbook 1999: Adult corrections*. Middletown, CT: Criminal Justice Institute, Inc.

Clear, T. R. (1994). *Harm in American penology: Offenders, victims, and their communities*. Albany, NY: State University of New York Press.

Cullen, F. T. (2002). Rehabilitation and treatment programs. In J. Q. Wilson & J. Petersilia (Eds.), *Crime: Public policies for crime control* (2nd ed., pp. 253-289). Oakland, CA: ICS Press.

Cullen, F. T., Fisher, B. S., & Applegate, B. K. (2000). Public opinion about punishment and corrections. In M. Tonry (Ed.), *Crime and justice: A review of research, Vol. 27* (pp. 1-79). Chicago: University of Chicago Press.

Cullen, F. T., & Gendreau, P. (2000). Assessing correctional rehabilitation: Policy, practice, and prospects. In J. Horney (Ed.), *Criminal justice 2000: Vol. 3. Policies, processes, and decisions of the criminal justice system* (pp. 109-175). Washington, DC: National Institute of Justice, U.S. Department of Justice.

Cullen, F. T., & Gendreau, P. (2001). From nothing works to what works: Changing professional ideology in the 21st century. *The Prison Journal, 81*, 313-338.

Cullen, F. T., Pealer, J. A., Fisher, B. S., Applegate, B. K., & Santana, S. A. (2002). Public support for correctional rehabilitation in America: Change or consistency? In J. Roberts & M. Hough (Eds.), *Changing attitudes to punishment: Public opinion, crime and justice* (pp. 128-147). New York: Taylor and Francis.

Cullen, F. T., Pratt, T. C., Miceli, S. L., & Moon, M. M. (2002). Dangerous liaison? Rational choice theory as the basis for correctional intervention. In A. R. Piquero & S. G. Tibbetts (Eds.), *Rational choice and criminal behavior: Recent research and future challenges*. New York: Routledge.

Cullen, F. T, Wright, J. P., & Applegate, B. K. (1996). "Control in the community: The limits of reform?" In A. T. Harland (Ed.), *Choosing correctional option that work: Defining the demand and evaluating the supply*. Thousand Oaks, CA: Sage.

DiIulio, J. J., Jr. (1991). *No escape: The future of American corrections*. New York: Basic Books.

Gendreau, P. (2000). 1998 Margaret Mead Award address: Rational policies for reforming offenders. In M. McMahon (Ed.), *Assessment to assistance: Programs for women in community corrections* (pp. 329-338). Lanham, MD: American Correctional Association.

Gendreau, P., Cullen, F. T., & Bonta, J. (1994). Intensive rehabilitation supervision: The next generation of community corrections? *Federal Probation, 58* (March), 72-78.

Gendreau, P., Goggin, C., Cullen, F. T., & Andrews, D. A. (2000). The effects of community sanctions and incarceration on recidivism. *Forum on Corrections Research, 12* (May), 10-13.

Gendreau, P., Goggin, C., Cullen, F. T., & Paparozzi, M. (2002). The common-sense revolution and correctional policy. In J. McGuire (Ed.), *Offender rehabilitation and treatment: Effective programs and policies to reduce re-offending* (pp. 359-386). Chichester, UK: John Wiley.

Glaze, L. E. (2003). *Probation and parole in the United States, 2002.* Washington, DC: Bureau of Justice Statistics, U.S. Department of Justice.

Glenn, D. (2003, October 24). Nightmare scenarios. *Chronicle of Higher Education,* pp. A14-17.

Glueck, S., & Glueck, E. (1950). *Unraveling juvenile delinquency.* New York: The Commonwealth Fund.

Gottfredson, M. D., & Hirschi, T. (1990). *A general theory of crime.* Stanford, CA: Stanford University Press.

Harrison, P. M., & Beck, A. J. (2003). *Prisoners in 2002.* Washington, DC: Bureau of Justice Statistics, U.S. Department of Justice.

Howell, J. C. (2003). *Preventing and reducing juvenile delinquency: A comprehensive framework.* Thousand Oaks, CA: Sage.

Irwin, J., & Austin, J. (1994). *It's about time: America's imprisonment binge.* Belmont, CA: Wadsworth.

Jones, M., & Ross, D. L. (1997). Is less better? Boot camp, regular probation, and rearrest in North Carolina. *American Journal of Criminal Justice, 21,* 147-161.

Latessa, E. J., Cullen, F. T., & Gendreau, P. (2002). Beyond correctional quackery: Professionalism and the possibility of effective treatment. *Federal Probation, 66,* (2), 43-49.

Lewis, M. (2003). *Moneyball: The art of winning an unfair game.* New York: W. W. Norton.

Lipsey, M. W. (1999). Can intervention rehabilitate serious delinquents? *Annals of the American Academy of Political and Social Science, 564,* 142-166.

Lutze, F. E. (1998). Are shock incarceration programs more rehabilitative than traditional prisons? A survey of inmates. *Justice Quarterly, 15,* 547-566.

Lutze, F. E., & Brody, D. (1999). Mental abuse and unusual punishment: Do boot camp prisons violate the Eighth Amendment? *Crime and Delinquency, 45,* 242-255.

MacKenzie, D. L. (2000). Evidence-based corrections: Identifying what works. *Crime and Delinquency, 46,* 457-471.

MacKenzie, D. L. (2002). Reducing the criminal activities of known offenders and delinquents: Crime prevention in the courts and corrections. In L. W. Sherman, D. P.

Farrington, B. C. Welsh, & D. L. MacKenzie (Eds.), *Evidence-based crime prevention* (pp. 330-404). New York: Routledge.

MacKenzie, D. L., & Hebert, E. E. (Eds.). (1996). *Correctional boot camps: A tough intermediate sanction*. Washington, DC: National Institute of Justice, U.S. Department of Justice.

MacKenzie, D. L., Shaw, J., & Gowdy, V. (1993). *An evaluation of shock incarceration programs in Louisiana*. Washington, DC: National Institute of Justice, U.S. Department of Justice.

MacKenzie, D. L., Wilson, D. B., Armstrong, G. S., & Gover, A. R. (2001). The impact of boot camps and traditional institutions on juvenile residents: Perceptions, adjustment, and changes. *Journal of Research in Crime and Delinquency, 38*, 279-313.

MacKenzie, D. L., Wilson, D. B., & Kider, S. B. (2001). Effects of correctional boot camps on offending. *Annals of the American Academy of Political and Social Science, 588*, 126-143.

McCorkle, R. C. (1995). Correctional boot camps and change in attitude: Is all this shouting necessary? A research note. *Justice Quarterly, 12*, 365-375.

McKelvey, B. (1977). *American prisons: A history of good intentions*. Montclair, NJ: Patterson Smith.

Morris, N., & Tonry, M. (1990). *Between prison and probation: Intermediate punishment in a rational sanctioning system*. New York: Oxford University Press.

Nisbett, R., & Ross, L. (1980). *Human inference: Strategies and shortcomings of social judgement*. Englewood Cliffs, NJ: Prentice Hall.

Parent, D. (2003). *Correctional boot camps: Lessons from a decade of research*. Washington, DC: National Institute of Justice, U.S. Department of Justice.

Petrosino, A., Turpin-Petrosino, C., & Buehler, J. (2003). Scared straight and other juvenile awareness programs for preventing juvenile delinquency: A systematic review of the randomized experimental evidence. *Annals of the American Academy of Political and Social Science, 589*, 41-62.

Rand, A. (1987). Transitional life events and desistance from delinquency and crime. In M. Wolfgang, T. P. Thornberry, & R. Figlio (Eds.), *From boy to man, from delinquency to crime* (pp. 134-162). Chicago: University of Chicago Press.

Rhine, E. E. (Ed.). (1998). *Best practices: Excellence in corrections*. Lanham, MD: American Correctional Association.

Salant, J. D. (2002, August 26). 6.6 million in U.S. prisons or on parole or probation. *The Cincinnati Enquirer*, p. A1.

Sampson, R. J., & Laub, J. H. (1993). *Crime in the making: Pathways and turning points through life*. Cambridge, MA: Harvard University Press.

Sampson, R. J., & Laub, J. H. (1996). Socioeconomic achievement in the life course of disadvantaged men: Military service as a turning point, circa 1940-1965. *American Sociological Review, 61*, 347-367.

Selcraig, B. (2000). Camp fear. *Mother Jones* (November-December), 64-71.

Sherman, L. W., Farrington, D. P., Welsh, B. C., & MacKenzie, D. L. (Eds.). (2002). *Evidence-based crime prevention*. New York: Routledge.

Stinchcomb, J. B., & Terry, W. C., III. (2001). Predicting the likelihood of rearrest among shock incarceration graduates: Moving beyond another nail in the boot camp coffin. *Crime and Delinquency, 47*, 221-242.

Thaler, R. H., & Sunstein, C. R. (2003, September 1). Who's on first? *The New Republic*, pp. 27-30.
Tonry, M. (1996). *Sentencing matters*. New York: Oxford University Press.
Trulson, C., Triplett, R., & Snell, C. (2001). Social control in a school setting: Evaluating a school-based boot camp. *Crime and Delinquency, 47,* 573-609.
Van Voorhis, P. (1987). Correctional effectiveness: The high cost of avoiding success. *Federal Probation, 51* (March), 59-62.
Vaughn, M. (1994). Boot camps. *The Grapevine, 2* (Fall), 2.
Welsh, B. C., & Farrington, D. P. (2001). Toward an evidence-based approach to preventing crime. *Annals of the American Academy of Political and Social Science, 578,* 158-173.
Wright, J. P., Carter, D., & Cullen, F. T. (in press). A life-course analysis of military service in Vietnam. *Journal of Research in Crime and Delinquency*.

AUTHORS' NOTES

Francis T. Cullen, PhD (Columbia University), is Distinguished Research Professor of Criminal Justice and Sociology at the University of Cincinnati. His most recent works include *Combating Corporate Crime: Local Prosecutors at Work, Criminological Theory: Context and Consequences,* and *Criminological Theory: Past to Present–Essential Readings*. His current research focuses on the impact of social support on crime, the measurement of sexual victimization, and rehabilitation as a correctional policy. He is President of the American Society of Criminology and a Past President of the Academy of Criminal Justice Sciences.

Kristie R. Blevins is a PhD candidate in criminal justice at the University of Cincinnati. Her publications and research interests are in the areas of correctional rehabilitation, fairness in the application of capital punishment, public attitudes toward and the effectiveness of gun laws, and the impact of southern culture on criminal justice.

Jennifer S. Trager is a PhD candidate in criminal justice at the University of Cincinnati. Her research interests are in the areas of cognitive-behavioral treatment, program effectiveness, evaluation research, and human development and crime.

Paul Gendreau, PhD (Queens University), is University Research Professor of Psychology and Director of the Center for Criminal Justice Studies at the University of New Brunswick, Saint John. He is a Past President of the Canadian Psychological Association. In his career, he has worked in criminal justice settings as an administrator, clinician, and consultant. He has published extensively, especially in articulating principles of effective intervention in response to the "nothing works doctrine." His research interests include the prediction of criminal behavior, the effects of prison life, and the evaluation of correctional programs.

Address correspondence to Francis T. Cullen, Division of Criminal Justice, PO Box 210389, University of Cincinnati, Cincinnati, OH 45221-0389 (E-mail: cullenft@email.uc.edu).

A Randomized Evaluation of the Maryland Correctional Boot Camp for Adults: Effects on Offender Antisocial Attitudes and Cognitions

OJMARRH MITCHELL

University of Nevada, Las Vegas

DORIS L. MACKENZIE

University of Maryland

DEANNA M. PÉREZ

Virginia Department of Corrections

ABSTRACT This research addresses the question: Does the military atmosphere of a treatment-oriented boot camp lead to greater reductions in antisocial attitudes and cognitions than a standard correctional facility that is also treatment-oriented? A self-report measure of antisocial attitudes and cognitions was collected from 118 inmates randomly assigned to a boot camp program or a standard correctional facility. Analyses of post-program data revealed no significant or substantive differences between groups suggesting that the combination of a military atmosphere and therapeutic programming may not be any more efficacious in reducing antisocial attitudes than the administration of similar therapeutic programming in traditional correctional facilities. *[Article copies available for a fee from The Haworth Document Delivery Service: 1-800-HAWORTH. E-mail* address: <docdelivery@haworthpress.com> Website: <http://www.HaworthPress.com> © 2005 by The Haworth Press, Inc. All rights reserved.]

KEYWORDS Boot camps, experimental design, antisocial attitudes, prison

INTRODUCTION

Considerable research has investigated the effectiveness of boot camps on offender recidivism. A recent comprehensive meta-analysis of this research found 44 independent boot camp/comparison sample contrasts (MacKenzie, Wilson, & Kider, 2001). Overall, this meta-analysis found little evidence to support the notion that boot camps are more effective in reducing the recidivism rates of program participants than traditional correctional methods (e.g., probation, jail). In fact, their analysis found no overall significant difference in recidivism between boot camp participants and comparison samples.

MacKenzie and colleagues' meta-analytic synthesis also revealed voids in the existing body of research. Specifically, MacKenzie and associates found that none of these evaluations assessed an *adult* correctional program utilizing an experimental design. Further, the internal validity of the five existing experimental evaluations of juvenile correctional boot camps was negatively affected by high attrition rates and/or the exclusion of a large number of program dropouts. Therefore, none of these 44 evaluations of boot camp programs achieved the highest rating of internal validity–a randomized experiment, uncompromised by selection bias.

Further, while the cumulative results from these studies support the conclusion that boot camps are no more effective in reducing offender recidivism, there is some evidence that suggests boot camps with a therapeutic orientation may be successful in reducing recidivism. Specifically, MacKenzie, Brame, McDowall, and Souryal (1995), in concordance with Wilson et al. (2001), found that while boot camps in general did not reduce recidivism, programs incorporating greater levels of therapeutic activities (e.g., drug treatment, academic education, life skills education) and programs targeting prison-bound offenders did significantly reduce recidivism in comparison to traditional correctional institutions. Such findings suggest that it is too early to definitively conclude that boot camp programs are ineffective at crime reductions, as it is possible that the integration of the boot camp model and therapeutic programming may produce a synergy capable of reducing recidivism.

To our knowledge, the current evaluation is the first fully randomized experimental evaluation of an adult boot camp program. The present research analyzes the effect of participation in a boot camp on antisocial attitudes, an intermediate measure of recidivism. Criminological theory and prior research has established that such antisocial attitudes are strongly related to criminal conduct and recidivism (Akers, 2000; Andrews & Bonta, 1998; Gendreau, Little, & Goggin, 1996). In fact, Gendreau and colleagues found that the strongest predictor of recidivism was "criminal needs," a concept that included antisocial attitudes.

Specifically, this research is designed to address the question: Does the military atmosphere of a treatment-oriented boot camp lead to greater reductions in antisocial attitudes and cognitions than a standard correctional facility that is likewise treatment-oriented? In other words, does the combination of the military model and therapeutic programming lead to greater reductions in future criminal behavior than a standard correctional facility that emphasizes treatment? Specifically, this evaluation is designed to assess whether the Herman L. Toulson Boot Camp is more effective in reducing antisocial attitudes and cognitions than the Metropolitan Transition Center correctional facility, which has a similar treatment orientation.

We hypothesize that therapeutic programming, when integrated into a military atmosphere, is more effective in reducing recidivism than the same programming provided in a traditional correctional environment. This expectation is based on our personal observation that the military atmosphere demands more active and attentive participation in therapeutic programming than that exhibited in traditional facilities. The authors' personal experiences from many years of observing boot camp programs leads us to believe that participants in boot camps are more actively engaged in the various therapeutic activities than similar programs administered in traditional facilities. From these observations, many offenders engaged in treatment programs in traditional facilities passively resist such programming by not paying attention, acting disruptively, sleeping, and so forth. In contrast, the military atmosphere of boot camps forbids such forms of passive resistance, and therefore we hypothesize treatment programs in such environments will provide greater reductions in future antisocial behavior.

Program Descriptions

The Herman L. Toulson Correctional Boot Camp (hereafter "TBC") for adult offenders was established in 1990, in an effort to reduce prison overcrowding and as a means to encourage inmates to become responsible, productive citizens. The TBC has a maximum program capacity of 430 male and female offenders; however, only male offenders are housed at the facility. Female offenders participating in the program are not actually housed at the TBC. Instead female offenders are transported to the facility from a nearby women's facility each morning.

Programmatically, the TBC is a three-phase, six-month regiment that integrates a strong treatment component, including academic education, life skills training, and substance abuse education/treatment, into a military atmosphere.

As with all correctional boot camps, the TBC is modeled to resemble military basic training. This training emphasizes military fundamentals such as facing movements, marching, rigorous physical training, and manual labor. The military atmosphere also requires that inmates wear uniforms and conduct themselves in accordance with strict boot camp rules.

In addition to this military component, three therapeutic elements are utilized at the TBC. First, academic education is stressed; all inmates without a high school diploma or GED receive adult academic education, focusing on helping inmates obtain a GED. Second, boot camp inmates are also required to participate in a group-based drug education/treatment program. The drug education program teaches inmates about addictions and how to identify them, examines the multiple facets of individual addictions, and helps offenders develop strategies for conquering their addictions. Third, inmates are required to take part in a life skills training program, which focuses on pro-social decision-making and problem solving. The life skills component is based on a cognitive-behavioral approach, whereby inmates are taught to modify antisocial, self-centered, impulsive thinking patterns. The focus is on challenging these cognitions by teaching inmates to reflect on the consequences of their behavior and practice new thinking patterns in role-playing exercises. TBC also provides inmates who already have either a high school diploma or GED an opportunity to participate in vocational training (e.g., introductory fiber-optics installation training taught by a local community college, carpentry, electrical work).

The daily schedule of boot camp inmates varies somewhat by phase. In all phases, a typical day at TBC camp begins at 5 a.m. The day begins with inmates cleaning themselves and their housing areas. Phase I focuses on physical activity and military drill, whereas the two latter phases emphasize work projects. At 6 a.m., breakfast service begins. In Phase I, after breakfast, inmates engage in a regimen of physical training (e.g., push-ups, jogging, running through an obstacle course) and barracks inspection. Around mid-morning, Phase I inmates attend academic education and drug treatment programs. In the afternoons, inmates in Phase I engage in military drill instruction, then more physical training and educational programs. In Phase II and III of the program, typically inmates are assigned to road crew, which requires inmates to remove litter from Maryland roadways from 7 a.m. to 3 p.m. In the evenings, inmates attend boot camp community meetings, job skills training, and have time set aside for academic study. In short, inmates incarcerated at the TBC are involved in some form of structured activity all day long; there is little to no idle time.

Participants in the boot camp program are compared to inmates incarcerated at the Metropolitan Transition Center (hereafter "MTC"), a standard correctional facility that offers male inmates similar academic education, life skills training, and substance abuse education and treatment, sans the military atmosphere. While these therapeutic programs are available to all inmates at

MTC, participation in these programs was mandatory for the inmates involved in this study as a condition of their MAP contracts. Thus, with the exception of the vocational training provided by the TBC to a limited number of inmates, the two facilities offer similar programs. The most salient difference between the two facilities is the inclusion of the military component at the TBC. Another salient difference between the programs is that the TBC provides services to women although these female offenders are not housed at the TBC, whereas the MTC neither houses nor provides services to female offenders.

Over the years, the mission of the MTC has evolved from that of a maximum security prison to a prison directed at preparing inmates for re-entry back to the community (Shugg, 1995). Currently the facility houses approximately 1,500 male offenders, all of whom are on pre-release status. Thus, inmates at MTC serve 18 months or less before their expected parole release date.

The typical day in the MTC also begins early; however, there is much less structure at this facility. The first wake-up call begins at 5:00 a.m. and breakfast service begins at 5:30 a.m., although many inmates choose to skip breakfast in order to sleep in. Inmates are typically locked down after breakfast until the first recreation period (9:30 a.m.). After recreation, some inmates participate in various programming activities such as education classes, drug education classes, and life skills training. Inmates not involved in these programs are assigned to various cleaning projects or are confined to their cells until lunch service begins. After lunch, inmates involved in the various treatment programs resume these activities, while other inmates are allowed another recreation period. Before dinner, there is another recreation period. After dinner, inmates are usually locked in their cells or dormitories. In short, inmates are involved in unstructured activities for most of the day. Inmates confined at MTC occupy their days by watching television, reading, sleeping, or playing games (e.g., dominoes, various card games) with other inmates.

The inmates at the MTC are not required to adhere to the same military code of conduct present at TBC. Inmates are not required to wear uniforms. Instead, inmates dress in their own clothes and shoes. Furthermore, interactions between inmates and staff (or visitors) lack the formality of similar interactions present at the TBC.

Eligibility Criteria

All offenders included in the present evaluation had to be accepted into the boot camp program as "Part IA" offenders.[1] Further, because the comparison facility only accommodated males, the evaluation was forced to constrain the research sample to only male offenders. To be classified by the Maryland Division of Correction as a Part IA offender, inmates had to be less than 36 years of age, serving their first adult term of incarceration,[2] serving a sentence for a non-violent offense, serving a sentence of 5 years or less, and physically and psychologically fit to participate in the program. Inmates meeting these criteria were asked to volunteer for the program by entering into a Mutual Agreement Program (MAP) contract with the Maryland Parole Commission and the Maryland Division of Corrections. The MAP contract dictates the program components and conditions the inmate must complete in order to be paroled. Standard conditions of these MAP contracts dictate that offenders must engage in academic education, life skills training, drug education/treatment, and avoid infractions of facility rules. If the inmate completes the conditions stipulated by the MAP contract, they are guaranteed an early parole release date–typically six months after entry into the boot camp. That is, in exchange for completing these conditions, the offender's sentence is reduced to six months (the length of the boot camp program); this sentence reduction results in inmates being released anywhere from 6 to 18 months early.

It is important to note, however, that final determination of program eligibility is made by the Maryland Parole Commission. The Parole Commission interviews each inmate determined to be statutorily eligible for the program based on the above criteria. In some instances, the Parole Commission will reject inmates who meet the stated program eligibility criteria. Further, in rare instances, the Parole Commission and an inmate will enter into a MAP agreement that requires the inmate to complete a sentence longer than 6 months.

METHOD

This study is a randomized experimental evaluation of Maryland's only correctional boot camp for adult offenders. The evaluation of this program is designed to qualitatively and quantitatively evaluate whether a correctional boot camp for adults with a treatment orientation produces more favorable outcomes than a traditional correctional facility that also emphasizes treatment, but does not have a military component. The evaluation of TBC is ongoing. The full evaluation will compare and contrast inmate experiences while incarcerated in the two facilities, inmate perceptions of program effectiveness, and recidivism rates of the experimental and control groups. The present analysis focuses on assessing the boot camp program's effect on an intermediate measure of program effectiveness. Specifically, the current analysis provides a preliminary assessment of the TBC's effect on antisocial attitudes and cognitions.

Random Assignment Procedure

Male inmates who were classified as Part IA offenders and who were determined to be eligible for the boot camp program by the Parole Commission were randomly assigned to either the TBC or the MTC by the research team. Random assignment was accomplished via a random number generator, which assigned inmates to the two facilities using simple random assignment.

Random assignment decisions were final. Neither inmates nor correctional staff members were allowed to override the random assignment decision. Furthermore, inmates were not allowed to decline participation in the random assignment procedure; all male inmates classified as Part IA offenders and with approved MAP contracts were included in this evaluation. To date, no deviations from the random assignment procedure have occurred.

Data Collection

At the beginning of each month, a new platoon of eight to twenty inmates was drawn into the research sample. As the first step in the data collection procedure, the research team coded pertinent information from each offender's Division of Corrections file. These files contained data on offender demographics, current offense, current sentence, prior criminal history (arrests and convictions), and scheduled release date. The data collection process also included two 45-minute self-report surveys. The first self-report survey ("baseline survey") was administered just prior to the commencement of the MAP contract (i.e., program start date), typically 3 to 4 days before program start. Further, inmates were not told their facility assignment until after the baseline survey was complete. The second survey ("exit survey") was administered just prior to program completion, typically about a week before inmates were released.

These self-report surveys serve three primary purposes. First, the surveys are a valuable source of background data, such as employment history, education, drug use history, and prior criminal behavior. Second, these surveys were designed to assess change in antisocial attitudes and cognitions. The baseline and exit surveys contain identical scales designed to measure antisocial attitudes, values, and feelings. Third, the exit survey asked inmates a series of questions designed to measure their perceptions of their conditions of confinement. Specifically, inmates were asked to assess the safety of their facility and to rate how helpful the various treatment programs were in preparing them for the future.

The baseline survey was administered prior to program commencement date. Specifically, while inmates were awaiting final program eligibility decisions, they were housed at the TBC in a separate "staging" area reserved for inmates awaiting eligibility decisions. Inmates in the staging area were not allowed to participate in the regular boot camp activities; they were held in this area pending a final eligibility determination.

Once a month, around the time program eligibility status decisions were made, trained survey facilitators solicited participation from inmates eligible for inclusion in the study (Part IA offenders) to complete a 45-minute voluntary, self-report survey. The inmates were advised of their rights as participants in the evaluation and were asked to sign informed consent forms. The self-report survey was administered to each incoming platoon and they were interviewed as a group. The survey was read aloud to aid inmates with reading deficiencies.

The exit survey was also administered once a month by the same group of trained survey facilitators. Approximately one week before inmates were released to the community, the survey facilitators traveled to both facilities. There, the survey facilitators gathered the outgoing group of inmates and asked each inmate to participate in the exit survey. As with the baseline survey, inmates were advised of their rights as participants in the evaluation and signed reminder informed consent forms. Generally, inmates were usually eager to participate in the survey and provide details of their experiences while incarcerated. Once again, the survey was read aloud as an aid to inmates with reading difficulties.

Data collection began in January of 2002 and is ongoing. As of September 2003, a total of 195 inmates have met the eligibility criteria for inclusion in this evaluation; 93 (48%) of these offenders were assigned to the TBC and the remaining 102 (52%) were assigned to the MTC. Of the 195 inmates included in the random assignment portion of this evaluation, 193 (99%) agreed to participate in the baseline self-report survey. At the time of this writing, all inmates asked to participate in the exit survey have completed the self-report survey.[3] This research focuses on the 118 inmates who have completed both the baseline and exit surveys with a focus on assessing change in antisocial attitudes and cognitions.

A small number of inmates in the evaluation have had their MAP contracts revoked. The MAP contracts that all inmates must sign to participate in the TBC program (and hence our evaluation of the boot camp) outline clear grounds for termination of the MAP contract. In essence, the MAP contract stipulates that inmates convicted of any infraction resulting in 30 or more days of segregation, convicted of more than two infractions at any one institution, charged with escape, charged with a new criminal offense, or re-classified to a higher security level will have their MAP contract terminated. Upon the termination of the MAP contract, the inmate's full sentence is reinstated, i.e., the inmate's guaranteed parole release date is withdrawn and the inmate is released in accordance to standard parole release practices. These rules apply to inmates housed in both TBC and MTC.

Currently, six offenders (3%) have had their MAP contracts terminated for violating the conditions of the agreement. Five of the terminations occurred at the TBC and one termination occurred at the MTC. All of the inmates were terminated because of disciplinary infractions (e.g., fighting, possessing contraband, and failure to participate in one or more the program components described above). The higher rate of terminations evident at the boot camp facility appears to be attributable to the fact that the boot camp places more demands on its inmates (e.g., participation in physical therapy) and has

Table 1: Description of Survey Data Attrition

	TBC (n = 93)	MTC (n = 102)
Full Sample	93 (48%)	102 (52%)
Refused to participate in survey	1	1
Still serving sentence	30	29
Terminated from program	6	1
Released prior to exit survey	2	4
Too much missing data	5	3
Valid survey data (time 1 and 2)	49 (43%)	64 (57%)

closer supervision of inmates than the MTC (see Table 1 for a description of sample attrition). The differential rates of attrition are somewhat troublesome, as selection bias becomes an issue to the extent that attriters are different in important ways to non-attriters. However, given the low rates of attrition, the potential distorting effects of selection bias are believed to be minimal.

Measures

The measure of antisocial attitudes utilized in the present analysis is a subscale of the Self-Appraisal Questionnaire (SAQ). The SAQ is a 72-item self-report survey designed to predict recidivism (Loza, Dhaliwal, Kroner, & Loza-Fanous, 2000). The SAQ has seven subscales Criminal Tendencies (CT), Antisocial Personality Problems, Conduct Problems, Criminal History, Alcohol/Drug Abuse, Antisocial Associates, and Anger. The 27-item CT scale is particularly important for the current research, as this scale is designed to assess "antisocial attitudes, beliefs, behaviors, and feelings" (Loza et al., 2000: 360). Prior theory and research has established that such attitudes are strongly related to criminal conduct and recidivism (Akers, 2000; Andrews & Bonta, 1998; Gendreau, Little, & Goggin, 1996). These antisocial attitudes and cognitions are particularly suitable for study not only because they have been found to be strongly related to recidivism but also because they are a dynamic, mutable factor that can be targeted by correctional interventions (Gendreau et al., 1996). Furthermore, the SAQ as a whole and its subscales have been found to be reliable in a sample of incarcerated offenders (Loza et al., 2000) and several studies have demonstrated the SAQ's predictive validity in samples of incarcerated offenders (Kroner & Loza, 2001; Loza et al., 2000; Loza & Loza-Fanous, 2000, 2001).

RESULTS

Research Sample

The present analysis includes the 118 inmates who were randomly assigned to the two experimental conditions and who have been released back into the community. After list-wise deletion of cases with missing data on more than 15% of the 27-item CT scale, 113 inmates remained for the following analysis (49 inmates from TBC and 64 inmates from MTC). Ninety-seven of these inmates had no missing data; mean imputation of missing data was used to estimate 16 inmates' score on the measure of antisocial attitudes. By analyzing a data set of this limited size, all but relatively large differences will not be detected at conventional levels of statistical significance. In fact, analyses indicate that in order to achieve statistical power of 0.80, we would need to observe a between-group standardized mean difference effect size of approximately 0.54 (two-tailed, $\alpha = 0.05$). Thus, it needs to be emphasized that the current analysis lacks the statistical power necessary to detect small to moderate between-group differences.

From Table 1, it is apparent that the research sample is highly homogeneous; the overwhelming majority of the offenders in this evaluation were young African-Americans from Baltimore City, convicted of drug offenses. Chi-square and t-test procedures were utilized to compare the two experimental conditions. Given the random assignment process and the high degree of homogeneity apparent in this sample, it is not surprising that the two groups of inmates are highly similar. In fact, none of the comparisons between the two groups at program entry were statistically significant using a conventional α of 0.05 or a statistically more powerful α of 0.10.

The mean age of the combined sample of offenders was roughly 23 years old, and this did not vary meaningfully across groups. Similarly, over 85% of the combined sample of offenders were African-Americans and this also did not vary substantially across groups. Moreover, the vast majority of offenders (90%) were convicted of drug offenses (i.e., drug sales or violations of probation for an original drug conviction) with similar proportions from both groups serving sentences for drug crimes. As might be expected, given the research sample's involvement in the drug trade, a high percentage of both the experimental and control groups self-reported drug use in the 12 months prior to their incarceration. The majority of respondents reported marijuana use (76%) in the past 12 months, and substantially fewer respondents reported use of cocaine, heroin, or other drugs (15%).

In spite of the fact that one of the program eligibility criteria required that all offenders be serving their first extended term of incarceration, most of the offenders in the sample have substantial criminal histories. The mean number of prior arrests and prior convictions were 4.5 and 1.5, respectively, based on official criminal history record checks of adult records. Self-reports also indicated substantial criminal histories. On average, offenders reported nearly 7 lifetime arrests (including juvenile arrests) and 38% reported having spent time in a juvenile reformatory (i.e., training school, reformatory, group home).

Perhaps most important, comparisons of the experimental and control conditions also indicated there were no significant differences on either the measure of antisocial attitudes (i.e., the Criminal Tendencies scale) or SAQ total score at program entry (see top portion of Table 2). Both of these measures revealed that the control condition had somewhat greater mean levels of criminal tendencies than the experimental condition at program entry. However, while these differences were not significantly different, the observed differences are non-negligible. In fact, transforming the observed mean differences on the SAQ Criminal Tendencies subscale into a standardized mean difference effect size produces an effect size of -0.32. Given this effect size, we believe that a prudent post-program analysis must account for the possibility that the two groups may have pre-existing differences on our measure of antisocial attitudes.

Post-Program Comparisons

Just prior to being released back into the community both groups of inmates were surveyed a second time (exit survey). Among other measures, the exit survey re-assessed inmates' antisocial attitudes with the SAQ. Given the strong relationship between antisocial attitudes and criminal behavior, it was expected that if the boot camp program is to be effective in reducing future criminality, then the program should also reduce antisocial attitudes in comparison to the control condition. Thus, antisocial attitudes serve as an intermediate outcome in this evaluation, mediating the relationship between boot camp participation and recidivism.

The lower portion of Table 2 reports the results of a test of the hypothesis that the boot camp program (TBC) is more effective in reducing antisocial attitudes than a standard correctional facility (MTC). By comparing baseline and exit scores on the Criminal Tendencies subscale of the SAQ, it is apparent that neither program, in absolute terms, was successful in reducing antisocial attitudes. In fact, inmates in both programs reported somewhat higher mean levels of antisocial attitudes upon release than at entry into the evaluation (Table 3).

In relative terms, however, inmates released from the boot camp reported lower antisocial attitudes in comparison to inmates released from the standard correctional facility. A *t*-test of post-program means reveals that the observed differences were not statistically significant at conventional levels of statistical significance [$t(111) = 1.78, p = 0.08$]. These observed mean differences translate into a standardized mean difference effect size of -0.34. If there had been no evidence of pre-existing group differences, then these results would provide some support for our hypothesis. However, given that the two groups exhibited non-trivial pre-existing differences at program entry, we also

Table 2: Sample Characteristics by Experimental Condition

Variable	TBC (*n* = 49)	MTC (*n* = 64)
Mean Age (*SD*)	22.94 (3.70)	23.33 (4.16)
Race		
African-American	43 (88%)	54 (84%)
White	6 (12%)	10 (16%)
Marital Status		
Married/Cohabitate	23 (47%)	25 (39%)
Single/Divorced/Separated	26 (53%)	39 (61%)
Education		
8th Grade or Less	5 (10%)	3 (5%)
9th Grade	10 (20%)	12 (19%)
10-11th Grade	19 (39%)	30 (47%)
High School Grad/GED	10 (20%)	13 (20%)
More than High School	5 (10%)	6 (9%)
Employment Status		
Full-Time	18 (40%)	27 (45%)
Part-Time/Irregular	14 (31%)	15 (25%)
Unemployed	13 (29%)	18 (30%)
County of Residence		
Baltimore City	35 (71%)	42 (66%)
Baltimore County	2 (5%)	3 (4%)
Prince George's County	2 (4%)	1 (2%)
Other Counties	10 (20%)	18 (28%)
Any Drug Use, Past 12 Months		
Yes	40 (83%)	49 (77%)
No	8 (17%)	15 (23%)
Incarcerated on a Drug Offense		
Yes	44 (90%)	58 (91%)
No	5 (10%)	6 (9%)
Mean Age at First Arrest (*SD*)	15.57 (2.45)	16.37 (4.88)
Mean Number of Self-Reported Arrests, Lifetime (*SD*)	7.30 (4.37)	6.48 (5.86)
Mean Number of Official Arrests, Adult Only (*SD*)	4.49 (4.63)	4.56 (3.59)
Mean Number of Prior Convictions (*SD*)	1.59 (1.24)	1.56 (1.31)
Sentence Length, in Months (*SD*)	42.59 (10.81)	43.06 (11.39)

* $p < 0.10$; ** $p < 0.05$

Table 3: Antisocial Attitudes by Experimental Condition

Variable	TBC (*n* = 49) Mean (*SD*)	MTC (*n* = 64) Mean (*SD*)
Program Entry		
SAQ Criminal Tendencies	10.58 (4.18)	12.14 (5.24)
SAQ Total Score[a]	27.27 (8.67)	28.08 (10.37)
Program Exit		
SAQ Criminal Tendencies	11.39 (3.99)	12.98 (5.22)
Gain Score SAQ Criminal Tendencies	0.80 (4.94)	0.85 (3.78)

* $p < 0.10$; ** $p < 0.05$
[a] SAQ Total Score excludes the SAQ Anger scale in order to make these scores comparable to SAQ scores reported in previous research (e.g., Loza et al., 2000).

compared gain scores from the two groups and conducted a *t*-test on these gain scores (see Table 2). From this analysis of group gain scores, it is apparent that the two groups did not exhibit statistically significant differential rates of change [$t(87.3$ unequal variances$) = 0.05$, $p = 0.96$], with a corresponding standardized mean difference effect size of -0.01. Clearly, in both statistical and substantive terms, the between-group differences on gain scores are negligible; therefore, the authors' hypothesis was not supported in these preliminary data.

DISCUSSION

This research began with the hypothesis that the integration of therapeutic programming into the military atmosphere of a correctional boot camp program would reduce antisocial attitudes and cognitions more effectively than the same therapeutic programming administered in a standard correctional facility. Based on the authors' observations of boot camp programs, we expected that participants in boot camp programs would be more actively engaged in such programs in comparison to participants in traditional correctional facilities. As a consequence of this heightened level of active participation, we expected therapeutic programming administered within a boot camp to produce greater treatment benefits than very similar treatment programs administered in a standard correctional facility. Further, we hypothesized that reductions in antisocial attitudes and cognitions are a key intermediate outcome mediating the relationship between boot camp participation and reductions in subsequent criminal behavior.

A preliminary analysis of the experimental data suggests that this hypothesis was not supported. Inmates were randomly assigned to either the boot camp program condition or the control condition. Prior to the administration of the treatment program, comparisons of the two groups of offenders indicated that these groups did not display any statistically significant differences; however, on the key dependent variable (antisocial attitudes as measured by the Criminal Tendencies subscale of the SAQ) the two groups displayed a non-trivial difference at program entry. At the conclusion of the treatment program, the two groups continued to display differences in antisocial attitudes of the same magnitude as at program entry. Therefore, based on these preliminary data, we cannot conclude that the combination of a military atmosphere and therapeutic programming produced greater treatment benefits than the same therapeutic programming administered without a military component.

Proponents of boot camp programs often promote boot camps as an effective means to reduce recidivism (e.g., Clark & Aziz, 1996; MacKenzie & Hebert, 1996), whereas critics of boot camps contend that these programs are not only ineffective, but may also promote increased criminal behavior (Morash & Rucker, 1990; Sechrest, 1989). Assuming that the predictive validity of the SAQ holds in this sample, our findings offer little support to either side of this debate. Thus, these results comport with the findings from the cumulative body of existing research regarding the effectiveness of boot camp programs in reducing recidivism (see MacKenzie et al., 2001).

The current study's findings must be tempered by several factors. First and foremost, these results are preliminary and may not hold after data collection is complete. Second, the current research did not actually assess offender criminal behavior–only criminal tendencies. It is entirely possible that, in spite of the similarity between groups on our measure of antisocial attitudes, the two groups could still differ on rates of recidivism. Continued data collection and analyses are necessary before more firm conclusions can be drawn.

NOTES

1. Other classifications of offenders also participate in the boot camp program; however, this evaluation focuses on Part IA offenders, who are the most common type of offender accepted into the program.

2. Incarceration is defined as a period of post-conviction confinement of 60 days or more.

3. Six inmates were released before research staff were able to solicit participation. Further, the sample is limited to 118 because not all 193 offenders interviewed at baseline have expired the 6 months thus far and thus have not completed the exit survey.

REFERENCES

Akers, R.L. (1998). *Social learning and social structure: A general theory of crime and deviance*. Boston, MA: Northeastern University Press.

Andrews, D.A., & Bonta, J. (1992). *The psychology of criminal conduct*. Cincinnati, OH: Anderson.

Clark, C.L., & Aziz, D.L. (1996). Shock incarceration in New York State: Philosophy, results, and limitations. In D.L. MacKenzie & E.E. Hebert (Eds.), *Correctional boot camps: A tough intermediate sanction* (pp. 39-68). Washington, DC: U.S. Department of Justice, National Institute of Justice.

Gendreau, P., Little, T., & Goggin, C. (1996). A meta-analysis of the predictors of adult offender recidivism: What works! *Criminology, 34*, 575-607.

Kroner, D.G., & Loza, W. (2001). Evidence for the efficacy of self-report in predicting nonviolent and violent criminal recidivism. *Journal of Interpersonal Violence, 16*, 168-177.

Loza, W., Dhaliwal, G., Kroner, D.G., & Loza-Fanous, A. (2000). Reliability, construct, and concurrent validities of the Self-Appraisal Questionnaire. *Criminal Justice and Behavior, 27*, 356-374.

Loza, W., & Loza-Fanous, A. (2001). The effectiveness of the Self-Appraisal Questionnaire in predicting offenders' postrelease outcome: A comparison study. *Criminal Justice and Behavior, 28*, 105-121.

Loza, W., & Loza-Fanous, A. (2000). Predictive validity of the Self-Appraisal Questionnaire (SAQ): A tool for assessing violent and nonviolent release failures. *Journal of Interpersonal Violence, 15*, 1183-1191.

MacKenzie, D.L., Brame, R., McDowall, D., & Souryal, C. (1995). Boot camp prisons and recidivism in eight states. *Criminology, 33*, 327-357.

MacKenzie, D.L., & Hebert, E.E. (1996). *Correctional boot camps: A tough intermediate sanction*. Washington, DC: U.S. Department of Justice, National Institute of Justice.

MacKenzie, D.L., Wilson, D.B., & Kider, S.B. (2001). Effects of correctional boot camps on offending. *The Annals of the American Academy of Political and Social Sciences, 578*, 126-143.

Morash, M., & Rucker, L. (1990). Critical look at the idea of boot camp as a correctional reform. *Crime & Delinquency, 36*, 204-222.

Sechrest, D.D. (1989). Prison "boot camps" do not measure up. *Federal Probation, 53*, 15-20.

Shugg, W. (2001). *A monument to good intentions: The Maryland State Penitentiary, 1804-1995*. Chambersburg, PA: Alan C. Hood and Company.

AUTHORS' NOTES

Ojmarrh Mitchell is an assistant professor in the Criminal Justice Department at the University of Nevada, Las Vegas. His research interests include sentencing and corrections, drugs and crime, and race and crime. He has recently completed a meta-analytic synthesis of the race and sentencing literature and an evaluation of the national Breaking the Cycle Demonstration Project.

Doris L. MacKenzie is Director of the Evaluation Research Group and Professor in the Department of Criminology and Criminal Justice at the University of Maryland. Her recent work focuses on examining the effectiveness of correctional programs and offender behavior.

Deanna M. Pérez is a Senior Research Analyst with the Virginia Department of Corrections, where she is responsible for coordinating evaluations of institutional and community corrections programs in the state. Previously, she managed a study to assess drug treatment needs among arrestees, and worked on evaluations of drug treatment programs for criminal justice clients, as well as delinquency and drug abuse prevention programs. Her research interests include evaluations of correctional interventions, drug abuse and crime, and violent behavior. She is working on her doctorate in the Department of Criminology and Criminal Justice at the University of Maryland.

Address correspondence to Ojmarrh Mitchell, Department of Criminal Justice, University of Nevada, Las Vegas, 4505 Maryland Parkway–Box 5009, Las Vegas, NV 89154-5009.

Survival Analysis of Recidivism of Male and Female Boot Camp Graduates Using Life-Course Theory

BRENT B. BENDA

University of Arkansas at Little Rock

NANCY J. HARM

University of Arkansas at Little Rock

NANCY J. TOOMBS

North Little Rock, Arkansas

ABSTRACT This was a five-year follow-up study of 572 male and 120 female graduates of a boot camp in the South. The purpose was to examine what elements of life-course theory predict recidivism (felony conviction or parole violation), gender differences in predictors, and some issues regarding the effects of boot camp. Special emphasis was on perceptions of the boot camp experience by inmates, and on how sexual and physical abuses during different stages of the life span predict recidivism.

Cox's Proportional-Hazards Model indicated that certain favorable perceptions of the boot camp program were associated with decreased hazard rates of recidivism, even after considering factors considered to be ameliorating experiences in life-course theory. Childhood sexual abuse, sexual and physical maltreatments in adolescence, and current sexual assaults are related to increases in the hazard rates of recidivism. In support of life-course theory, ameliorating experiences, such as having a conventional partner and full-time employment, did significantly reduce the hazard rates of most predictors studied. Finally, several gender differences relevant to questions about the utility and humanity of boot camps were discussed. *[Article copies available for a fee from The Haworth Document Delivery Service: 1-800-HAWORTH. E-mail address: <docdelivery@haworthpress.com> Website: <http://www.HaworthPress.com> © 2005 by The Haworth Press, Inc. All rights reserved.]*

KEYWORDS Boot camp, recidivism, life-course theory, gender differences, sexual and physical abuses

INTRODUCTION

There is a well-established pattern that, for most offenses and offenders, crime rates increase with advances in age during adolescence, reaches a pinnacle at entry into adulthood, and then decline thereafter (Hirschi & Gottfredson, 1983). Contrasting explanations have been proffered for this curvilinear relationship (Kruttschnitt, Uggen, & Shelton, 2000). Hirschi and Gottfredson (1983, pp. 554-562), for example, argue that desistance, or the cessation, of acts of criminality simply occurs as a result of the "inexorable aging of the organism." In contrast, Sampson and Laub's (1993) explanation of desistance from crime is based on a social control theory that transitions–such as marriage, having children, employment, and attaining education–often are "turning points" in life-course trajectories (Elder, 1985). These transitions can be "turning points" from a life-course trajectory of criminal behavior to law-abiding pursuits (Sampson & Laub, 1990, 1992, 1993, 1996; Uggen, 2000; Warr, 1998).

Sampson and Laub attribute desistance from an unlawful lifestyle to the establishment or augmentation of informal social controls through bonding to loved ones and commitment to responsibilities and achievements such as having a family, education, and employment (Cernkovich & Giordano, 2001; Farrington, 1995; Farrington & West, 1995; Horney, Osgood, & Marshall, 1995). Their (Sampson & Laub, 1993) position is that although many offenders do possess general propensities toward crime (Gottfredson & Hirschi, 1990), changes in life circumstances can be a critical "turning point" that alters one's life trajectory from criminality to conventionality (Bushway, Piquero, Broidy, Cauffman, & Mazerolle, 2001; Giordano, Cernkovich, & Rudolph, 2002; Piquero, Brame, Mazerolle, & Haapanen, 2002; Simons, Stewart, Gordon, Conger, & Elder, 2002; Uggen, 2000). Life course theory is a useful explanation because the majority of adolescents desist from criminal behavior as they enter adulthood (Blumstein, Cohen, Roth, & Visher, 1986; Visher, Lattimore, & Linster, 1991): The explanation not only provides an understanding of the desistance process, it also identifies possible targets for invention that might accelerate the process (Andrews & Bonta, 1998). For example, meaningful educational or training opportunities and satisfactory employment may encourage commitments to conventionality that represent "turning points" away from a criminal lifestyle (Cullen & Gendreau, 2001; Cullen, Wright, & Chamlin, 1999).

Historically, studies of cessation from criminal trajectories have focused on males. Recently, a few studies have investigated the effects of social bonds on desistance from crime among young women (Alarid, Burton, & Cullen, 2000; Simons, Stewart, Gordon, Conger, & Elder, 2002; Uggen & Kruttschnitt, 1998). Alarid et al. (2000) studied women and men who had been sentenced for their first felony conviction to shock probation for three months. They found that social bonds–attachments to family, partner, and friends; involvement in conventional activities, and law-abiding beliefs–were more relevant to criminal behavioral among women than among men. Weak parental attachment was a significant predictor of greater involvement in crime (violent, property, and drug crimes) among women, less involvement in conventional activities predicted more drug and violent offenses, and marriage or living with a man was associated with increases in drug and/or property offenses. Alarid et al. found that parental attachment and conventional activities were inversely related to unlawful acts, which support Laub and Sampson's (1993) life-course theory that social bonding leads to desistance from crime. However, they also found that attachment to a partner was positively related to criminal activity, a finding that could be seen as contrary to life-course theory. Alarid et al. suggested that this finding might be interpreted as association with criminally oriented partners (Akers & Sellers, 2004).

On the other hand, Uggen and Kruttschnitt (1998) found only one predictor that differed significantly between men and women in National Supported Work Demonstration Project (Hollister, Kemper, & Maynard, 1984): each additional year of education cuts women's risks of self-reported illegal earnings by 18% but increases men's risk by 2%. Conversely, they observed that several covariates have significantly different effects on avoidance of arrest according to gender: The effects are much larger for women than for men. For example, present use of illegal drugs and prior criminal history increase the risk of arrests more than twice as much for women as for men. Uggen and Kruttschnitt suggest these gender differences may be due to differential labeling and sanctioning of women and men (Lutze & Murphy, 1999).

In extending Warr's (1998) findings that marriage increases the likelihood of desistance from crime through termination of affiliations with criminals, Simons et al. (2002) concluded that association with offenders is diminished only if one's partner is committed to a conventional lifestyle. Additionally, while living with a partner who engages in unlawful behavior enhances the probability of crime for men and women, these romantic relationships exert a greater negative influence on women. Association with peers involved in criminal activities has the strongest influence on unlawful behavior of men, influencing both the choice of a romantic partner and involvement in crime. Simons et al. also found that job satisfaction was positively related to desistance from crime only among men.

In summary, there is a paucity of research on possible gender differences in application of life-course theory (Elder, 1985; Sampson & Laub, 1993) to criminal patterns and desistance. Existing studies offer conflicting evidence regarding the nature and extend of gender differences in elements of the theory relevant to continuation or cessation of unlawful behavior. For example, there are studies of male offending that have found no relationship between intimate partnerships and men's likelihood of engaging in crime (Alarid et al., 2000). Other researchers find that marriage, especially for men, acts as a social bond that facilitates desistance from crime (Horney et al., 1995; Laub, Sampson, & Nagin, 1998; Laub & Sampson, 1993; Sampson & Laub, 1993). More recent research has found that romantic relationships encourage desistance from crime only insofar as they diminish affiliations with criminals (Simons et al., 2002; Warr, 1998). Furthermore, there is evidence that intimate partners, paramours or spouses, discourage criminal associations and, thereby, unlawful acts only to the extent that partners embrace conventionality (Griffin & Armstrong, 2003). This latter observation may apply more to women than to men because women are more influenced by intimate partners, whereas men are more inclined to follow the lead of peer associates (Griffin & Armstrong, 2003; Haney, 1996; Steffensmeier & Allan, 1996).

Purpose of the Present Study

The purpose of the present study is fourfold: (a) to examine possible gender differences in elements of life-course theory (Sampson & Laub, 1993; Benda, 2003; Benda, Toombs, & Peacock, 2003a) as predictors of criminal recidivism among boot camp graduates, (b) to determine if there are gender differences in how perceptions of the boot camp program predict recidivism, (c) to investigate gender differences in the prediction of recidivism of abuses that occur at different stages of the life span, and (d) to open dialog about the possible detrimental effects of boot camp. Boot camps have been severely criticized for summary punishments that include physical abuse, degrading verbal confrontations, and threats of being returned to prison where sexual victimization would likely be experienced (Lutze & Brody, 1999; Morash & Rucker, 1990; Welch, 1997). The ultramasculine environments of boot camps promote aggression, toughness, bravado, intimidation, and coercion (Lutze, 1998; Lutze & Murphy, 1999; Morash & Rucker, 1990). Lutze (1996) finds that while inmates in boot camp were better adjusted and held more positive attitudes toward the program and staff than their counterparts in prison, the former report greater feelings of isolation and helplessness than those incarcerated in traditional prisons. Morash and Rucker (1990, p. 206) ask "Why would a method that has been developed to prepare people to go to war, and as a tool to manage legal violence, be considered as having ... potential in deterring or rehabilitating offenders?"

Having examined how perceptions of the boot camp program predict recidivism in prior research (Benda, Toombs, & Peacock, 2002), the authors are especially interested in possible gender differences in these predictors. While no studies have been located that examine gender differences in predictors of recidivism among boot camp graduates, there is evidence that infractions while incarcerated, including violence toward staff, is significantly related to elevated recidivism rates among women (Bonta, Pang, & Wallace-Caprette, 1995). There also are clues in the general literature on recidivism of incarcerated women about possible predictors that fit the life-course perspective (Feinman, 1994; Chesney-Lind, 1995; Griffin & Armstrong, 2003; Loper, 2002; MacKenzie & Li, 2002). Approximately three-fourths of women incarcerated in federal prisons, and sixty percent in state prisons, in 1998 were charged with drug offenses, which is about a sixty percent increase since 1990 (Greenfeld & Snell, 1999). In a study of incarcerated parents, Mumola (2000) observed that mothers were twice as likely as fathers to have committed their crime while under the influence of drugs.

Personal histories of incarcerated female drug users and distributors reveal sequelae of sexual and physical abuse. Browne, Miller, and Maguin (1999) observed that nearly three-fourths of women interviewed in a maximum-security prison reported childhood physical abuse and that over half indicated sexual abuse. Siegel (1996) found that maltreated women were more than five times more likely to be arrested for drug offenses than were non-abused women from a demographically matched sample. Hirsch (2001) indicated that women interviewed with a drug felony conviction reported abusive relationships throughout their life span. Hirsch noted that women were selling illegal drugs to support their substance use and abuse. The suggested life trajectory seems to be one of cumulative victimization, chemical use to anesthetize painful memories, addiction, and criminal behavior to afford illicit drugs.

While the precise sequential pattern of experiences that lie between childhood abuse and drug and other felonious offenses has yet to be identified, there is evidence that early sexual and physical assaults have protracted effects extending into adulthood (Weeks & Widom, 1998; Widom, 1996, 2001). Abuses at different stages of the life span have rarely been investigated (Cicchetti & Toth, 1995; Ireland, Smith, & Thornberry, 2002). However, it is logically plausible that more proximal abuse is a stronger predictor of recidivism than childhood maltreatment, or there may be a cumulative effect of abuses over an extended period of time. Also, there is a paucity of studies that examine the differential effects of sexual and physical abuse on criminal recidivism (Thornberry, Ireland, & Smith, 1999). Gender differences in these various relationships between abuses and crime in adulthood have not been examined.

Life-Course Theory and Gender Differences in Predictors of Recidivism

Although Sampson and Laub (1993) do not discuss gender in their life-course theory, prior research and experiential observation provide hints that gender differences in what factors are relevant to longitudinal patterns of crime are likely (Downen & Andrews, 1999; Griffin & Armstrong, 2003; Uggen & Kruttschnitt, 1998). For example, our experience suggests that women's perceptions of boot camp may not be a correlate of recidivism because of the canceling effects of opposing positions: Some women seem to be grateful for boot camp because it allows them quicker access to their children due to earlier visitation and release than is typically true of a traditional prison sentence. Other women find the ultramasculine environments too stressful and intimidating because of the aggressive and degrading verbal confrontations and threats from staff. Psychological examinations suggest that women with histories of abuse are especially vulnerable to adverse reactions to attention-riveting confrontations by staff (Lutze & Symons, 2003).

Women are more likely to be sexually assaulted than are men at each stage of the life span (Bassuk, Melnick, & Browne, 1998; Finkelhor & Dziuba-Leatherman, 1994). Because women are at greater risk of sexual and physical victimizations than are men, a recent retrospective National Comorbidity Survey indicates that women have more depression, anxiety, and suicidal thoughts and attempts (Molnar, Buka, & Kessler, 2001). Because of the relationships between these factors, it is anticipated that abuses and psychological problems are more likely to be predictors of recidivism among women than among men (Andrews & Bonta, 1998; Gover, 2004; Weeks & Widom, 1998; Widom, 1996, 2001). We have no hypotheses regarding gender differences in use and sales of drugs because of the rapid rise in participation in these crimes among women (Uggen & Kruttschnitt, 1998).

In accord with life-course theory (Elder, 1985; Sampson & Laub, 1993), childhood abuses are thought to result from fractured attachments to caregivers (Benda, 2001a, 2002a).

Close attachments, in contrast, foster acceptance of caregiver monitoring and refrain from unlawful behaviors and associations because of the emotional pain these undesirable actions and affiliations would cause loved ones (Paternoster, Dean, Piquero, Mazerolle, & Brame, 1997; Patterson, Crosby, & Vuchinich, 1992; Simons, Whitbeck, Conger, & Conger, 1991; Wright, Caspi, Moffitt, & Silva, 2001). Because young women tend to maintain closer ties with their families, and are more influence by familial dynamics, we expect that caregiver attachment and monitoring will be more inversely related to criminal recidivism among them than among men. Evidence indicates that men are much more influenced in their unlawful behavior by peer association and gangs (Battin, Hill, Abbott, Catalano, & Hawkins, 1998; Lizotte, Krohn, Howell, Tobin, & Howard, 2000; Zhang, Welte, & Wieczorek, 1999). Gangs are considered to be different than peer association conceptually (Battin et al., 1998; Lizotte et al., 2000). Gangs have more formal rituals, expectations, and sanctions, and are more organized around criminal behavior than are delinquent peer associations which occur more spontaneously and episodically with little or no organization or expectations about participation (Hagedorn, 1994). Battin et al. (1998) find that gangs have influences on crime in addition to those of peer affiliations.

There is a complex nexus of gang membership, drug use, and carrying weapons that cannot be disentangled in the present research (Blumstein, 1995a, 1995b; Lizotte et al., 2000; Zhang et al., 1999). Peer associations, gangs, use and selling of drugs, and regular carrying of weapons are further manifestations of deficient informal social control (Kruttschnitt et al., 2000; MacKenzie, Wilson, Armstrong, & Gover, 2001). The expectation is that peer association, gang membership, and regular possession of weapons will be more relevant to the recidivism of men than of women (Benda, 2001a, 2002a, 2002b; Benda & Toombs, 2002).

A primary tenet of life-course theory (Sampson & Laub, 1993) is that persons, who have had adversities such as abuse, or engaged in undesirable behavior such as crime, can have ameliorating experiences that represent "turning points" from a life of crime to conventionality (Bushway et al., 2001; Piquero et al., 2002). Rather than try to formulate hypotheses based on possible gender differences found in the literature, we have elected to simply explore whether there are differences between men and women in predictors considered as ameliorating experiences. Based on life-course theory, the expectation is that higher education, regular full-time employment, living with a conventional partner (spouse or paramour), having children, and positive social relationships will be inversely related to recidivism.

Although the most comprehensive study to date indicates no clear-cut effectiveness of boot camps in reducing recidivism (MacKenzie, Brame, McDowall, & Souryal, 1995), it is possible that inmates' perceptions of the boot camp program are related to criminal recidivism (Benda, 2001b; Benda et al., 2002; Gover, MacKenzie, & Styve, 2000; Stinchcomb & Clinton, 2001; Wood & Grasmick, 1999). It is also plausible that life-course events overshadow any boot camp experiences in the prediction of recidivism. It should be noted at this juncture that this is a preliminary study to examine how well elements of life-course theory and perceptions of boot camp predict criminal recidivism. The study is not designed to test a theoretical model, or the nature of interrelationships between predictors. Statistical interactions are examined to detect gender differences that have been discussed.

METHOD

Sample

The present study consists of a convenience sample of 601 male and 120 female graduates from the only boot camp for adults in a southern state. Participation in the boot camp studied was an option to prison offered to eligible inmates. To be officially eligible for boot camp, inmates had to meet five criteria: (a) be a first-time referral to the adult correctional system in this state, (b) be sentenced to ten or less years, (c) have no recorded violent offenses in the adult correctional system, (d) have an IQ above seventy, and (e) have no physical or psychological problems, including drug addiction, that would preclude military training. Correctional counselors screened persons at the Diagnostic Unit. The drop-out rate was approximately 20 percent at the time of the study. Characteristics of the sample were shown in Table 1. Noteworthy gender differences showed that women were much more likely than men to have been sexually and physically abused in childhood and recently. Men were more likely to be gang members and to regularly carry a weapon than women.

Procedure and Data

A staff psychologist, who had eight research associates available to monitor each table of five respondents to clarify wording or to answer questions, administered the two questionnaires. The two questionnaires were administered on separate Sundays to make the task more manageable for inmates, and hopefully to enhance the accuracy of responses. Research associates were available to interview inmates who could not read the questionnaires. The questionnaire was administered approximately three weeks into the 105-day program to allow military discipline to develop, as well as trust in the psychologist who administered the questionnaires, since she also did mental health classes and counseling at this boot camp. While respondents did record their Department of Correction ID number for a recidivism study, they were assured of confidentiality by telling them that names would not be associated with ID numbers on the questionnaires, and none of the information provided by them was shared with anyone in the Department of Correction (DOC) except in aggregate form. Participation in the study was voluntary, and only six persons refused participation during the study period.

About 85 percent of the items on the questionnaires had no missing information, and most of the others were missing from one to ten cases. No variable was missing more than five percent of the cases.

Table 1: Characteristics of the Sample (N = 721)

	Men (N = 601) Mean	SD	Women (N = 120) Mean	SD
Age (in years)	25.3	5.1	24.2	4.0
Age first arrest (in years)	14.2	1.7	15.9	2.6
Education	11.4	2.0	12.1	2.2
Number of children	1.9	1.2	2.0	1.4

	Frequency	Percent	Frequency	Percent
Race				
Caucasian	278	46.3	48	40.0
African American	306	50.9	68	56.7
Asian American	2	0.3	0	0.0
Hispanic American	6	1.0	3	2.5
Other	9	1.5	1	0.8
Childhood sexual abuse				
Yes	306	50.9	96	80.0
No	290	48.3	18	15.0
Missing	5	0.8	6	5.0
Childhood physical abuse				
Yes	264	43.9	87	72.5
No	332	55.3	25	20.8
Missing	5	0.8	8	6.7
Current sexual abuse				
Yes	15	2.5	52	43.3
No	576	95.8	60	50.0
Missing	10	1.7	8	6.7
Current physical abuse				
Yes	32	5.3	59	49.2
No	557	92.7	56	46.7
Missing	12	2.0	5	4.1
Living with conventional partner				
Yes	438	72.9	75	62.5
No	163	27.1	45	37.5
Full-time employment (past 3 years)				
Yes	408	67.9	73	60.8
No	193	32.1	47	39.2
Gang member				
Yes	432	71.9	67	55.8
No	169	28.1	53	44.2
Regularly carry weapon				
Yes	361	60.1	34	28.3
No	240	39.9	80	66.7
Missing			6	5.0
Sell drugs				
Yes	408	67.9	79	65.8
No	186	31.0	36	30.0
Missing	7	1.1	5	4.2

Outcome or Dependent Variable

The DOC number assigned to inmates allowed a determination of whether or not boot camp graduates had any arrests or parole violations during the five-year follow-up study. All of the inmates were on parole after release from boot camp for the duration of their sentence. In approximately 65 percent of the cases, parole extended over the entire study; for almost all graduates, parole lasted at least three years. Parole entailed weekly contact for the first six months and monthly contact after this initial period, with random drug screens and additional unannounced visits. In short, the parole supervision was more intense and personal than is often true for persons released from prison. Although census surveys in the state indicate little migration from the state, there is no information about persons who left the state and committed felonies elsewhere (Arkansas Institute for Economic Advancement, 1999). This is a common flaw of recidivism studies because attempts to contact former inmates would be very expensive in several ways and the validity of responses about crime would be suspect.

There were 26 of 601 male inmates, or 4.3 percent, for whom there was no follow-up information. Presumably, those 26 graduates failed to report to a parole officer as required and disappeared from DOC. Three other cases (.3 percent of 575 graduates) were missing the number of days in the community, despite having other data recorded. The analyses of the 5-year follow-up data on recidivism, as a result, were based on 572 male boot camp graduates. No women were missing follow-up information. Hence, there was a relatively low "no response" rate for a criminal recidivism study (Andrews & Bonta, 1998). Every graduate was followed for 5 years, which meant individualized follow-up periods.

Of the 572 male graduates for whom data on number of days in the community was recorded, 352 persons, or 61.5 percent, were recidivists. Recidivism was defined as a return to the Department of Corrections for a new conviction for a felony or parole violation. Twenty percent of the men were returned to DOC for a parole violation. Fifty women, or 41.7 percent, were recidivists, and 15 percent of the female graduates were parole violators. Misdemeanors were not the reason for any type of recidivism.

Questionnaires and Prediction Measures

The Addiction Severity Index (ASI) (McLellan et al., 1992) was administered on a separate day from other measures presented in the following paragraphs. The ASI has reports of good reliability and validity (see review, Rosen, Henson, Finney, & Moos, 2000). The ASI provided information on residence (0 = rural < 10,000 versus 1 = urban > 10,000); years of education; the number of days in the month prior to incarceration they were drunk on alcohol; composite score on close relationships with children, family, friends, and spouse/sexual partner; composite score on psychiatric status (e.g., depression, anxiety, violent tendencies, suicide ideation, suicide attempts); sexually abused in the past year; physically abused in the past year; number of children; and employment pattern that characterizes most of the past 3 years (0 = full-time, 1 = other). Full-time employment was defined as working 40 or more hours a week. The ASI manual has formulae for deriving composite scores (McLellan et al., 1992). Other sociodemographic factors added to the ASI were age of onset of crimes listed in an earlier article in this journal (Benda, Toombs, & Peacock, 2003a), and race (0 = white, 1 = person of color).

Attachment was measured by two distinct variables of attachment to female and to male caregivers (4-point scales): (1) How much did you like being with ___; (2) how close did you feel to ___; (3) how much did you want to be like your ___, and (4) how much did you enjoy spending time with ___. However, since the distributions were similar, the two summated scores were added and divided by 2 (α = .88).

Caregiver monitoring was measured with five items (four-point scales, ranging from "very little" to "very much") asking how closely caregivers supervised: (a) spending money, (b) peer associations, (c) movies and parties, (d) how late you stay out, and (e) school activities (during childhood and adolescence). Caregiver attachment and monitoring were taken from Marcos and Bahr (1988) (α = .87).

Physical and sexual abuses were each measured with two items (four-point Likert scales, ranging from "never" to "more than ten times") asking how often respondents had been abused before 12 years of age (childhood abuse): (a) by a caregiver, and (b) by someone other than a caregiver. Two items each were also asked about sexual and physical abuses during the year before incarceration in boot camp, at a later point in the questionnaire, by: (1) partner, (2) other person. Physical abuse was defined as any physical contact that resulted in severe cuts, bruises, welts, or other marks that took a few days to disappear; in concussions or breaking of bones; or in scalding or burns. Sexual abuse was defined as any touching of the genitals, and oral or anal intercourse that was non-consensual.

Peer association was measured with five items (five-point scales, ranging from "none" to "more than ten") asking how many of your best friends: (a) have ever been arrested, (b) use illegal drugs regularly, (c) consume three or more drinks of alcohol in a day regularly, (d) steal regularly, and (e) have used a weapon on another person (α = .82).

The most common measure of gang membership is a single-item asking about whether one is a member of a formal gang (Battin et al., 1998; Klein, 1995; Lizotte et al., 2000). *Gang membership* in the present study was a single item (coded: 0 = no, 1 = yes) asking whether respondents are members of a formal gang (i.e., a group formally organized for criminal purposes which has a designated hierarchy, name, colors, symbols, graffiti, and allegiance to each other). Since staff at the boot camp was familiar with the local gangs, only inmates who indicated they were members of known gang were recorded as gang members (Klein, 1995). *Carrying weapons* was measured with two items (five-point scales, ranging from "never" to "all the time") asking if they: (a) carry a gun most of the time, (b) or carry other weapons such as knives, brass knuckles, chains, shanks, or ball bats most of the time (Lizotte et al., 2000).

Drug use was measured by six items asking inmates how often they had used: (a) barbiturates (chlordiazepoxide, diazepam, glutethimide, meprobamate, methaqualone), (b) amphetamine (other psychostimulate, Methytpheniadate, Ritalin, intravenous Methedrine, Desoxun, diet pills), (c) opiates (heroin, Paregoric, Meperidine, Methadone, Morphine, opium, opium alkaloids and derivatives, (d) cocaine, (e) hallucinogens (LSD, Mescaline, MDA, DMT, PCP, STP, Psilocybin), or (f) solvents (α = .89). *Selling drugs* was measured with a single item asking if they had sold any of these drugs. All items asking about drug use and selling illicit drugs have the same five-point scale (1 = none, 2 = 1 or 2 times, 3 = 3 to 5 times, 4 = 6 to 9 times, and 5 = 10 times or more). Street names were provided for all drugs to be sure of mutual understanding, such as speed, yellow jackets, crank, pink hearts, and cross tops for amphetamines.

Measures of perceptions of the boot camp environment are based on Toch's (1977) argument that needs for safety, structure, support, helpful feedback, and stimulation are requisite to changing inmates' criminal behavior. All measures had four-point Likert scales, ranging from "strongly disagree" to "strongly agree." *Perception of benefits of the boot camp program* was measured with eight items asking if the program is: (a) helping you, (b) making you a better person, (c) useless, (d) causing you to re-evaluate your commitments to your family, (e) an experience that will cause you to stop crime, (f) causing you to think about being more responsible to others, (g) causing you to become more criminal, and (h) leading you to plan for employment (α = .85). *Feeling safe* was measured by five items asking: (a) if you feel safe in boot camp, (b) do you feel that you are "put down" or "disrespected" by officers in boot camp, (c) are you called names to disrespect you such as "boy," "sissies," and "chum bag," (d) do you think officers use physical abuse to intimidate inmates, and (e) have you been physically abused or seen an inmate abused by an officer (α = .86)? *Staff support* is measured with seven items asking if: (a) you would ask staff for help, (b) you think staff dislike inmates, (c) staff are fair, (d) you try to talk to staff to solve problems, (e) you like some of the staff, (f) you think staff are stupid, and (g) staff are trying to help you (α = .83). *Stimulation* is measured by 5 items (same 4-point scale) asking if: (a) the boot camp is depressing, (b) challenges you to think about your life, (c) is worthwhile because it is getting you into good physical shape, (d) if the program is doing more harm than good, and (e) the program is a challenging experience (α = .88). *Perception of change* from the boot camp experience is measured by four items asking if: (a) this incarceration will keep you from using drugs, (b) this incarceration will stop you from committing crimes, (c) this incarceration will keep you from selling drugs, and (d) this incarceration has caused you to be a better person ($\alpha = .84$).

It is plausible that many inmates choose boot camp instead of prison simply because the period of time incarcerated is shorter, even though the environment and expectations in boot camp are more regimented and demanding in terms of physical exertion and behavioral expectations. *Expedience* was measured with two items (4-point scale from strongly disagree to strong agree) asking: (a) if the boot camp program was chosen because it was for a briefer period of time than serving one's sentence in prison, and (b) if boot camp was selected only because it was a faster way to get back out on the streets than going to prison.

Finally, the boot camp staff reliably recorded any *infractions* committed because they were considered to be a critical element in instilling discipline in the program. The gamut of infractions were very wide, ranging from forgetting to salute or answer "yes sir or madam" to disorderly behavior or assault.

Statistical Analyses

An examination of a correlation matrix and tests for tolerance and the variance inflation factor (VIF) did not reveal problems with multicollinearity (Freund & Wilson, 1998). The primary analyses are Cox's proportional hazard model because this procedure is not based on any assumption concerning the nature or shape of the underlying survival distribution (Lee, 1980; Wu & Tuma, 1994; Yamaguchi, 1991). The model assumes that the underlying hazard rate (rather than survival time) is a function of the independent variables (Allison, 1984, 1995). The model may be written as:

$$h\{(t), (z1,z2,....,zm)\} = h0(t)*exp(b1*z1 +....+bm*zm),$$

In which: h(t,...) denotes the resultant hazard, given the values of the m covariates for the respective case (z1,z2,....,zm) and the respective survival time (t). The term h0(t) is called the baseline hazard; it is the hazard for the respective individual when all independent variable values are equal to zero. This model is made linear by dividing both sides of the equation by h0(t) and then taking the natural logarithm of both sides: $log\{h\{(t), (z....)\}/h0(t)\} = b1*z1+....+bm*zm$, which provides a linear model that can be estimated (Lee, 1980; Wu & Tuma, 1994; Yamaguchi, 1991).

FINDINGS

Nonparametric Analysis of Survival Curves

The standard life table methods (Namboodiri & Suchindran, 1987) are used to examine the time until the first felony arrest or parole violation of men and women, who graduated from boot camp (Figure 1). These approaches are nonparametric in the sense that they make no distributional assumptions about recidivism. The survival distributions for men and for women are compared. The horizontal axis represents time in months and the vertical axis represents the cumulative proportion of those at risk of recidivism who have not been arrested or received a parole violation. The statistical difference in the survival curves for men and for women is assessed with a log-rank test of survival-curve equality. Visually and statistically it may be seen that the two curves differ significantly: For example, after one year approximately 85 percent of the males are not recidivists, whereas about 95 percent of the females have not been arrested for a felony or received a parole violation.

Cox's Proportional Hazards Models

Cox's proportional hazards models are conducted in the complete sample, using statistical interactions to examine gender differences, because of the relative small number of women available at the time of the study. The first

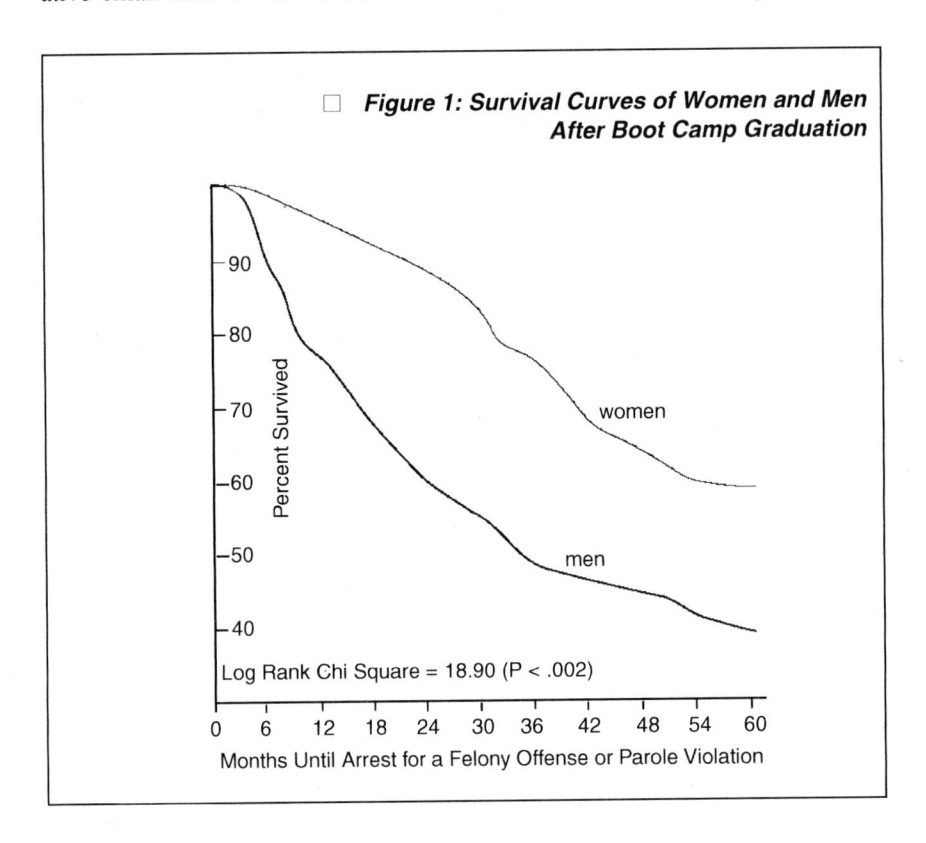

Figure 1: Survival Curves of Women and Men After Boot Camp Graduation

Log Rank Chi Square = 18.90 (P < .002)

Months Until Arrest for a Felony Offense or Parole Violation

Cox's proportional hazards model (Table 2) is a hierarchical analysis, where hypothesized ameliorating experiences are added in the second hierarchy to predictors considered in the first hierarchy. In Cox regression, the baseline hazard rate (HR) describes the risk of when the event (i.e., felony arrest or parole violation) will occur. A value greater than 1 reflects a greater hazard rate of recidivism (i.e., felony arrest or parole violation) for each unit of change in the predictor variable, and a beta value less than 1 reflects a smaller hazard rate of recidivism at each unit of change in the predictor variable. Continuous data are standardized to normalize distributions and to make coefficients more meaningful. The estimated betas give the magnitude of effect of each predictor on the log odds (logit) of the hazard of recidivism. Taking antilogs (exponents) of the estimated betas converts the effects to the odds of the hazard of recidivism. For example, the effect of age on recidivism is $-.25$ (Table 2),

Table 2: Cox's Proportional-Hazards Model of Recidivism

	Beta	Hazard Rate	Beta	Hazard Rate	Beta	Hazard Rate	Beta	Hazard Rate
Model 1 – Women (N = 120)								
Low self-control	.50**	1.65						
Model 2 – Men (N = 120)								
Low self-control	.75**	2.11						
Model 3 – Gender (0 = women) (both N's = 120) and self-control								
Gender	.59**	1.80	.27**	1.31				
Low self-control			.42**	1.52				
Model 4 – Age (N = 240)								
Age	−.51**	.60 (1.67)						
Model 5 – Age and self-control (N = 240)								
Age	−.51**	.60	−.12	.89 (1.12)				
Low self-control			.39**	1.48				
Model 6 – Gender, age and self-control (N = 240)								
Gender					.57**	1.77	.26**	1.29
Age					−.48**	.62	−.11	.90
Low self-control							.35**	1.42

Note: The reciprocal rate is shown in parentheses (1 per hazard rate). Age is standardized. The two samples used for Models 1 and 2 are combined for Models 4-6.
*P < .05; **P < .01

which when exponentiated indicated that the odds of the hazard of recidivism decreases by .76 for each unit (i.e., one standard deviation) increase in age, which is a 24 percent decrease (1 − .76 = .24).

Before ameliorating experiences are considered, the first hierarchy of the analysis shows that race is the only insignificant (alpha = 0.05) predictor. However, when ameliorating experiences are added to the analysis, psychiatric problems, gang membership, regular carrying of weapons, alcohol consumption, other drug use, illicit drug sales, feel safe at boot camp, perceived change in self during boot camp, and viewing boot camp as an expedient way of gaining early release from incarceration also are not significant predictors.

According to the size of the hazard rate of recidivism, the strongest predictors of recidivism (HR's > 2), irrespective of gender, are regular carrying of weapons, gang membership, and infractions in boot camp. However, only the latter predictor remains significant after ameliorating experiences are considered in the second hierarchy. In the second hierarchy, the strongest predictors are factors labeled as ameliorating experiences. For example, the reciprocal hazard rate (1/hazard rate) of recidivism is 2.70 if the pattern of employment over the past three years is less than full-time (1/.37 = 2.70). The reciprocal hazard rate allows direct comparisons with the more numerous positive relationships, and each ameliorating experience has a reciprocal hazard rate above two, which is larger than any other rates in Table 2. The Wald chi-square statistic shows that there are many significant changes in the effects (Betas) of predictors after the ameliorating experiences are added to the analysis. It should be noted that graduates who perceive benefits from the boot camp program, think the staff is supportive, and believe the experience is stimulating are less likely to be a recidivist.

In Table 3, the perceptions of boot camp are replaced with sexual and physical abuse measures pertaining to childhood (< 12 years of age) and currently (within the past year). Before considering ameliorating experience, both forms of abuse are significant at each stage of the life span. After introducing the ameliorating experiences in the second hierarchy of the analysis, childhood and current physical abuse are not significant predictors of recidivism. These latter findings per se suggest that early sexual abuse may have more lasting effects on unlawful behavior than physical maltreatment. However, the findings are heavily influenced by the greater prevalence of men.

In Table 4 are presented the significant interactions between gender (coded: 0 = men, 1 = women) and other predictors. Interactions between gender and each factor in the study are considered in separate analyses. In each analysis, an interaction between gender and a predictor is added to the main effects of all other study factors. Only the statistically significant interactions from these analyses are shown, owing to space limits. Based on the coding of gender, the first interaction shown in Table 4 indicates that women are 19 percent (1.19 − 1 = .19) more likely than men to be a recidivist if they have psychiatric problems.

Table 3: Cox's Proportional-Hazards Model of Recidivism (N = 692)

	First Hierarchy		Second Hierarchy		
	Beta	Hazard Rate	Beta	Hazard Rate	
Race (0 = white)	.10	1.10	.06	1.06	
Residence (0 = rural)	.55**	1.68	.53**	1.69	
Attachment to caregivers	−.36**	0.70	−.13	0.88	SC
Caregiver monitoring	−.60**	0.55	−.56**	0.57	
Criminal peer associations	.66**	1.90	.57**	1.77	SC
Ameliorating experiences					
Conventional partner (0 = yes)	−.69**	0.50	−.37**	0.69	SC
Number of children	−.91**	0.40	−.73**	0.48	SC
Years of education	−.65**	0.52	−.36**	0.70	SC
Employment (0 = full-time)	−.87**	0.42	−.69**	0.50	SC
Supportive relationships	−.89**	0.41	−.65**	0.52	SC
Age	−.37**	0.69	−.08	0.92	SC
Gender (0 = women)	.55**	1.75	.23**	1.26	SC
Low self-control			.29**	1.33	
−2 log likelihood	201.73**		190.01**		
Model chi-square			11.72*		

Note: Hazard rates based on standardized data (one unit change is one standard deviation for each predictor). Codes for dichotomous data (e.g., race) are shown. SC is significant (α = 0.05) change according to Wald chi-square tests.
*P < .05; **P < .01

Since attachment is inversely related to recidivism, the minus Beta indicates that women are 20 percent less likely to return to DOC if they have higher attachment to caregivers than are men. Men are 18 percent (1/.85) more likely than are women to be a recidivist if they are in a gang. Men are almost twice as likely as women to return to DOC if they regularly carry a weapon, and 25 percent more likely to return if they drink alcohol more often.

Table 4: Cox's Proportional-Hazards Model of Recidivism: Gender Interaction (N = 692)

	First Hierarchy Beta	Hazard Rate	Second Hierarchy Beta	Hazard Rate	
Race (0 = white)	.10	1.10	.04	1.04	
Residence (0 = rural)	.55**	1.68	.51**	1.67	
Attachment to caregivers	−.36**	0.70	−.11	0.90	SC
Caregiver monitoring	−.60**	0.55	−.53**	0.59	
Criminal peer associations	.66**	1.90	.53**	1.70	SC
Ameliorating experiences					
Conventional partner (0 = yes)	−.69**	0.50	−.34**	0.71	SC
Number of children	−.91**	0.40	−.65**	0.52	SC
Years of education	−.65**	0.52	−.30**	0.74	SC
Employment (0 = full-time)	−.87**	0.42	−.65**	0.52	SC
Supportive relationships	−.89**	0.41	−.60**	0.55	SC
Gender (0 = women)	.55**	1.75	.01	1.01	SC
Age	−.37**	0.69	−.06	0.94	SC
Self-control	.02	1.02			
Gender * Low self-control			.23**	1.26	
−2 log likelihood	198.44**		180.41**		
Model chi-square			18.03**		

Note: Hazard rates based on standardized data (one unit change is one standard deviation for each predictor). Codes for dichotomous data (e.g., race) are shown. SC is significant ($\alpha = 0.05$) change according to Wald chi-square tests.
*P < .05; **P < .01

Interactions show that women are far more likely than are men to return to DOC if they have been sexually or physically abused during the year prior to incarceration in boot camp.

However, a caveat is needed that a much larger percentage of women than of men have experienced recent sexual and physical abuse. Women have a lower probability of return to DOC than men if they are living with a convention partner (spouse or paramour), have more children, and have stronger supportive relationships.

DISCUSSION

This study of 572 male and 120 female graduates of a boot camp found that 61.5 percent of the men and 41.7 percent of the women either were arrested for a felony or had a parole violation during the 5-year follow-up period. Twenty percent of the men and 15 percent of the women were parole violators. The survival curves for men and women were found to significantly differ with a log-rank chi-square test of survival.

There is a paucity of studies of recidivism of women who have graduated from boot camps. Also, there are few studies of gender differences in recidivism based on a theoretical framework (Kruttschnitt et al., 2000; MacKenzie, Wilson, Armstrong, & Gover, 2001). Yet, these studies can be useful to offender rehabilitation because theory offers an explanation for how or why factors contribute to unlawful behavior and many theoretical factors are amenable to planned change (Andrews & Bonta, 1998). The present study is based on life-course theory (Laub & Sampson, 1993; Sampson & Laub, 1993). Sampson and Laub are in basic agreement with another well-received control theory (Gottfredson & Hirschi, 1990) that some individuals have propensities toward crime as a result of adverse experiences early in life, such as insecure attachments, lack of caregiver monitoring, and abuse. However, Sampson and Laub postulate that people begin to control natural urges for unlawful acts when they find relationships or employment they do not want to jeopardize by criminal behavior.

In support of life-course theory, this study finds that having a relationship with a conventional partner (spouse or paramour), more children, higher education, full-time employment, and supportive relations with family, friends, children and others is associated with a lower likelihood of recidivism. What is especially noteworthy about these findings is that these ameliorating experiences are significant predictors even after the strongest known predictors of criminal recidivism are simultaneously considered (Akers & Sellers, 2004; Andrews & Bonta, 1998; Blumstein et al., 1986). In fact, the findings suggest that each of these ameliorating experiences decreases the hazard rate of recidivism by at least a half. For example, full-time employment lowers the hazard rate of recidivism by .37. Almost all other employment conditions are sporadic, part-time employment; there is less than one percent of the inmates who were in school or some vocational training. The hazard rates for ameliorating experiences are the largest rates found in this study (e.g., the reciprocal hazard rate for the smallest is $1/.54 = 1.85$). Other large hazard rates are associated with having an urban residence and greater abuse currently and in adolescence.

The entry of these ameliorating experiences into the analyses reduces the effects of many factors significantly. Most notably, the effects of gang membership, regular carrying of weapons, alcohol consumption, other drug use, and selling of illicit drugs are reduced to insignificance. These reductions in effects of well-documented strong predictors of recidivism provide support for the life-course explanation that even those persons, who have exhibited signature behaviors that they are motivated by criminal propensities, can take an alternate path in life toward conventionality, if they become involved in bonds that alter their motivations (Agnew, 1995). A caring relationship with a spouse or paramour who is living a conventional life and disapproves of crime, children who need a responsible parent, supportive relationships that can bolster one in the time of need, and security that comes from education and full-time employment can be the bonds that insulate women and men from temptations that are natural to human urges (Sampson & Laub, 1993).

Even with the ameliorating experiences in the analysis, three factors measuring perceptions of the boot camp program remain significant predictors of predictors of recidivism. Perception of benefits from the program, of staff support, and of stimulation (e.g., causes you to think about life, is challenging) are inversely related to recidivism. These are perceptions that were reported about three weeks after entering the program, and it is certainly possible that some respondents gave "socially acceptable" responses. However, experience suggests that "socially acceptable" responses are more likely to come from sociopathic inmates who know how to "play the role of a model inmate," but have high recidivism rates (Kroner & Mills, 2001). At the same time, inmates' perceptions are not objective indicators of program effectiveness. These findings regarding perceptions of aspects of the boot camp experience do raise some interesting questions about a prevalent perspective that these programs only ill-treat or brutalize inmates and have adverse effects.

An investigation that examines the experiences of inmates in the boot camp program to establish whether certain assumptions made in the literature are accurate would be welcome. Ultimately, experimental designs are needed that compare boot camp programs to alternative brief interventions on several outcomes are needed to assess effectiveness. These experimental studies should have indicators of all activities involved in the program, and of well-documented feelings, attitudes, beliefs, and behaviors associated with various unlawful acts (Andrews & Bonta, 1998; Benda, Corwyn, & Toombs, 2001).

This study also finds that sexual and physical abuses at each stage of life studied are positive predictors of recidivism before considering ameliorating experiences. Childhood and current sexual abuse are positively associated with recidivism, irrespective of gender. These abuses remain significant predictors of recidivism even after considering the ameliorating experiences. These findings should not get lost in a morass of significant predictors observed in this study because they suggest that childhood abuse is somehow related to criminal recidivism in adulthood. Establishing the linkage between early abuse and later criminality is very difficult, especially in a cross-sectional study, because of the concomitant familial, personality, and relational problems. Clearly, prospective studies of abuse and unlawful behavior are immensely important (Horwitz, Widom, McLaughlin, & White, 2001).

Meanwhile, serious consideration needs to be given to incarcerating persons, who have a history of abuse, in boot camp programs where there is maltreatment of inmates (Lutze & Brody, 1999). Demeaning verbal assaults, torturous physical demands, and threats of sexual abuse if sent back to prison trigger painful memories and psychological devastation that lies beyond the grasp of staff that are inflicting the torment. Even if staff or administrators are indifferent to the psychological damage that maltreatment of inmates causes, they should think of the grounds for lawsuits discussed by Lutze and Brody (1999). Hopefully, however, the findings of this study will evoke human compassion for suffering as well as fear of lawsuits.

The most poignant findings are the significant interactions with gender of factors that should be examined in policies of sending women to boot camp. The findings show women with psychiatric problems (e.g., depression, anxiety, suicidal thoughts), and who are currently (within the past year) being physically or sexually abused, are at greater risk of recidivism. While we do not have measures of program effects, or enough women in the sample to examine interactions between these afflictions and abuses, knowledge of psychology suggests that boot camps may be exacerbating ill feeling that accompany psychiatric problems and victimization. A sophisticated analysis of the psychological effects of boot camp programs on persons, who have been abused and suffer psychiatric problems, possibly would produce evidence that makes these interventions appear barbaric to open-minded correctional officials. This study suggests that the effects of current sexual and physical abuse on recidivism among women may be reduced by living with a partner (spouse of paramour) who engages in conventional behavior, having children, and supportive relationships. However, the positive relationships between current abuses and recidivism remain significant after considering these ameliorating circumstances.

In conclusion, this preliminary study raises some serious questions about the possible detrimental effects of militaristic correctional intervention, especially if the regimen involves verbal and physical insults and maltreatment, for at least some inmates. These findings need to be replicated with stronger designs that have multiple measures and sources of information on the various aspects of the program and their effects on psychological, social, and behavioral outcomes. Longitudinal and experimental designs are needed to answer the question of whether boot camps have beneficial or detrimental effects. A major concern that needs to be addressed is whether many persons sent to boot camp could be deterred from crime without disrupting the bonding processes that may actually be the most important contributors to the desistance from criminal careers. It is quite possible that incarcerating certain persons is actually creating problems for the very processes, such as partnerships and employment, that are the primary sources of desistance from crime.

REFERENCES

Agnew, R. A. (1995). Testing the leading crime theories: An alternative strategy focusing on motivational processes. *Journal of Research in Crime and Delinquency, 32,* 363-398.

Akers, R. L., & Sellers, C. S. (2004). *Criminological theories: Introduction and evaluation* (4th ed.). Los Angeles, CA: Roxbury.

Alarid, L., Burton, V., & Cullen, F. (2000). Gender and crime among felony offenders: Assessing the generality of social control and differential association theories. *Journal of Research in Crime and Delinquency, 32,* 171-199.

Allison, P. D. (1984). *Event history analysis.* Newbury Park, CA: Sage.

Allison, P. D. (1995). *Survival analysis using the SAS system.* Cary, NC: SAS Institute, Inc.

Andrews, D. A., & Bonta, J. (1998). *The psychology of criminal conduct* (2nd ed.). Cincinnati, OH: Anderson.

Arkansas Institute for Economic Advancement (1999). *Arkansas net migration by age, race and county.* University of Arkansas at Little Rock, AR: author.

Bassuk, E. L., Melnick, S., & Browne, A. (1998). Responding to the needs of low-income and homeless women who are survivors of family violence. *Journal of the American Medical Women's Association, 53,* 57-64.

Battin, S. R., Hill, K. G., Abbott, R. D., Catalano, R. F., & Hawkins, J. D. (1998). The contribution of gang membership to delinquency beyond delinquent friends. *Criminology, 36,* 93-115.

Benda, B. B. (2001a). Conceptual model of assets and risks: Unlawful behavior among adolescents. *Adolescent & Family Health, 3,* 123-131.

Benda, B. B. (2001b). Factors that discriminate between recidivists, parole violators, and nonrecidivists in a 3-year follow-up of boot camp graduates. *International Journal of Offender Therapy and Comparative Criminology, 45,* 711-729.

Benda, B. B. (2002a). A test of three competing theoretical models of delinquency using structural equation modeling. *Journal of Social Service Research, 29,* 55-91.

Benda, B. B. (2002b). Religion and violent offenses among youth entering boot camp: Structural equation model. *Journal of Research in Crime and Delinquency, 39,* 92-101.

Benda, B. B. (2003). Survival analysis of criminal recidivism of boot camp graduates using elements from general and developmental explanatory models. *International Journal of Offender Therapy and Comparative Criminology, 47,* 89-101.

Benda, B. B., Corwyn, R. F., & Toombs, N. J. (2001). Recidivism among adolescent serious offenders: Prediction of entry into the correctional system. *Criminal Justice and Behavior, 28,* 588-613.

Benda, B. B., Toombs, N. J., & Peacock, M. (2002). Ecological factors in recidivism: A survival analysis of boot camp graduates after three years. *Journal of Offender Rehabilitation, 35,* 63-85.

Benda, B. B., Toombs, N. J., & Peacock, M. (2003a). Discriminators of types of recidivism among boot camp graduates in a 5-year follow-up study. *Journal of Criminal Justice, 37*, 43-75.

Benda, B. B., Toombs, N. J., & Peacock, M. (2003b). An examination of competing theories in predicting recidivism of adult offenders five years after graduation from boot camp. *Journal of Offender Rehabilitation, 37*, 43-75.

Blumstein, A. (1995a). Violence by young people: Why the deadly nexus? *National Institute of Justice Journal, 3*, 1-9.

Blumstein, A. (1995b). Youth violence, guns, and the illicit-drug industry. *Journal of Criminal Law and Criminology, 86*, 10-36.

Blumstein, A., Cohen, J., Roth, J. A., & Visher, C. A. (Eds.) (1986). *Criminal careers and "career criminals."* Washington, DC: National Academy Press.

Bonta, J., Pang, B., & Wallace-Capretta, S. (1995). Predictors of recidivism among incarcerated female offenders. *The Prison Journal, 75*, 277-294.

Bushway, S. D., Piquero, A. R., Broidy, L. M., Cauffman, E., & Mazerolle, P. (2001). An empirical framework for studying desistance as a process. *Criminology, 39*, 491-515.

Cernkovich, S. A., & Giordano, P. C. (2001). Stability and change in antisocial behavior: The transition from adolescence to early adulthood. *Criminology, 39*, 371-410.

Chesney-Lind, M. (1995). Rethinking women's imprisonment: A critical examination of trends in female incarceration. In B. R. Price & N. Skoloff (Eds.), *The criminal justice system and women*. New York: McGraw-Hill.

Cicchetti, D., & Toth, S. L. (1995). A developmental psychopathology perspective on child abuse and neglect. *Journal of the American Academy of Child & Adolescent Psychiatry, 34*, 541-564.

Cullen, F. T., & Gendreau, P. (2001). From nothing works to what works: Changing professional ideology in the 21st century. *The Prison Journal, 81*, 313-338.

Cullen, F. T., Wright, J. P., Chamlin, M. B. (1999). Social support and social reform: A progressive crime control agenda. *Crime and Delinquency, 45*, 188-207.

Dowden, C., & Andrews, D. A. (1999). What works for female offenders: A meta-analytic review. *Crime and Delinquency, 45*, 438-453.

Elder, G. H. Jr. (Ed.) (1985). *Life course dynamic: Transitions and trajectories*. Ithaca, NY: Cornell University Press.

Farrington, D. P. (1995). The development of offending and antisocial behavior from childhood: Key findings from the Cambridge Study in Delinquent Development. *Journal of Child Psychology and Psychiatry, 36*, 1-36.

Farrington, D. P., & West, D. J. (1995). Effects of marriage, separation and children on offending by adult males. In J. Hagen (Ed.), *Delinquency and disrepute in the life course* (pp. 249-281). Greenwich, CT: JAI.

Feinman, C. (1994). *Women in the criminal justice system*. Westport CT: Praeger.

Finkelhor, D., & Dziuba-Leatherman, J. (1994). Children as victims of violence: A national survey. *Pediatrics, 94*, 413-420.

Freund, R. J., & Wilson, W. J. (1998). *Regression analysis: Statistical modeling of a response variable*. New York: Academic Press.

Giordano, P. C., Cernkovich, S. A., & Rudolph, J. L. (2002). Gender, crime, and desistance: Toward a theory of cognitive transformation. *The American Journal of Sociology, 107*, 990-1064.

Gottfredson, M., & Hirschi, T. (1990). *A general theory of crime*. Palo Alto, CA: Stanford University Press.

Gover, A. L. (2005). Native American ethnicity and childhood maltreatment as variables in perceptions and adjustments to boot camp vs. "traditional" correctional settings. *Journal of Offender Rehabilitation, 40*(3/4), 177-198.

Gover, A. R., MacKenzie, D. L., & Styve, G. J. (2000). Boot camps and traditional correctional facilities for juveniles: A comparison of the participants, daily activities, and environments. *Journal of Criminal Justice, 28*, 53-68.

Greenfeld, L., & Snell, T. L. (1999). Bureau of Justice Statistics Special Report: Women offenders (175688). Washington, DC: US Department of Justice Office of Justice Programs.

Griffin, M. L., & Armstrong, G. S. (2003). The effect of local life circumstances on female probationers' offending. *Justice Quarterly, 29*, 213-225.

Hagedorn, J. M. (1994). Neighborhoods, markets, and gang drug organization. *Journal of Research in Crime and Delinquency, 31*, 264-294.

Hirsch, A. E. (2001). The world was never a safe place for them: Abuse, welfare reform and women with drug convictions. *Violence Against Women, 7*, 159-175.

Hirschi, T., & Gottfredson, M. R. (1983). Age and the explanation of crime. *American Journal of Sociology, 89*, 552-584.

Hollister, R. G., Jr., Kemper, P., & Maynard, R. A. (1984). The National Supported Work Demonstration. Madison: University of Wisconsin Press.

Horney, J., Osgood, D. W., & Marshall, I. H. (1995). Criminal careers in the short-term: Intra-individual variability in crime and its relation to local life circumstances. *American Sociological Review, 60*, 655-73.

Horwitz, A. V., Widom, C. S., McLaughlin, J., & White, H. R. (2001). The impact of childhood abuse and neglect on adult mental health: A prospective study. *Journal of Health and Social Behavior, 42*, 184-201.

Ireland, T. O., Smith, C. A., & Thornberry, T. A. (2002). Developmental issues in the impact of child maltreatment on later delinquency and drug use. *Criminology, 40*, 359-399.

Klein, M. W. (1995). *The American street gang*. New York: Oxford University Press.

Kroner, D. G., & Mills, J. F. (2001). The accuracy of five risk appraisal instruments in predicting institutional misconduct and new convictions. *Criminal Justice and Behavior, 28*, 450-470.

Kruttschnitt, C., Uggen, C., & Shelton, K. (2000). Predictors of desistance among sex offenders: The interaction of formal and informal social controls. *Justice Quarterly, 17*, 61-88.

Laub, J. H., Sampson, R. J., & Nagin, D. S. (1998). Trajectories of change in criminal offending: Good marriages and the desistance process. *American Sociological Review, 63*, 225-38.

Laub, J. H., & Sampson, R. J. (1993). Turning points in the life course: Why change matters in the study of crime. *Criminology, 31*, 301-325.

Lee, E. T. (1980). *Statistical methods for survival data analysis*. Belmont, CA: Lifetime Learning Publications.

Lizotte, A. J., Krohn, M. D., Howell, J. C., Tobin, K., & Howard, G. J. (2000). Factors influencing gun carrying among young urban males over the adolescent-young adult life course. *Criminology, 38*, 811-834.

Loper, A. B. (2002). Adjustment to prison of women convicted of possession, trafficking, and non-drug offenses. *Journal of Drug Issues, 32*, 1033-1051.

Loza, W., Dhaliwal, G., Kroner, D. G., & Loza-Fanous, A. (2000). Reliability, construct, and concurrent validities of the self-appraisal questionnaire. *Criminal Justice and Behavior, 27*, 356-374.

Lutze, F. E. (1996). Does shock incarceration provide a supportive environment for the rehabilitation of offenders? A study of the impact of a shock incarceration program on inmate adjustment and attitudinal change. Unpublished doctoral dissertation. Pennsylvania State University, Harrisburg.

Lutze, F. E. (1998). Are shock incarceration programs more rehabilitative than traditional prison? A survey of inmates. *Justice Quarterly, 15*, 547-66.

Lutze, F. E., & Brody, D. C. (1999). Mental abuse as cruel and unusual punishment: Doboot camp prisons violate the eighth amendment? *Crime and Delinquency, 45*, 242-255.

Lutze, F. E., & Murphy, D. W. (1999). Ultramasculine prison environments and inmates' adjustment: It's time to move beyond the "boys will be boys" paradigm. *Justice Quarterly, 16*, 709-734.

Lutze, F. E., & Symons, M. L. (2003). The evolution of domestic violence policy through masculine institutions: From discipline to protection to collaborative empowerment. *Criminology & Public Policy, 2*, 319-331.

MacKenzie, D. L., Brame, R., McDowall, D., & Souryal, C. (1995). Boot camp prisons and recidivism in eight states. *Criminology, 33*, 327-357.

MacKenzie, D. L., & Li, S. D. (2002). The impact of formal and informal control on the criminal activities of probationers. *Journal of Research in Crime and Delinquency, 39*, 243-278.

MacKenzie, D. L., Wilson, B. D., Armstrong, G. S., & Gover, A. R. (2001). The impact of boot camps and traditional institutions on juvenile residents: Perceptions, adjustment, and change. *Journal of Research in Crime and Delinquency, 38*, 279-313.

Marcos, A. C., & Bahr, S. J. (1988). Control theory and adolescent drug use. *Youth & Society, 13*, 395-425.

McLellan, A. T., Kushner, H., Merger, D., Peters, R., Smith, L., Grissom, G., Pett, H., & Argeriou, M. (1992). The fifth edition of the Addiction Severity Index. *Journal of Substance Abuse Treatment, 9*, 199-213.

Molnar, B. E., Buka, S. L., & Kessler, R. C. (2001). Child sexual abuse and subsequent psychopathology: Results from the National Comorbidity Survey. *American Journal of Public Health, 91*, 753-760.

Morash, M., & Rucker, L. (1990). A critical look at the idea of boot camp as a correctional reform. *Crime & Delinquency, 36*, 204-222.

Mumola, C. (2000). Incarcerated parents and their children (NCJ 182335). Washington, DC: US Department of Justice Office of Justice Programs.

Namboodiri, K., & Suchindran, C. M. (1987). *Life table techniques and their applications*. New York: Academic.

Paternoster, R., Dean, C., Piquero, A. R., Mazerolle, P., & Brame, R. (1997). Continuity and change in offending careers. *Journal of Quantitative Criminology, 13*, 231-266.

Patterson, G. R., Crosby, L., & Vuchinich, S. (1992). Predicting risk for early police arrest. *Journal of Quantitative Criminology, 8*, 335-355.

Piquero, A. R., Brame, R., Mazerolle, P., & Haapanen, R. (2002). Crime in emerging adulthood. *Criminology, 40*, 137-169.

Rosen, C. S., Henson, B. R., Finney, J. W., & Moos, R. M. (2000). Consistency of self-administered and interview-based Addiction Severity Index composite scores. *Addiction, 95*, 419-425.

Sampson, R. J., & Laub, J. H. (1990). Crime and deviance over the life course: The salience of adult social bonds. *American Sociological Review, 55*, 609-27.

Sampson, R. J., & Laub, J. H. (1992). Crime and deviance in the life course. *Annual Review of Sociology, 18*, 63-84.

Sampson, R. J., & Laub, J. H. (1993). *Crime in the making: Pathways and turning points through life.* Cambridge, MA: Harvard University Press.

Sampson, R. J., & Laub, J. H. (1996). Socioeconomic achievements in the life course of disadvantaged men: Military service as a turning point, 1940-1965. *American Sociological Review, 61*, 347-367.

Simons, R. L., Stewart, E., Gordon, L. C., Conger, R. D., & Elder, G. H. (2002). A test of life-course explanations for stability and change in antisocial behavior from adolescence to young adulthood. *Criminology, 40*, 401-434.

Simons, R. L., Whitbeck, L. B., Conger, R. D., & Conger, K. (1991). Parenting factors, social skills, and value commitment as precursors to school failure, involvement, with deviant peers, and delinquent behavior. *Journal of Youth and Adolescence, 20*, 645-663.

Steffensmeier, D., & Allan, E. (1996). Gender and crime: Toward a gendered theory of female offending. *Annual Review of Sociology, 22*, 459-487.

Stinchcomb, J. B., & Terry, W. C. (2001). Predicting the likelihood of rearrest among shock incarceration graduates: Moving beyond another nail in the boot camp coffin. *Crime and Delinquency, 47*, 221-243.

Thornberry, T. P., Ireland, T. O., & Smith, C. A. (2001). Thee importance of time: The varying impact of childhood and adolescent maltreatment on multiple outcomes. *Development and Psychopathology, 13*, 957-979.

Toch, H. (1977). *Living in prison: The ecology of survival.* New York: Free Press.

Uggen, C. (2000). Work as a turning point in the life course of criminals: A duration model of age, employment, and recidivism. *American Sociological Review, 65*, 529-546.

Uggen, C., & Kruttschnitt, C. (1998). Crime in the breaking: Gender differences in desistance. *Law and Society Review, 32*, 339-366.

Visher, C. A., Lattimore, P. C., & Linster, L. R. (1991). Predicting the recidivism of serious youthful offenders using survival models. *Criminology, 29*, 329-366.

Warr, M. (1998). Life-course transitions and desistance from crime. *Criminology, 36*, 183-216.

Weeks, R., & Widom, C. S. (1998). Self-reports of early childhood victimization among incarcerated adult male felons. *Journal of Interpersonal Violence, 13*, 346-356.

Welch, M. (1997). A critical interpretation of correctional boot camps as normalizing institutions: Discipline, punishment, and the military model. *Journal of Contemporary Criminal Justice, 13*, 184-205.

Widom, C. S. (1996). Crime and childhood sexual abuse. *American Journal Psychiatry, 156,* 1223-1230.
Widom, C. S. (2001). Alcohol abuse as risk factor for and consequence of child abuse. *Alcohol Research and Health, 25,* 52-58.
Wood. P. B., & Grasmick, H. G. (1999). Toward the development of punishment equivalencies: Male and female inmates rate the severity of alternative sanctions compared to prison. *Justice Quarterly, 16,* 19-51.
Wright, B. R. E., Caspi, A., Moffitt, T. E., & Silva, P. A. (2001). The effects of social ties on crime vary by criminal propensity: A life-course model of interdependence. *Criminology, 39,* 321-351.
Wu, L. L., & Tuma, M. B. (1994). Assessing bias and fit of global and local hazard models. *Sociological Methods and Research, 19,* 354-87.
Yamaguchi, K. (1991). *Event history analysis.* Newbury Park, CA: Sage.
Zhang, L. J., Welte, W., & Wieczorek, W. F. (1999). Youth gangs, drug use, and delinquency. *Journal of Criminal Justice, 27,* 101-109.

AUTHORS' NOTES

Dr. Brent B. Benda is a professor in the School of Social Work at the University of Arkansas at Little Rock. He has published numerous articles on crime and delinquency, substance abuse, adolescent sexual behavior, and homelessness in journals such as *Journal of Research in Crime and Delinquency, Criminal Justice and Behavior, Journal of Criminal Justice, Journal of Social Service Research, Social Work Research, Journal of Youth and Adolescence, Journal of Adolescence, Youth & Society,* and, of course, several in the *Journal of Offender Rehabilitation.*

Many of these articles are co-authored with Dr. Nancy J. Toombs, who was a psychologist at the boot camp studied. Currently, she is in private practice and teaches psychology courses at the University of Arkansas at Little Rock.

Dr. Nancy J. Harm is an associate professor in the School of Social Work at the University of Arkansas at Little Rock.

Address correspondence to Dr. Brent Benda, School of Social Work, University of Arkansas at Little Rock, Little Rock, AR 72204 (E-mail: BBBENDA@UALR.EDU).

Self-Control, Gender, and Age: A Survival Analysis of Recidivism Among Boot Camp Graduates in a 5-Year Follow-Up

BRENT B. BENDA

University of Arkansas at Little Rock

NANCY J. TOOMBS

North Little Rock, Arkansas

ROBERT FLYNN CORWYN

University of Arkansas at Little Rock

ABSTRACT This study of 572 male and 120 female graduates of a boot camp investigates the potency of self-control as a predictor of recidivism in comparison to gender, age, and elements of life-course theory. It also examines whether the effects of self-control on recidivism are commensurate within the categories of gender. Recidivism is defined as a felony conviction or parole violation in a 5-year follow-up period. Cox's Proportional-Hazards Models indicate that self-control, gender, and age are significant predictors of recidivism when they are considered separately, and self-control and gender remain significant predictors when they are analyzed simultaneously. Furthermore, analyses show that low self-control is a stronger predictor of recidivism among men than women. Low self-control is a significant predictor of recidivism after elements of life-course theory are added to an analysis that also includes age and gender. Implications of these findings for self-control theory are discussed. *[Article copies available for a fee from The Haworth Document Delivery Service: 1-800-HAWORTH. E-mail address: <docdelivery@haworthpress.com> Website: <http://www.HaworthPress.com> © 2005 by The Haworth Press, Inc. All rights reserved.]*

KEYWORDS Boot camps, recidivism, self-control theory, gender differences

INTRODUCTION

The most widely cited (Vazsonyi & Killias, 2001) general theory of crime (Gottfredson & Hirschi, 1990, p. 117) posits that the operation of a single mechanism, low self-control, accounts for all forms of crime and "analogous behaviors" such as smoking, gambling, reckless driving, imprudent sex, and cheating on exams. General theory (Gottfredson & Hirschi, 1990) rests on the foundational assumption that humans naturally desire pleasure or self-gratification. Gottfredson and Hirschi (1990, p. 90) assume that crime and analogous behaviors typically are expedient means of self-gratification. The theory also assumes people differ in levels of self-control due to socialization. Self-control is gendered by caregiver attachment and monitoring (Benda, 2002a; Hay, 2001). Attachment fosters a desire to restrain natural impulses to avoid causing emotional pain to caregivers, and monitoring reinforces an internalizing of caregivers' expectations regarding obedience (Benda, 2001, 2002b; Benda & Corwyn, 2000). Low self-control is basically the product of weak external control and limited feelings of closeness to caregivers. Gottfredson and Hirschi (1990) do not specify the nature of interrelationships between caregiver attachment and monitoring and self-control. The emphasis on self-control implies that attachment and monitoring recede into the background and become irrelevant to crime once the level of self-control has been established (Hay, 2001; Pratt & Cullen, 2000).

Gottfredson and Hirschi (1990, p. 232) state that self-control accounts for individual differences in criminal and analogous behaviors, albeit they do not view self-control as deterministic: Self-control is the mechanism that regulates natural urges for self-gratification. In any situation, however, low self-control results in criminal or analogous behaviors only when the opportunity to engage in these behaviors is present. Although Gottfredson and Hirschi do link self-control to opportunity in the commission of these behaviors, the logic of their theory accords more significance to self-control in accounting for individual differences in crime and analogous behaviors (Pratt & Cullen, 2000). Opportunity refers to structural conditions of access and availability.

For example, substance use depends on access to and availability of drugs. However, as Pratt and Cullen (2000, p. 933) observe, there are ubiquitous opportunities for self-gratification. Gottfredson and Hirschi do not clarify the concept "opportunity," and they do not specify the nature of the relationships between opportunity, self-control, and crime or analogous behaviors (LaGrange & Silverman, 1999). Instead, their real emphasis is on self-control over natural urges for pleasure.

Low self-control is conceptualized as a stable construct manifested as propensities for hedonistic self-gratification (Gottfredson & Hirschi, 1990, p. 91): Individuals with low self-control are impulsive, prefer easy or simple tasks, seek risky experiences, choose physical rather than cognitive activities, are self-centered and insensitive to the needs of others, and lose their temper easily (Grasmick, Tittle, Bursik, & Arneklev, 1993). These propensities are evident by ten years of age, and they remain the primary motivations for criminal and analogous behaviors throughout the life span (see review, Pratt & Cullen, 2000). Stated succinctly, variation in criminal and analogous behavior between and within individuals can be fully accounted for by weak self-control. As Gottfredson and Hirschi state:

> Criminal acts are a subset of acts in which the actor ignores the long-term negative consequences that flow from the act itself (e.g., the health consequences of drug use), from the social or familial environment (e.g., spouses reaction to infidelity), or from the state (e.g., the criminal justice response to robbery). . . . The property of individuals that explains variance in the likelihood of engaging in such acts we call "self-control." (Pp. 1-2)

Self-control has "consequences" for the personal development and social functioning as well. According to Gottfredson and Hirschi (1990), however, any relationship between these "social consequences" and subsequent crime or analogous behaviors is spurious, and will disappear once levels of self-control are controlled. They are clear on this controversial point: "Lack of perseverance in school, in a job, or in an interpersonal relationship is simply different manifestations of the personal factors assumed to cause crime in the first place. Taking up with delinquent peers is another example of an event without causal significance" (Gottfredson & Hirschi, 1990, p. 251 and pp. 154-168). Limited educational attainment, sporadic employment, problems in relationships, association with criminals, and unlawful behavior are consequences of low self-control. When the positive relationship between low self-control and criminal behavior is considered, other theoretical factors cease to have relevance to this behavior (Tittle, Ward, & Grasmick, 2003).

Gottfredson and Hirschi (1990; Hirschi & Gottfredson, 1995) postulate that the effects of self-control on crime are commensurate across all sociodemorgaphic categories as well (Tittle et al., 2003). The effect of self-control is thought to be universal and robust, accounting for most if not all of the variance in crime within all social categories. Even if self-control does not account for most of the variance in unlawful behavior, it should explain equivalent amounts of variance within social categories–the effects of self-control should not be conditioned on these categories (Tittle et al., 2003). Also, self-control should account for any relationship between sociodemographic factors and offending.

Purpose of the Study

The purpose of the present study is fourfold: (a) to see if self-control predicts continuation of criminal behavior among graduates of a boot camp for adults in a 5-year follow-up period, (b) to investigate any differences in self-control according to gender and age, (c) to examine interactions between gender and self-control, and age and self-control, and (d) and to determine if elements of life-course theory predict recidivism when self-control is simultaneously considered. Gender and age are the strongest predictors of crime and recidivism, and so represent the severest challenge to claims of the universality of the relationship between self-control and criminal behavior. If self-control is as robust as Gottfredson and Hirschi (1990) maintain, the relationships between these sociodemographic factors and recidivism should be reduced to insignificance when they are considered simultaneously with self-control. Also, the relationship between self-control and recidivism should be commensurate within categories of gender and age.

Another strong competitor to self-control in predicting criminal behavior is peer association (Akers & Sellers, 2004; Benda & Toombs, 2002; Benda, Corwyn, & Toombs, 2001; Benda, Toombs, & Peacock, 2002, 2003; Pratt & Cullen, 2000). The three strongest predictors of crime, in descending order, is often reported to be gender, age, and peer associations (Akers & Sellers, 2004; Andrews & Bonta, 1998; Empey, Stafford, & Hay, 1999). Weak and ineffectual caregiver attachment and monitoring are theorized to be responsible for low self-control and drifting into affiliations with criminals (Cochran, Wood, Sellers, Wilkerson, & Chamlin, 1998; Gibbs, Giever, & Martin, 1998; Hay, 2001; Polakowski, 1994; Simons, Wu, Conger, & Lorenz, 1994).

In contrast, life-course theory (Sampson & Laub, 1993) posits that there are ameliorating experiences that represent "turning points" in one's life trajectory that can lead to desistance from crime. Based on prior research on life-course theory, the expectation is that higher education, regular full-time employment, living with a conventional partner (spouse or paramour), having children, and positive social relationships will be related to a desistance from criminal behavior among these boot camp graduates (Benda, 2003; Benda et al., 2003; Bushway, Piquero, Broidy, Cauffman, & Mazerolle, 2001; Giordano, Cernkovich, & Rudolph, 2002; Piquero, Brame, Mazerolle, & Haapanen, 2002; Simons, Stewart, Gordon, Conger, & Elder, 2002; Uggen, 2000). In other words, these ameliorating experiences are hypothesized to be "turning points" from a life trajectory of criminality to conventionality.

In summary, this is an exploratory study of the relative prediction of recidivism of self-control in comparison to two of the strongest sociodemographic predictors and several ameliorating experiences from life-course theory. This is a preliminary prediction study and not a test of theory.

METHOD

Sample

The present study consists of a convenience sample of 601 male and 120 female graduates from the only boot camp for adults in a southern state. Participation in the boot camp studied was an option to prison offered to eligible inmates. To be officially eligible for boot camp, inmates had to meet five criteria: (a) be a first-time referral to the adult correctional system in this state, (b) be sentenced to ten or less years, (c) have no recorded violent offenses in the adult correctional system, (d) have an IQ above seventy, and (e) have no physical or psychological problems, including drug addiction, that would preclude military training. Correctional counselors screened persons at the Diagnostic Unit. The drop-out rate was approximately 20 percent at the time of the study. Characteristics of the sample are shown in Table 1.

Procedure and Data

A staff psychologist, who administered the two questionnaires, had eight research associates available to monitor each table of five respondents to clarify wording or to answer questions. Research associates were available to interview inmates who could not read the questionnaires.

The two questionnaires were administered on separate Sundays to make the task more manageable for inmates, and hopefully to enhance the accuracy of responses. The questionnaire was administered approximately three weeks into the 105-day program to allow military discipline to develop, as well as trust in the psychologist who administered the questionnaires, since she also did mental health classes and counseling at this boot camp. While respondents did record their Department of Correction ID number to determine recidivism at a later date, they were assured of confidentiality by telling them that names would not be associated with ID numbers on the questionnaires, and none of the information provided by them was shared with anyone in the Department of Correction (DOC) except in aggregate form. Participation in the study was voluntary, and only six persons refused participation during the study period.

Table 1: Characteristics of the Sample (N = 721)

	Men (N = 601) Mean	SD	Women (N = 120) Mean	SD
Age (in years)	25.3	5.1	24.2	4.0
Age first arrest (in years)	14.2	1.7	15.9	2.6
Education	11.4	2.0	12.1	2.2
Number of children	1.9	1.2	2.0	1.4

	Frequency	Percent	Frequency	Percent
Race				
Caucasian	278	46.3	48	40.0
African American	306	50.9	68	56.7
Asian American	2	0.3	0	0.0
Hispanic American	6	1.0	3	2.5
Other	9	1.5	1	0.8
Childhood sexual abuse				
Yes	306	50.9	96	80.0
No	290	48.3	18	15.0
Missing	5	0.8	6	5.0
Childhood physical abuse				
Yes	264	43.9	87	72.5
No	332	55.3	25	20.8
Missing	5	0.8	8	6.7
Current sexual abuse				
Yes	15	2.5	52	43.3
No	576	95.8	60	50.0
Missing	10	1.7	8	6.7
Current physical abuse				
Yes	32	5.3	59	49.2
No	557	92.7	56	46.7
Missing	12	2.0	5	4.1
Living with conventional partner				
Yes	438	72.9	75	62.5
No	163	27.1	45	37.5
Full-time employment (past 3 years)				
Yes	408	67.9	73	60.8
No	193	32.1	47	39.2
Gang member				
Yes	432	71.9	67	55.8
No	169	28.1	53	44.2
Regularly carry weapon				
Yes	361	60.1	34	28.3
No	240	39.9	80	66.7
Missing			6	5.0
Sell drugs				
Yes	408	67.9	79	65.8
No	186	31.0	36	30.0
Missing	7	1.1	5	4.2

About 85 percent of the items on the questionnaires had no missing information, and most of the others were missing from one to ten cases. No variable was missing more than five percent of the cases.

Outcome or Dependent Variable

The DOC number assigned to inmates allowed a determination of whether or not boot camp graduates had any arrests or parole violations during the five-year follow-up study. All of the inmates were on parole after release from boot camp for the duration of their sentence. In approximately 65 percent of the cases, parole extended over the entire study; for almost all graduates, parole lasted at least three years. Parole entailed weekly contact for the first six months and monthly contact after this initial period, with random drug screens and additional unannounced visits. In short, the parole supervision was more intense and personal than is often true for persons released from prison. Although census surveys in the state indicate little migration from the state, there is no information about persons who left the state and committed felonies elsewhere (Arkansas Institute for Economic Advancement, 1999). This is a common flaw of recidivism studies because attempts to contact former inmates would be very expensive in several ways and the validity of responses about crime would be suspect.

There were 26 of 601 male inmates, or 4.3 percent, for whom there was no follow-up information. Presumably, those 26 graduates failed to report to a parole officer as required and disappeared from DOC. Three other cases (.3 percent of 575 graduates) were missing the number of days in the community, despite having other data recorded. The analyses of the 5-year follow-up data on recidivism, as a result, were based on 572 male boot camp graduates. No women were missing follow-up information. Hence, there was a relatively low "no response" rate for a criminal recidivism study (Andrews & Bonta, 1998). Every graduate was followed for 5 years, which meant individualized follow-up periods.

Of the 572 male graduates for whom data on number of days in the community was recorded, 352 persons, or 61.5 percent, were recidivists. Recidivism was defined as a return to the Department of Corrections for a new conviction for a felony or parole violation. Twenty percent of the men were returned to DOC for a parole violation. Fifty women, or 41.7 percent, were recidivists, and 15 percent of the female graduates were parole violators. Misdemeanors were not the reason for recidivism of any type.

Questionnaires and Prediction Measures

The Addiction Severity Index, or ASI (McLellan et al., 1992), was administered on a separate day from other measures presented in the following paragraphs. The ASI has reports of good reliability and validity (see review,

Rosen, Henson, Finney, & Moos, 2000). The ASI provided information on age; years of education; marriage to or living with conventional partner (0 = conventional, 1 = engages in crime); composite score on close relationships with children, family, friends, and spouse/sexual partner; suicide ideation; suicide attempts; number of children; and employment pattern that characterizes most of the past 3 years (0 = full-time, 1 = other). Full-time employment was defined as working 40 or more hours a week. The ASI manual has formulae for deriving composite scores (McLellan et al., 1992). Information also was collected on race. Since data showed that whites and African Americans comprised about 92 percent of the data, race was a dichotomy (0 = white, 1 = person of color).

Attachment was measured by two distinct variables of attachment to female and to male caregivers (4-point scales): (1) How much did you like being with ___; (2) how close did you feel to ___; (3) how much did you want to be like your ___, and (4) how much did you enjoy spending time with ___. However, since the distributions were similar, the two summated scores were added and divided by 2.

Caregiver monitoring was measured with five items (four-point scales, ranging from "very little" to "very much") asking how closely caregivers supervised: (a) spending money, (b) peer associations, (c) movies and parties, (d) how late you stay out, and (e) school activities (during childhood and adolescence). Caregiver attachment and monitoring were taken from Marcos and Bahr (1988).

Physical and sexual abuses were each measured with two items (four-point Likert scales, ranging from "never" to "more than ten times") asking how often respondents had been abused before 12 years of age (childhood abuse): (a) by a caregiver, and (b) by someone other than a caregiver. The same two items were also asked about sexual and physical abuses during adolescence at a later point in the questionnaire. Physical abuse was defined as any physical contact that resulted in severe cuts, bruises, welts, or other marks that took a few days to disappear; in concussions or breaking of bones; or in scalding or burns. Sexual abuse was defined as any touching of the genitals, and oral or anal intercourse that was non-consensual.

Peer association was measured with five items (five-point scales, ranging from "none" to "more than ten") asking how many of your best friends: (a) have ever been arrested, (b) use illegal drugs regularly, (c) consume three or more drinks of alcohol in a day regularly, (d) steal regularly, and (e) have used a weapon on another person.

Self-Control Measure

Hirschi and Gottfredson (1993, p. 48) argued that the best measures of self-control were based on behavior. Presumably, the behaviors selected were indicative of propensities to engage in risk-taking. These dichotomous (0 = no,

1 = yes) behaviors were selected from the ASI (McLellan et al., 1992): (1) illegal income, (2) arrests for disorderly conduct or public intoxication, (3) driving while drunk, (4) major traffic tickets in the past year, (5) car wrecks in the past year, (6) living with someone who has a alcohol/drug problem, and (7) attempted suicide in lifetime. On the ASI, inmates also were asked how many days in the past month they were: (1) drunk on alcohol, and (2) used other drugs (methadone; opiates/analgesics; barbiturates; sedatives, hypnotics, tranquilizers; cocaine, amphetamines/methamphetamines; marijuana; hallucinogens; inhalants; and club drugs (e.g., GHB or gamma-hydroxybutyrate, MDMA or ecstasy, Rohypnol). Street names were provided for drugs to be certain of mutual understanding.

The boot camp staff reliably recorded any infractions committed because they were considered to be a critical element in instilling discipline in the program. The gamut of infractions was very wide, ranging from forgetting to salute to disorderly behavior or assault. Finally, respondents were asked whether they regularly carry a concealed weapon, sold drugs, shared a needle in using drugs, and had unprotected sex (dichotomies of 0 = no versus 1 = yes). All items were factor analyzed with principal components, using a varimax rotation, and then they were standardized (Z-scores). The self-control scale was derived by multiplying the factor loading for each item by its Z-score, and summing across all items, which results in a scale with a mean of 0 and a standard deviation of 1 (Tittle et al., 2003). Items of the self-control measure were scaled so higher scores indicate low self-control.

The well-conceived and validated Grasmick self-control scale (Grasmick et al., 1993) was not available in this study. Tittle et al. (2003), however, found that behavioral measures were stronger predictors of various forms of crime than the Grasmick self-control scale.

Statistical Analyses

An examination of a correlation matrix and tests for tolerance and the variance inflation factor (VIF) do not reveal problems with multicollinearity (Freund & Wilson, 1998). The primary analyses are Cox's proportional hazard model because this procedure is not based on any assumption concerning the nature or shape of the underlying survival distribution (Lee, 1980; Wu & Tuma, 1994; Yamaguchi, 1991). The model assumes that the underlying hazard rate (rather than survival time) is a function of the independent variables (Allison, 1984, 1995). The model may be written as:

$$h\{(t), (z1,z2,....,zm)\} = h0(t)*exp(bl*z1 +....+bm*zm),$$

In which: h(t,...) denotes the resultant hazard, given the values of the m covariates for the respective case (z1,z2,....,zm) and the respective survival time (t). The term h0(t) is called the baseline hazard; it is the hazard for the respective individual when all independent variable values are equal to zero. This model is made linear by dividing both sides of the equation by h0(t) and then taking the natural logarithm of both sides: log{h{(t), (z....)}/h0(t)} = b1*z1+....+bm*zm, which provides a linear model that can be estimated (Lee, 1980; Wu & Tuma, 1994; Yamaguchi, 1991).

FINDINGS

The first two Cox's proportional hazards models (Models 1 and 2) in Table 2 are bivariate analyses of the effects of self-control on recidivism (arrest for felony or parole violation) in the 5-year follow-up of women and men who

Table 2: Cox's Proportional-Hazards Model of Recidivism

	Beta	Hazard Rate	Beta	Hazard Rate	Beta	Hazard Rate	Beta	Hazard Rate
Model 1 – Women (N = 120)								
Low self-control	.50**	1.65						
Model 2 – Men (N = 120)								
Low self-control	.75**	2.11						
Model 3 – Gender (0 = women) (both N's = 120) and self-control								
Gender	.59**	1.80	.27**	1.31				
Low self-control			.42**	1.52				
Model 4 – Age (N = 240)								
Age	−.51**	.60 (1.67)						
Model 5 – Age and self-control (N = 240)								
Age	−.51**	.60	−.12	.89 (1.12)				
Low self-control			.39**	1.48				
Model 6 – Gender, age and self-control (N = 240)								
Gender					.57**	1.77	.26**	1.29
Age					−.48**	.62	−.11	.90
Low self-control							.35**	1.42

Note: The reciprocal rate is shown in parentheses (1 per hazard rate). Age is standardized. The two samples used for Models 1 and 2 are combined for Models 4-6.
*P < .05; **P < .01

graduated from boot camp. To allow direct comparisons of the effects (Beta) of self-control between women and men in equal sample sizes, a simple random sample of 120 men is selected from the original 572 male graduates. A Wald chi-square shows that the effects of self-control do significantly differ by gender, and it can be seen that self-control is a stronger predictor for men (Beta = .75) than for women (Beta = .50). In Cox regression, the baseline hazard rate describes the risk of when the event (i.e., felony arrest or parole violation) will occur. A value greater than 1 reflects a greater hazard rate of recidivism for each unit of change in the predictor variable, and a beta value less than 1 a smaller hazard rate of recidivism at each unit of change in the predictor variable. The estimated betas give the magnitude of effect of each predictor on the log odds (logit) of the hazard of recidivism. Taking antilogs (exponents) of the estimated betas converts the effects to the odds of the hazard of recidivism. For example, the effect of self-control on recidivism of women is .50 (Table 2), which when exponentiated indicated that the odds of the hazard of recidivism increase by 1.65 for each unit (i.e., one standard deviation) increase in low self-control, which is a 65 percent increase (1.65 − 1 = .65). The hazard rate of recidivism rises 111 percent for men for every standard deviation increase in low self-control.

The third Cox's proportional hazards model shows that adding low self-control to gender in a second hierarchy does not reduce the effects on recidivism of gender to insignificance. Model 4 shows that the hazard rate of recidivism declines .60 with every standard deviation in advance in age, or increases 1.67 for every standard deviation decrease in age (1 per hazard rate). Age ceases to be a significant (alpha = 0.05) predictor of recidivism with the introduction of low self-control in the second hierarchy of Model 5. Although gender and age are both relevant predictors when analyzed together, age ceases to be a significant predictor after low self-control is entered simultaneously in the equation (Model 6).

Table 3 shows the hierarchical proportional hazards model, where low self-control is added to the analysis of sociodemographic characteristics (race, residence) and elements of life-course theory (Sampson & Laub, 1993). Continuous data are standardized to normalize distributions and to make coefficients more meaningful. The statistically significant changes (SCs), based on Wald's chi-square, in effects (Betas) between the first and second hierarchies indicate that low self-control reduces the prediction of recidivism of most factors analyzed. Race is not a significant predictor, and the addition of low self-control does not significantly affect the prediction of residence and caregiver monitoring. While the introduction of low self-control reduces the prediction of age to insignificance, and significantly diminishes the effects of gender, men are 33 percent more likely to be recidivists than are women.

Examining the statistical interaction between gender and self-control in the second hierarchy of the proportional hazards model shown in Table 4 indicates that this interaction significantly reduces the effects of most study fac-

Table 3: Cox's Proportional-Hazards Model of Recidivism (N = 692)

	First Hierarchy Beta	Hazard Rate	Second Hierarchy Beta	Hazard Rate	
Race (0 = white)	.10	1.10	.06	1.06	
Residence (0 = rural)	.55**	1.68	.53**	1.69	
Attachment to caregivers	−.36**	0.70	−.13	0.88	SC
Caregiver monitoring	−.60**	0.55	−.56**	0.57	
Criminal peer associations	.66**	1.90	.57**	1.77	SC
Ameliorating experiences					
Conventional partner (0 = yes)	−.69**	0.50	−.37**	0.69	SC
Number of children	−.91**	0.40	−.73**	0.48	SC
Years of education	−.65**	0.52	−.36**	0.70	SC
Employment (0 = full-time)	−.87**	0.42	−.69**	0.50	SC
Supportive relationships	−.89**	0.41	−.65**	0.52	SC
Age	−.37**	0.69	−.08	0.92	SC
Gender (0 = women)	.55**	1.75	.23**	1.26	SC
Low self-control			.29**	1.33	
−2 log likelihood	201.73**		190.01**		
Model chi-square			11.72*		

Note: Hazard rates based on standardized data (one unit change is one standard deviation for each predictor). Codes for dichotomous data (e.g., race) are shown. SC is significant ($\alpha = 0.05$) change according to Wald chi-square tests.
*P < .05; **P < .01

tors, and it shows that men who have low self-control are 26 percent more likely to be arrested for a felony or have a parole violation than men with higher self-control. The likelihood ratio compares the likelihood function for the full model to the likelihood function if all coefficients except the intercept are 0. The resulting statistic follows a chi-square distribution when the null hypothesis is true. A chi-square table, with K-1 degrees of freedom, with K being the number of estimators in the model, is used to ascertain the probability. The likelihood ratio statistic is labeled −2 log likelihood. A significant reduction in the −2 likelihood chi-square with the addition of predictors indicates improvement in model fit. A reduction is considered significant if the difference in −2 log likelihood chi-square is greater than the critical value for the chi-square distribution and corresponding degrees of freedom lost (or number of parameters added). This test can be used to determine if models are im-

Table 4: Cox's Proportional-Hazards Model of Recidivism: Gender Interaction (N = 692)

	First Hierarchy Beta	Hazard Rate	Second Hierarchy Beta	Hazard Rate	
Race (0 = white)	.10	1.10	.04	1.04	
Residence (0 = rural)	.55**	1.68	.51**	1.67	
Attachment to caregivers	−.36**	0.70	−.11	0.90	SC
Caregiver monitoring	−.60**	0.55	−.53**	0.59	
Criminal peer associations	.66**	1.90	.53**	1.70	SC
Ameliorating experiences					
Conventional partner (0 = yes)	−.69**	0.50	−.34**	0.71	SC
Number of children	−.91**	0.40	−.65**	0.52	SC
Years of education	−.65**	0.52	−.30**	0.74	SC
Employment (0 = full-time)	−.87**	0.42	−.65**	0.52	SC
Supportive relationships	−.89**	0.41	−.60**	0.55	SC
Gender (0 = women)	.55**	1.75	.01	1.01	SC
Age	−.37**	0.69	−.06	0.94	SC
Self-control	.02	1.02			
Gender * Low self-control			.23**	1.26	
−2 log likelihood	198.44**		180.41**		
Model chi-square			18.03**		

Note: Hazard rates based on standardized data (one unit change is one standard deviation for each predictor). Codes for dichotomous data (e.g., race) are shown. SC is significant ($\alpha = 0.05$) change according to Wald chi-square tests.
*P < .05; **P < .01

proved with the inclusion of additional parameters, and is referred to as the model chi-square. The model chi-squares in Tables 3 and 4 show that the predictors added in the second hierarchy increased the fit of the model.

DISCUSSION

This investigation of boot camp graduates found that 61.5 percent of the 572 men and 41.7 percent of the 120 women were convicted of a felony or violated parole in a 5-year follow-up period of study. Twenty percent of the men and 15 percent of the women were parole violators. Bivariate Cox's proportional hazards models indicated low self-control has a higher hazard rate of recidivism among men than among women (2.11 versus 1.65). The finding of gender differences in the hazard rate of recidivism is not synchronous with the assumption of commensurate effects of self-control across all social categories made by Gottfredson and Hirschi (1990). Nor did this study find support for the supposition of self-control accounting for the relationship between gender and recidivism. Gender remained a significant predictor of recidivism after self-control was simultaneously considered in the analysis, and even after age was added to the equation. At the same time, the addition of self-control did significantly reduce, according to a Wald chi-square test, the effects of gender on recidivism (Betas are .59 and .27). Further analysis indicated that men with low self-control are 26 percent more likely to be a recidivist than are men who have stronger self-control. These findings simply do not support Gottfredson and Hirschi's (1990) universality claim that self-control has equivalent effects within social groupings such as gender.

In contrast, age ceases to be a significant predictor of recidivism once self-control is entered in the same analysis, which is in agreement with the assumption of universality. Hirschi and Gottfredson (1983, pp. 554-562) argue that variation in crime across the life span is the result of the "inexorable aging of the organism" and, therefore, does not need to be explained by theory. Rather, self-control is robust enough to account for any difference in criminality according age, even though self-control does not explain it. Further, after considering major sociodemographic and theoretical predictors, self-control continues to be significantly associated with the recidivism of boot camp graduates over a five-year follow-up period. This latter finding provides support for at least a moderated claim that self-control is a key factor in persistence in crime. However, the present study certainly does not indicate that self-control is the sole, or even the primary, predictor of continuation in unlawful behavior. The findings suggest that a more modest role may need to be assigned to self-control in explaining the trajectory of criminal patterns over the life span. This observation is consistent with conclusions drawn by other researchers who have conducted similar research (Burton, Cullen, Evans, Alarid, & Dunaway, 1998; LaGrange & Silverman, 1999; Tittle et al., 2003). Accumulating evidence suggests that self-control is an important (Pratt & Cullen, 2000), but less prominent factor in the sequelae of unlawful behavior than proposed by Gottfredson and Hirschi (1990).

In fact, analyses in the present study indicate that ameliorating experiences, identified in life-course theory (Sampson & Laub, 1993), are stronger predictors of recidivism than self-control. For example, persons who have a pattern of full-time employment in the three years before incarceration in the boot camp are half as likely to be a recidivist as their counterparts. This 50 percent decrease in probability of recidivism compares to a 33 percent greater likelihood of recidivism with each unit (standard deviation) increase in low self-control (1.33 − 1 = .33). Analyses not shown due to space limits and redundancy indicate that self-control does not account for any of the ameliorating experiences seen in Table 4.

Taken together, the findings of the present study provide clues that self-control is likely a vital element of a more elaborate explanation than the one postulated by Gottfredson and Hirschi. (1990). The analyses presented offer preliminary support for incorporating the concept of self-control in life-course theory, adjusting for the overstated claims of potency.

In conclusion, the discussion of the implications of this study should not be interpreted as disapprobation, and certainly not rejection, of the importance of the concept of self-control to predicting or explaining the continuation of unlawful behavior. The consistent and compelling support for the relationship between low self-control and various forms of unlawful and unacceptable behavior (Pratt & Cullen, 2000; Tittle et al., 2003) is testimony to the merit of this concept. However, the preponderance of evidence is beginning to show that self-control is more likely an important conceptual element of an explanation than a theory per se. More research is needed to verify the findings because of limitations of the present study. Indeed, a prospective rather than a retrospective study is needed to establish temporal order of experiences. Also, multiple measures of self-control would be more convincing, especially since the validity of the measure used is not established. Variation in self-control also could be restricted in a sample of people who have been incarcerated for crime. Certainly, similar analyses must be performed in a variety of samples with different measures and outcomes before definitive statements are made in regard to the potency of self-control. However, the diversity of first admissions to the adult correctional system would seem to lessen the likelihood of restricted variation, and distribution and standard deviation actually observed in this study do not indicate that this is a problem. Finally, having a sample from one boot camp limits the generalizability of the study.

REFERENCES

Akers, R. L., & Sellers, C. S. (2004). *Criminological theories: Introduction and evaluation* (4th ed.). Los Angeles, CA: Roxbury.

Alarid, L., Burton, V., & Cullen, F. (2000). Gender and crime among felony offenders: Assessing the generality of social control and differential association theories. *Journal of Research in Crime and Delinquency, 32,* 171-199.

Allison, P. D. (1984). *Event history analysis.* Newbury Park, CA: Sage.

Allison, P. D. (1995). *Survival analysis using the SAS system.* Cary, NC: SAS Institute, Inc.

Andrews, D. A., & Bonta, J. (1998). *The psychology of criminal conduct* (2nd ed.). Cincinnati, OH: Anderson.

Benda, B. B. (2001). Conceptual model of assets and risks: Unlawful behavior among adolescents. *Adolescent & Family Health, 3,* 123-131.

Benda, B. B. (2002a). A test of three competing theoretical models of delinquency using structural equation modeling. *Journal of Social Service Research, 29,* 55-91.

Benda, B. B. (2002b). Religion and violent offenses among youth entering boot camp: Structural equation model. *Journal of Research in Crime and Delinquency, 39,* 92-101.

Benda, B. B. (2003). Survival analysis of criminal recidivism of boot camp graduates using elements from general and developmental explanatory models. *International Journal of Offender Therapy and Comparative Criminology, 47,* 89-101.

Benda, B. B., & Corwyn, R. F. (2000). A theoretical model of religiosity and drug use with reciprocal relationships: A test using structural equation modeling. *Journal of Social Service Research, 26,* 43-67.

Benda, B. B., Corwyn, R. F., & Toombs, N. J. (2001). Recidivism among adolescent serious offenders: Prediction of entry into the correctional system. *Criminal Justice and Behavior, 28,* 588-613.

Benda, B. B., Toombs, N. J., & Peacock, M. (2002). Ecological factors in recidivism: A survival analysis of boot camp graduates after three years. *Journal of Offender Rehabilitation, 35,* 63-85.

Benda, B. B., Toombs, N. J., & Peacock, M. (2003). An examination of competing theories in predicting recidivism of adult offenders five years after graduation from boot camp. *Journal of Offender Rehabilitation, 37,* 43-75.

Burton, V. S., Jr., Cullen, F. T., Evans, T. D., Alarid, L. F., & Dunaway, R. G. (1998). Gender, self-control, and crime. *Journal of Research in Crime and Delinquency, 35,* 123-147.

Bushway, S. D., Piquero, A. R., Broidy, L. M., Cauffman, E., & Mazerolle, P. (2001). An empirical framework for studying desistance as a process. *Criminology, 39,* 491-515.

Cochran, J. K., Wood, P. B., Sellers, C. S., Wilkerson, W., & Chamlin, M. B. (1998). Academic dishonesty and low self-control: An empirical test of a general theory of crime. *Deviant Behavior, 19,* 227-255.

Empey, L. T., Stafford, M. C., & Hay, C. H. (1999). *American delinquency: Its meaning and construction* (4th ed.). Belmont, CA: Wadsworth.

Freund, R. J., &Wilson, W. J. (1998). *Regression analysis: Statistical modeling of a response variable.* New York: Academic Press.

Gibbs, J. J., Giever, D., & Martin, J. S. (1998). Parental management and self-control: An empirical test of Gottfredson and Hirschi's general theory. *Journal of Research in Crime and Delinquency, 35,* 40-70.

Giordano, P. C., Cernkovich, S. A., & Rudolph, J. L. (2002). Gender, crime, and desistance: Toward a theory of cognitive transformation. *The American Journal of Sociology, 107,* 990-1064.

Gottfredson, M., & Hirschi, T. (1990). *A general theory of crime.* Palo Alto, CA: Stanford University Press.

Grasmick, H., Tittle, C., Bursik, R. J., & Arneklev, B. J. (1993). Testing the core empirical assumptions of Gottfredson and Hirschi's general theory of crime. *Journal of Research in Crime and Delinquency, 30,* 5-29.

Hay, C. (2001). Parenting, self-control, and delinquency: A test of self-control theory. *Criminology, 39,* 707-736.

Heimer, K. (1996). Gender, interaction, and delinquency: Testing a theory of differential social control. *Social Psychology Quarterly, 59,* 39-61.

Heimer, K., & DeCoster, S. (1999). The gendering of violent delinquency. *Criminology, 37*, 277-317.

Hirschi, T. (1969). *Causes of delinquency.* Berkeley: University of California Press.

Hirschi, T., & Gottfredson, M. R. (1983). Age and the explanation of crime. *American Journal of Sociology, 89*, 552-584.

Hirschi, T., & Gottfredson, M. R. (1993). Commentary: Testing the general theory of crime. *Journal of Research in Crime and Delinquency, 30*, 47-54.

Hirschi, T., & Gottfredson, M. R. (1995). Control theory and the life-course perspective. *Studies on Crime and Crime-Prevention, 4*, 131-142.

LaGrange, T. C., & Silverman, R. A. (1999). Low self-concept and opportunity: Testing the general theory of crime as an explanation for gender differences in delinquency, *Criminology, 37*, 41-72.

Lee, E. T. (1980). *Statistical methods for survival data analysis.* Belmont, CA: Lifetime Learning Publications.

Marcos, A. C., & Bahr, S. J. (1988). Control theory and adolescent drug use. *Youth & Society, 13*, 395-425.

McLellan, A. T., Kushner, H., Merger, D., Peters, R., Smith, L., Grissom, G., Pett, H., & Argeriou, M. (1992). The fifth edition of the Addiction Severity Index. *Journal of Substance Abuse Treatment, 9*, 199-213.

Piquero, A. R., Brame, R., Mazerolle, P., & Haapanen, R. (2002). Crime in emerging adulthood. *Criminology, 40*, 137-169.

Polakowski, M. (1994). Linking self- and social control with deviance: Illuminating the structure underlying a general theory of crime and its relation to deviant activity. *Journal of Quantitative Criminology, 10*, 41-78.

Pratt, T. C., & Cullen, F. T. (2000). The empirical status of Gottfredson and Hirschi's general theory of crime: A meta-analysis. *Criminology, 38*, 931-960.

Rosen, C. S., Henson, B. R., Finney, J. W., & Moos, R. M. (2000) Consistency of self-administered and interview-based Addiction Severity Index composite scores. *Addiction, 95*, 419-425.

Sampson, R. J., & Laub, J. H. (1993). *Crime in the making: Pathways and turning points through life.* Cambridge, MA: Harvard University Press.

Sampson, R. J., & Laub, J. H. (1997). A life-course theory of cumulative disadvantage and the stability of delinquency. In T. P. Thornberry (ed.) *Developmental theories of crime and delinquency* (pp. 133-161). New Brunswick, NJ: Transaction Publishers.

Simons, R. J., Wu, C., Conger, R. D., & Lorenz, F. O. (1994). Two routes to delinquency: Differences between early and late starters in the impact of parenting and deviant peers. *Criminology, 32*, 247-274.

Simons, R. L., Stewart, E., Gordon, L. C., Conger, R. D., & Elder, G. H. (2002). A test of life-course explanations for stability and change in antisocial behavior from adolescence to young adulthood. *Criminology, 40*, 401-434.

Tittle, C. R., Ward, D. A., & Grasmick, H. G. (2003). Gender, age, and crime/deviance: A challenge to self-control theory. *Journal of Research in Crime and Delinquency, 40*, 426-453.

Uggen, C. (2000). Work as a turning point in the life course of criminals: A duration model of age, employment, and recidivism. *American Sociological Review, 65*, 529-546.

Vazsonyi, A. T., & Killias, M. (2001). Immigration and crime among youth in Switzerland. *Criminal Behavior and Justice, 28,* 329-366.

Wu, L. L., & Tuma, M. B. (1994). Assessing bias and fit of global and local hazard models. *Sociological Methods and Research, 19,* 354-87.

Yamaguchi, K. (1991). Event history analysis. Newbury Park, CA: Sage.

AUTHORS' NOTES

Dr. Brent B. Benda is a professor in the School of Social Work at the University of Arkansas at Little Rock. He has published articles on crime and delinquency, substance abuse, adolescent sexual behavior, and homelessness in journals such as *Journal of Research in Crime and Delinquency, Criminal Justice and Behavior, Journal of Criminal Justice, Journal of Social Service Research, Social Work Research, Journal of Youth and Adolescence, Journal of Adolescence, Youth & Society,* and, of course, several in the *Journal of Offender Rehabilitation.*

Some of these articles are co-authored with Dr. Nancy J. Toombs, who was a psychologist at the boot camp studied. Currently, she is in private practice and teaches psychology courses at the University of Arkansas at Little Rock.

Dr. Robert Flynn Corwyn is an assistant professor, Department of Psychology, University of Arkansas at Little Rock, who has published several articles with Dr. Benda.

Address correspondence to Dr. Brent Benda, School of Social Work, University of Arkansas at Little Rock, Little Rock, AR 72204 (E-mail: BBBENDA@UALR.EDU).

Rehabilitation Issues, Problems, and Prospects in Boot Camp. Pp. 133-152.
http://www.haworthpress.com/web/JOR
© 2005 by The Haworth Press, Inc. All rights reserved.
Digital Object Identifier: 10.1300/J076v40n03_07

Boot Camp Prisons as Masculine Organizations: Rethinking Recidivism and Program Design

FAITH E. LUTZE

Washington State University

CORTNEY A. BELL

Washington State University

ABSTRACT A number of studies have tested the effectiveness of boot camp prisons in reducing recidivism and results indicate that they have not been as successful as originally anticipated. While no two programs are comparable in terms of programming and treatment, most programs utilize a hypermasculine paramilitary prison structure to deter, punish, and rehabilitate. We argue that this structure is problematic in terms of the way in which it is used to instill and reinforce hypermasculine behaviors that have been found to be highly correlated with criminal behavior. After introducing the prison as a gendered organization and discussing the relationship of masculinity and crime, we review studies of boot camp prisons and relate these findings to specific masculine attributes of the boot camp to show how the organizational design may be ineffective in producing desired correctional outcomes. *[Article copies available for a fee from The Haworth Document Delivery Service: 1-800-HAWORTH. E-mail address: <docdelivery@haworthpress.com> Website: <http://www.HaworthPress.com> © 2005 by The Haworth Press, Inc. All rights reserved.]*

KEYWORDS Boot camps, hypermasculine environments, organization designs, gender

Boot camp prisons emerged in the 1980s as a means to get tough on young, male, nonviolent offenders who were perceived as needing structure and strict discipline in order to live a law abiding lifestyle. "Bad boys" were to be turned into respectful and responsible men through an intense, stark, paramilitary prison environment designed to deter, punish, and rehabilitate (see Lutze, 2001, 2003; Lutze & Murphy, 1999). Unfortunately, a recent review of boot camp prison research reports that "boot camps did not reduce recidivism regardless of whether the camps were for adults or juveniles or whether they were first generation programs with a heavy military emphasis or later programs with more emphasis on treatment" (MacKenzie, Wilson, & Kider, 2001; Parent, 2003, p. 4). After 20 years of operation and evaluation, most shock incarceration programs are unable to reduce recidivism at a rate greater than that of traditional prisons or probation. This failure has been primarily attributed to low dosage effects (short term stays–usually from 90 to 120 days), a lack of cognitive-based treatment programs, and the absence of aftercare programs (MacKenzie et al., 2003; Parent, 2003; Stinchcomb & Terry, 2001; Zachariah, 1996).

Current research suggests that making comparisons across programs is difficult because with the exception of military-like training, no two programs are alike in their design and implementation (MacKenzie et al., 2001; Parent, 2003). One similarity across programs that is rarely discussed in the boot camp prison literature is the hypermasculine prison environment and its potential effects on offender success (Lutze, 2002; Lutze & Murphy, 1999; Morash & Rucker, 1990; Welch, 1997). Morash and Rucker (1990) were the first to express concerns about subjecting young impressionable men to a military model designed to train soldiers to use aggression for the purposes of war. They argue that the institutional setting is instilling the very attributes found to be highly correlated with criminal offending. Thus, Morash and Rucker (1990) question the use of an aggressive paramilitary model in terms of its philosophical inconsistency with promoting prosocial behavior.

Moreover, Welch (1997) points out how the United States military no longer uses its traditional boot camp training due to adverse effects on behavior resulting from the use of aggression, humiliation, and intimidation. He challenges the use of a quasi-military approach to instill productive and socially valuable behaviors when there is a lack of research supporting the connection between intimidation style interventions and responsivity to treatment. Welch (1997) suggests that, rather than using the masculine-centered military model as a normalizing institution in correctional settings, prison officials should place more emphasis on education and treatment.

In support of Morash and Rucker's (1990) and Welch's (1997) argument, Lutze and Murphy (1999) found, in a study including both boot camp and traditional inmates, that those who defined the prison environment as more masculine reported "greater levels of assertiveness, isolation, helplessness, stress, and conflict with other inmates and with the staff" (p. 725). Furthermore, inmates in both prisons reported feeling less safe when they defined the environment as more coercive. Lutze and Murphy (1999) proposed that the gendered nature of prisons could potentially inhibit the effectiveness of rehabilitation and treatment programming.[1]

This study builds upon prior research by reviewing studies of boot camp prisons and relating these findings to masculine prison environments and their inability to reduce recidivism. We argue that the hypermasculine prison environment that exists in most prisons, and especially boot camp prisons, creates a milieu that has a tendency to mitigate the potential for creating long-term positive change in male offenders.[2] First, we define masculinity and its connection to criminal behavior. Second, we define masculine prison environments as implemented in boot camp prisons. Third, we discuss the connection between gendered prison environments and the individual attributes related to recidivism.

Ultimately, we argue that the interaction between the institutionalization of masculinity in boot camp prisons and individual level factors related to masculinity will help to explain the failure of boot camp prisons to reduce recidivism. To effectively rehabilitate offenders, boot camp prisons must target predictors of criminality in programming and treatment settings (see Andrews, Zinger, Hoge, Bonta, Gendreau, & Cullen, 1990; Harland, 1996). In order for correctional institutions to be successful in changing behavior, the interaction between masculine organizations and individualized masculine-based responses to incarceration needs to be fully understood. An environment steeped in masculine attributes and approaches will fail to reduce recidivism because it reinforces the very masculine qualities that highly correlate with criminal behavior.

MASCULINITY AND CRIME

Within a patriarchal society, masculinity is stereotypically described as strong, independent, dominant, aggressive, coercive, forceful, tough, rational, logical, competitive, and unemotional (Johnson, 1997; Kilmartin, 2000; Lorber, 2001; Schwartz & DeKeseredy, 1997). Masculinity represents those characteristics that are in direct opposition to femininity. Femininity is defined as feeble, erratic, emotional, dependant, subservient, and passive (Johnson, 1997; Kilmartin, 2000; Lorber, 2001). These sex roles differentiate appropriate behaviors for men and women. In patriarchal societies, masculine characteristics are related to the positive and the powerful in terms of social identity

(Johnson, 1997; Kilmartin, 2000; Lutze, 2003). In general, patriarchal society rejects and devalues behaviors, characteristics, and ideals associated with femininity.

Patriarchy is fundamental to understanding society in its relation to the value society places on masculinity. Johnson (1997) defines patriarchy as an oppressive society that is "male-dominated, male-identified, and male-centered" (p. 5). Patriarchy functions as a social system that penetrates all aspects of daily life, from individual and group level interaction, to the organizational structure of institutions. The male domination of patriarchal society is manifested where positions of power, authority, and decision-making are reserved almost exclusively for men and awards men a greater portion of prestige, wealth, power, and influence than women. Patriarchy, combined with a man's social standing as it relates to race, socio-economic status, sexual orientation and other social positions, functions to give some men greater power than other men and the inherent right to assert control over their behavior (Johnson, 1997; Kilmartin, 2000). Thus, depending on the situation and social position, men are often placed in positions to either assert their authority over, or to have to defend their masculinity from, other men.

Masculinities are developed through a process of learning and imitation where parents, peers, institutions, organizations, and society teach and train appropriate patterns of behavior (Haywood & Mac an Ghaill, 2003; Johnson, 1997; Kilmartin, 2000; Schwartz & DeKeseredy, 1997). Such support or peer networks construct, maintain, reinforce, and encourage the existence of masculine ideals (Haywood & Mac an Ghaill, 2003). Moreover, in many situations, if men do not adhere to these stringent masculine-gendered guidelines, or should publicly express feminine attributes, they are considered weak and vulnerable (Lutze, 2003). This is especially true in all-male organizations such as athletic teams, fraternities, gangs, and prisons (see Humphry & Kahn, 2000; Jackson, 1991; Lutze, 2003; Lutze & Murphy, 1999; Messner & Sabo, 1994; Schwartz & DeKeseredy, 1997). In all male groups, men are often pressured to contend with an "ultramasculine" or "hypermasculine" environment. Hypermasculinity is acting in extreme adherence to the masculine gender role in ways that over emphasize masculine attributes and diminish all things feminine (see Kilmartin, 2000).

It appears that when gender roles are exaggerated and their expression narrowly defined that negative consequences can occur. For example, certain behaviors are viewed positively, like independence, but when "help from others is needed to overcome personal problems such as drug and alcohol addiction or financial hardships," independence may get in the way of potential healing and productive behaviors (Lutze & Murphy, 1999, pp. 711-712). Additionally, aggressiveness and confrontation can be useful in some circumstances, but may be counterproductive when attempting to promote compromise. Behaviors such as these may cause domestic problems, public conflict, and even lead to crime (see Johnson, 1997; Kilmartin, 2000; Lorber, 2001).

Interestingly, criminologists have consistently identified gender as a primary predictor of criminal behavior where men and boys commit a disproportionate amount of crime (see Kempf-Leonard & Tracy, 2003; Krienert, 2003; Messerschmidt, 1997 for review). Hypermasculinity has been theoretically and empirically linked with criminality and delinquency (Cloward & Ohlin, 1960; Cohen, 1955; Collison, 1996; Parsons, 1964; Sutherland & Cressey, 1924; see Morash & Rucker, 1990), aggression (Pleck, 1981), sexual assault (Bohmer & Parrot, 1993; Herbert, 2002; Miedzian, 1993; Schwartz & DeKeseredy, 1997; Sanday, 1990) and violence (Adler & Polk, 1996; Bourgois, 1996; Brittan, 1989; Hatty, 2000; Kersten, 1996). Although earlier theorists did not directly consider masculinity as an important variable in defining delinquency, contemporary reviews of their work have categorized and identified the very attributes associated with criminality as being masculine in nature and meeting the definition of characteristically masculine descriptors (see Belknap, 2001; Krienert, 2003).

Some theorists argue that the use of criminal male accomplishment (referring to the status achieved by the toughness and courage it takes to perpetrate crime) is especially likely when an individual's masculinity is questioned (see Krienert, 2003). Messerschmidt (1993) argues that if traditional outlets (work, education, recreation) are unavailable for prescribing to stereotypical masculine behaviors, alternative resources (criminality) will be utilized instead. Krienert (2003) tested this hypothesis and reported that "violent incidents were more likely to include highly masculine men who had few traditional outlets to assert their masculinity" (p. 13). We argue that prison environments are designed to restrict alternative modes of adaption separate from hypermasculine responses to the prison and to other inmates. In stronger terms, prisons socially castrate males and their ability to adhere to healthy definitions of masculinity that allow for multiple modes of responding to their incarceration and to their potential for success.

BOOT CAMP PRISONS AS MASCULINE ORGANIZATIONS

Newton (1994) suggests that prisons are "amongst the most male-dominated of modern institutions" where men make up a disproportionate number of the prisoner population and the correctional and administrative staff (p. 194). She argues that the study of gender and masculinities as problematic sociological discourse in the prison setting is needed to explain the structure of the institution as a gendered organization. Additionally, the hierarchy and dominance so prevalent in prisons informs the function of masculinity as a tool used by prison staff to highlight their authority and undermine the power of the inmates and their inmate subculture (Newton, 1994; Sims, 1994).

Gender research on organizations show that masculine and feminine attributes become institutionalized in organizations through their design, organization, procedures and products. An organization refers to the "act and process of social organizing" (Hearn & Parkin, 2001, p. 1). A gendered organization is defined as the process and structure of social relations founded upon the interpretation of sex role stereotypes. In other words, an organization is gendered to the extent that it exhibits the gendered (1) division of labor and authority, (2) decision-making, (3) responsibilities, and (4) existence and occurrence of sex and violence (Hearn & Parkin, 2001). Additionally, within a gendered organization, gendered value systems are developed, highlighting the influential affect of organizational functioning (Mills, 1992).

Witz and Savage (1992) discuss the gendered nature of organizations as they are pivotal in the process of reinforcing and continuing gendered relations and patterns of gender in society. Such organizations affect interactions inside and outside of the organization (Mills, 1992). Carrabine and Longhurst (1998) posit the importance of organizational power relations as they involve the construction and reproduction of masculinities in prison with regard to prison management and the interaction between the "activities of the powerful and their interactions with the relatively powerless" (Carrabine & Longhurst, 1998, pp. 163-164). In other words, order is obtained by prison management and correctional officers through gendered power.

Research on traditional prison environments contend that prisons designed by men to punish other men are inherently designed to strip men of their masculinity (Carrabine & Longhurst, 1998; Lutze, 2003; Newton, 1994). Lutze (2003, pp. 186-187) argues that,

> to punish men is to strip them of their manhood–to dominate them, by stripping them of their independence, their ability to achieve legitimate success, their ability to work, their ability to compete, and of their heterosexuality. To be a male inmate is to have to maintain one's manhood in the face of institutionalized masculinity by maintaining some level of independence and dominance (if necessary through defiance) by being tougher, stronger and more aggressive than one's captors and other inmates, and by defending one's heterosexuality. Therefore, male prisons are in a constant state of men attempting to emasculate other men and men resisting that emasculation.

Thus, male inmate behavior often is in direct confrontation to the authority that is attempting to strip them of their masculinity (also see Carrabine & Longhurst, 1998; Newton, 1994). Inmates must not only defend their masculinity from the enforcement of organizational policies implemented by corrections officers, but also act in defense against other inmates seeking to assert their own masculinity within the group.

Newton (1994) suggests that many of the earlier works on prison culture and inmate adjustment were descriptions of how men must adjust their masculinity to the deprivations of the prison environment. She argues that Sykes'

(1958) "pains of imprisonment" (lack of liberty, goods and services, heterosexual relations, autonomy, and security) are directly tied to the importation of an offender's masculine status from outside the prison and their need to maintain their identity in the face of the prison's attack on their masculinity. Newton (1994) also maintains that the prison culture that develops as a result of the prisoner's code is possibly a "variant theme of male bonding" that can be "found in almost any male-dominated institution" (p. 196). Thus, the peer group culture that forms within the prison setting is masculine in nature and gendered because it reinforces ideas about proper male behavior (also see Schwartz & Dekersedy, 1997 for a related discussion). Although many boot camp prisons were designed to counter many of the negative attributes of the prison culture described by Sykes (1958) and others (see Lutze, 1998), they still create a climate that reinforces stereotypical male responses to incarceration.

The philosophy, goals, implementation strategies, and rehabilitative programming of shock incarceration programs have been designed "for men by men" (Lutze, 2002). Moreover, the environmental context of such sanctioning is defined by its prescription to hypermasculine ideals. It is this structural foundation of narrow masculinity that is of utmost concern when examining the organization of boot camp prisons (Lutze & Murphy, 1999; Morash & Rucker, 1990).

Boot camp prisons are masculine organizations in their use of a paramilitary design that emphasizes aggressive interaction, physical exercise, physical labor, corporal punishment, limited visitation with family, and limited contact with women. The masculine environment is experienced by inmates on two levels. First, the organizational level relates to program design and how it is interpreted and implemented by primarily male correctional officers and applied to male inmates (organization/CO-to-inmate). Second is the individual/group level, in which inmates must also defend their masculinity within a group of male inmates (inmate-to-inmate).[3] Therefore, it is important to consider both the influence of organizational factors as well as individual level interactions on behavior when examining the gendered nature of a prison environment.

Communication through aggressive interaction and confrontation. Images of aggressive confrontation in boot camp prisons are abundant. Supporters of boot camp prisons are quick to promote images to the media of tough, mean-looking, drill-sergeants, in smokey-bear hats, yelling instructions inches away from an offender's face (see Lutze & Brody, 1999). Aggressive confrontation is envisioned as a means to confront inmate denial and manipulative behavior related to their criminality and to their lifestyle. It also serves the purpose of letting offenders know unconditionally who is in charge. Inmates are to respond assertively, but subserviently and respectfully, in response to staff comments by yelling with a resounding "yes or no sir." In some programs, inmates are expected to loudly ask permission to pass a staff member in the hallway, to enter the mess hall to eat, and to participate in general activities. Yelling is also a common part of participating in physical education and responding to the administration of corporal punishments.

From an organizational perspective, this approach is supported as a means to focus the offender's attention and to let him know who is in charge so that he may concentrate on changing his behavior. From a gendered perspective, however, this process of communication helps to establish the vertical hierarchy between men–it establishes who has power and who does not. For inmates to pause and ask permission to eat or merely pass through the hall is to constantly remind them of their subservient, weaker position.

Corporal punishment. Corporal punishment in BCP is generally proposed as a means to immediately address infractions and to hold inmates accountable for inappropriate behavior. In general, most corporal punishments are through short bursts of physical exercise such as pushups, sit-ups, running, or some test of endurance and strength (Mackenzie et al., 2001). Some punishments, however, are longer in duration and, at times, humiliating. For instance, some boot camp prisons make inmates carry logs on their backs, carry items (such as boots) with them for days, or wear signs that signify the extent of their infraction (see Lutze & Brody, 1999).

From a gendered perspective, it is not surprising that corporal punishment would center around physical strength and humiliation. Physical strength is central to masculinity. Additionally, the use of aggression, coercion, and forcefulness serves to achieve dominance (Kilmartin, 2000). Therefore, in a masculine-dominated (and male-centered) organization, male officers assert their masculinity by way of corporal punishments, assuming that other men are physically and mentally tough enough to handle the strain and humiliation; and if not, the perception then becomes that they have failed as men. It is the individual masculinity of the man who is questioned versus the "treatment" approach that is used. Unfortunately, this approach to the use of communication and corporal punishment conveys that an effective way to get what you want from others is to use aggressive confrontation to establish dominance–two attributes that may be dangerous if internalized by those prone to commit crime.

Physical education. Athleticism and physical health are often promoted as an important foundation for positive behavioral change. Many physical challenge programs, such as Outward Bound, are based on this philosophy. Physical education and wellness are viewed as a key component of many boot camp prison programs because many adult offenders, especially drug users, have lived destructive lifestyles. Exercise has been theoretically promoted as a means to enhance self-esteem, reduce stress, and build pro-social interaction through teamwork. Although the causal connection between exercise and pro-social activities is tenuous, there is still tremendous support for such approaches in boot camp prisons (see Corriea, 1997).

Physical exercise in boot camp prisons comes through traditional means such as morning calisthenics, weightlifting, and sport; and through less traditional means such as military drills, long distance runs, hard labor, and corporal punishments. Whether the causal relationship between exercise and the instilling of pro-social activities is still tenuous, the instillation of healthy habits through exercise is not an unreasonable goal for boot camp prisons. Exercise in most boot camp prisons, however, melds exercise with punishment. Through a gendered perspective, exercise in boot camp prison becomes an activity that is used to build physical strength because men should be strong, while at the same time it is used as a punishment to physically and mentally dominate and subordinate weaker men. It then becomes practically impossible to sort out the positive from the negative effects of exercise in boot camp prisons.

Physical or hard labor. A culturally reinforced aspect of patriarchal societies says that men work to support their families. Prisons have often equated work to rehabilitation and punishment (see Christianson, 1998; Pisciotta, 1994; Rothman, 1971 for historical reviews). Research has shown that meaningful work in prison is significantly related to success after release (Gendreau & Ross, 1987; Petersillia, 2003). In boot camp prisons, inmate labor is generally framed as a means to instil a strong work ethic and to provide valuable services to the institution and the inmates who live there.

The menial nature of most boot camp prison work, however, often conveys subservience and at times is equated with slave labor. For instance, farm labor is conducted with hand tools instead of machinery, non-motorized push mowers to cut the grass instead of tractors, tooth brushes to clean bathrooms, and other primitive methods to conduct menial labor. Most boot camp prisons do not provide vocational training opportunities where valuable skills may be used or practiced. Research has shown that boot camp prison inmates' attitudes toward work become more negative over time (Lutze, 2001). From a gendered perspective, work in the boot camp prison is used as a means to humiliate men instead of a means to empower or restore them to their traditional masculine status as productive individuals.

Family and contact with women. A separation from women is fundamental to the organizing structure of boot camp prisons. Women are underrepresented as correctional staff, and if present, usually hold positions within the secretarial, treatment and education realms. One could argue that women are seen as unsuitable drill sergeants, incapable of dominating, aggressing, and ordering male inmates into law-abiding subservience and subordination. Instead, their tasks are more central to nurturing change and support.

Schwartz and DeKeseredy (1997) argue that men-only space creates environments that breed exaggerated sex-role stereotypes and aggression directed toward women. Lack of privacy, personal space, and contact with females creates an increased need for inmates to demonstrate their masculinity. Within the prison setting, this translates into increased homophobia to counter threats of identifying with homosexuality. Moreover, all-male populations support and encourage the devaluation of anything feminine (Sanday, 1990; Schwartz &

DeKeseredy, 1997). This is manifested through the negative use of female language to insult and degrade. For instance, inmates failing to express their superior masculinity are labeled "sissies," "women," and "girls" (Lutze & Brody, 1999).

Additional interaction with women is denied because many boot camp prisons only allow inmates minimal contact with their family despite research that suggests that contact with family significantly relates to reduced recidivism (Petersilla, 2003). Boot camp prison administrators necessitate this practice because the inmate is an emotional and financial burden to his family and so contact should be kept to a minimum. Supported by the masculine notion of independence and stoic unemotionalism, it is expected that inmates give priority to solving their own problems instead of relying on others.

THE RELATIONSHIP BETWEEN MASCULINITY AND RECIDIVISM

Now that we have established boot camp prisons as inherently masculine organizations, it is necessary to look at what population of boot camp graduates recidivate. In other words, is there a connection between the masculinity present in boot camp prisons and those inmates who re-offend? Only a few studies of recidivists from boot camp prisons have looked at individual level attributes and success after release. These studies, when analyzed through a gendered perspective, lend support to our argument that masculine organizations, such as prisons, may in fact interact with individual-level characteristics of inmates to significantly affect recidivism.

Research on masculinity and behavior shows that younger males are more likely to be in competition with other males for status related to work, athletics, and women (see Kilmartin, 2000). They are more likely than older men to publicly express their masculine identity through the use of aggression and other high risk behaviors (i.e., consumption of alcohol and drugs, sports, etc.) to achieve status. The notion is that as many men become older they are more secure in their masculinity as life events, such as education, work, marriage, children, and financial stability, substantiate a change in their social status. Changes related to life events and status may also allow men to express a broader range of behaviors and emotions considered less masculine because they no longer feel obliged to compete directly with other males. Recent research on those who recidivate after boot camp prison appears to reflect this same pattern in the expression of masculinities over men's life span.

For instance, boot camp prisons tend to admit young, drug and alcohol using males who participate in high risk behaviors with their peers. Several studies by Benda and his colleagues report individual level differences in the types of offenders admitted to a boot camp prison and differences between groups after release. Toombs, Benda, and Tilmon (1999) report young drug offenders sentenced to boot camp prison as lacking interpersonal skills and displaying action-oriented, impulsive, nonreflective characteristics. Additionally, the drug offenders externalize blame to others and reward acts of personal power and toughness. In another study, Toombs, Benda, and Corwyn (2000) conducted a discriminate analysis on violent inmates in a boot camp for nonviolent offenders. Their analysis reports weapon carrying, peer association with violent peers, and alcohol consumption as the three highest predictors of violence.

These same attributes appear to be predictors of recidivism. In a discriminate analysis of boot camp graduates, Benda (2001) reported that non-recidivists, recidivists, and parole violators varied in terms of the factors associated with each group. Benda (2001) found recidivists to be younger (also see Stinchcomb & Terry, 2001), have earlier crime and drug use, be influenced by negative peer groups who engage in criminal behavior, and associate more frequently with negative peers, than the other two groups of boot camp graduates.

Benda, Tombs, and Peacock (2002) used Gottfredson and Hirschi's (1990 as cited in Benda et al., 2002) general theory of crime as their theoretical framework to hypothesize that measures of self-control (impulsivity, instant gratification, risk-seeking, physical versus mental activity, self-centeredness, and low frustration tolerance) can be used to predict who is most likely to recidivate from a boot camp prison. They found aggression, immaturity (refers to attitudes and behaviors of an "egoistic child"), denial, and peer influence (all associated with masculinity) to be among the strongest significant predictors of re-offending, with age at first offense and aggression being the strongest predictors, followed by immaturity. In a later study, Benda (2003) found low self-control, lack of social skills, criminal and gang peer associations, gang membership, drug use, and weapon carrying as positively associated with recidivism.

In contrast to recidivists, Benda (2001) found non-recidivists to be older, have higher levels of self-efficacy, higher resilience, higher self-esteem, greater expectations for the future, and positive overall experiences in boot camp overall. Interestingly, other researchers have also found similar findings of positive attitudinal change in boot camp prisons, but they have not connected those findings directly to recidivism (see Lutze, 2001; MacKenzie & Shaw, 1990; MacKenzie & Souryal, 1995). Benda's (2001) findings provide some support for the differentiation of masculine responses based on one's age or contentedness with oneself over time. Benda's (2001) findings also suggest that for younger offenders, hypermasculinity compensates for male insecurity leading to the greater likelihood that those individuals will participate in high risk behaviors directly related to offending (see Kilmartin, 2000). Relatedly, more general evidence from MacKenzie and Souryal's (1994) multisite study suggest that programs with more hours committed to treatment report lower rates of recidivism. This may be an indication that some programs are more adequately tempering the hypermasculine environment and/or individual commitment to stereotypes of masculinity. These findings strongly suggest that there is an interaction between the masculine nature of the prison environment and the individual characteristics of the offenders.

Unfortunately, prior research has not tested the interaction between specific attributes of the environment and individual adherence to hypermasculine beliefs and behaviors. While sociological research on organizations and gender consider masculinity as it affects individual behavior within organizations, there are no studies to date that attempt to operationalize measures of the prison setting as they relate to masculinity. The closest attempt to test the relationship between the masculine organization and its effect on inmates was conducted by Lutze and Murphy (1999). Their research, however, was unable to include *individual level* measures of masculinity and how they may influence inmate experiences in the prison environment. In order to determine the effects of masculine organizations on inmate behavior and future criminality, future research will need to test the relationship between individual level measures of masculinity and how individuals respond to the group and to the organization. Based on existing research, however, we predict that individual males will respond to the prison environment in direct relationship to their acceptance of traditional sex-role stereotypes.

RECOMMENDATIONS FOR CHANGE

It is quite apparent that boot camp prisons rest upon a masculine structure that reinforces and perpetuates masculine values and stereotypically masculine ideologies. This structure creates an environment that uses gendered power to establish a vertical hierarchy between those men with authority and those without. While boot camp prisons utilize treatment, rehabilitation, and additional programming designed to instill pro-social behaviors, the structure is flawed. In other words, the components of boot camp prisons are not inherently bad, but the way in which they are used to emasculate their participants counters much of the good that may come from completing the program. We propose that boot camp prisons may be greatly improved by reducing or eliminating the attributes of the environment steeped in negative stereotypes of masculinity. Programs will need to (1) reconceptualize the importance of inmate adjustment to future success, (2) reconsider how program components are implemented, and (3) reconsider how treatment is framed in the boot camp prison setting.

Adjustment. Inmates' adjustment to the prison environment is considered important in terms of whether offenders will be amenable to treatment and to their success after release (see Goodstein & Wright, 1989). Boot camp prison reformers primarily attempted to address inmate adjustment by mitigating the importation of negative street behaviors through demanding respect, administering discipline, and coercing appropriate behavior through strict parameters on verbal and body language. Boot camp prisons are fairly successful in addressing many of the negative adjustment strategies used by inmates to adjust to traditional prison (see Lutze, 2001; MacKenzie & Shaw, 1990; MacKenzie & Souryal, 1995). In spite of these successes in instilling positive adjustment, some negative adjustment still lingers, such as increases in conflict, isolation, and feelings of helplessness (see Lutze, 2001; Lutze & Murphy, 1999; MacKenzie & Shaw, 1990).

Many boot camp prisons, however, fail to realize that what is being imported from the street is adherence to lifestyles grounded in hypermasculinity (see Newton, 1994). Survival in poor communities often means being tough enough to defend yourself from others (see Baskin & Sommers, 1998; Shakur, 1993). Critics of the application of feminist oriented approaches to treating men might argue that teaching men to be more in touch with their emotions, less aggressive, and more dependant on others is unrealistic because offenders must leave prison and return to communities that are still entrenched in hypermasculine approaches to resolving conflict. There is evidence from the traditional prison literature that suggest that men can learn to cope maturely with the negative aspects of the prison environment (Johnson, 2002).

Johnson (2002) defines mature coping as an inmate's ability to deal with problems by achieving autonomy and security without the use of deception or violence in caring for the self and others. Thus, if boot camp prisons do not exacerbate hypermasculinity, and instead focus on enhancing inmates' mature coping skills, offenders may be able to return to unstable communities and survive without engaging in negative behaviors. Johnson (2002) also discovered that inmates who maturely cope with the prison environment create niches that provide a space and relationship with others in which offenders can be themselves. It is possible, if done correctly, that boot camp prisons can become the prison niche that fosters positive coping and amenability to change. This can be achieved through simple changes in the existing structure of most boot camp prison programs.

Restructuring of program components. Lutze (2003) argues that the original reformers who created and implemented boot camp prisons had good intentions in their desire to eradicate many of the negative aspects of traditional prisons and their effects on inmates. We argue that many aspects of boot camp prisons are positive and should remain, however, their implementation has been denigrated by counterproductive stereotypes about how men should be treated. For instance, many masculine attributes are positive, and when placed in a broader context of healthy power relations, can be beneficial to rehabilitation. Therefore, boot camp prisons should be aggressive in confronting negative inmate attitudes and behaviors, eliminating manipulative behavior, and imparting strength (physical and mental), assertiveness and independence, through programs such as work, education, physical well-being and exercise. As presented earlier, however, boot camp prisons are co-opted through hypermasculine definitions of power and authority that emphasize *power over others* versus the *empowerment of others* (see Zaplan, 1998).

All aspects of the programs should be directly connected to cognitive-based change and implemented in a way that empowers inmates to accomplish the program goals and reduce their likelihood to recidivate (see Harland, 1996; MacKenzie, 1997, 2000). Thus, work should be meaningful and teach new skills instead of being menial and humiliating. Exercise should be connected to physical health and not punishment and hard labor. Corporal punishments, if they remain, should be directly connected to the behavior or thought process that lead to the infraction and not just an exercise in humiliation. Programs should also increase contact with family so that intimate communication with significant others can be maintained and included in the offender's current process of change and creation of future plans. Gender equality should also be addressed in presenting women in positions of power among custody and treatment staff. This will help to counter the hypermasculine notion that all things feminine should be avoided or minimalized. Each of these changes will assist treatment programs in being more fully utilized, practiced, and rewarded in all aspects of the prison experience, and not just during treatment.

Treatment. Treatment programs in boot camp prisons have generally been criticized for failing to use cognitive-based approaches. For example, some programs provide drug and alcohol *education* but not *treatment*. Thus, inmates are taught about the negative consequences of addition, but not how to change their mental, physical or social behavior to cure their addiction. Some boot camp prisons, however, do provide meaningful treatment programs that work with offenders to address addiction, family, relationships, personal wellness, spiritual wellness, and education (see Clark & Aziz, 1996; Clark, Aziz, & MacKenzie, 1994; Lutze, 2001). Each of these treatments attempt to replace negative thought processes and behaviors with more positive ones.

Recent research regarding women's prisons argues that programs that are gender sensitive and empowering may still fail, or will be less effective, due to the coercive nature of the prison setting in which they occur (see Lutze, 2003; Zaplan, 1998). We suggest that this is also the case for men in boot camp prisons. What men learn in treatment about enhancing communication, dealing with emotions (especially anger), and the vulnerable feelings that come with personal change is not respected or supported in the public, nontreatment settings of the institution. Furthermore, what inmates learn in treatment cannot be openly practiced or their vulnerability will be viewed as weakness and the potential for victimization by others, both staff and inmates, is increased (see Lutze & Murphy, 1999 for a related discussion).

Another issue that affects the treatment of men in prison is the notion that, not only are men tough enough to handle a coercive and aggressive environment, but that they need to be "torn down" first. Some might argue that offenders who go to prison are oftentimes already torn down by their pre-prison experiences (see Austin & Irwin, 2001; Petersillia, 2003). In women's boot camp prisons, concerns have been expressed that the confrontational nature of the communication and the application of corporal punishment may mirror abusive relationships that many women have been exposed to prior to incarceration (see Lutze, 2003; Marcus-Mendoza et al., 1998). We suggest that this same risk applies to men. First, many of the men admitted to prison have experienced violence as children and adults. They also experience the hardships of living in poverty (see Austin & Irwin, 2001; Petersillia, 2003). Moreover, the hypermasculine prison environment is just more of the same in reinforcing the abuse and hierarchy of male aggression that confronted them before prison. Second, many men in prison may also be violent toward women in their personal relationships. The confrontational nature of the boot camp prison replicates this same pattern of abuse for men, only in this situation supporting them as perpetrators.

Obviously, the narrow definition of what will work with men and how it should be administered can have dire consequences in either enhancing their own victimization or in supporting their perpetration of crime. If boot camp prison administrators hope to be effective in reducing recidivism then they will have to give serious consideration to restructuring their programs and administering treatment in a way that considers the powerful influence of gender on behavior.

CONCLUSION

Boot camp prisons possess many positive attributes that have the potential for creating positive attitudinal change, adjustment, and beneficial expectations for the future. These programs are, however, delivered in the context of an environment steeped in hypermasculinity, masculine ideals, and hegemonic stereotypes. Thus, they have failed to address the negative power relations between a hypermasculine prison organization and the masculinity of individual men and the effects this dynamic may have on post-prison behavior. Additionally, the connection has not been made between the production of masculinities within a tainted prison setting and success after release.

Future prison programs must begin to consider the power of gendered relations in terms of program delivery, treatment implementation, empowerment, and inmate adjustment in molding behavior and influencing program outcomes. This interaction must be considered at the organizational and individual level if programs hope to advance change, promote pro-social behaviors, target criminality, and influence recidivism rates in the post-prison experience.

NOTES

1. The connection between the gendered nature of prisons and its effects on female inmates has been broadly discussed (see Zaitzow & Thomas, 2003; Zaplan, 1998 for extensive reviews of the literature). Similar discussions are only beginning to take place about men's prisons.

2. Our discussion focuses on male institutions because boot camp prisons were originally designed by men for men and only admitted women after demands were made for equal treatment (see Marcus-Mendoza, Klien-Saffran, & Lutze, 1998).

3. Schwartz and DeKeseredy (1997) argue that homogenous male populations who hold and support similar belief systems will legitimate and encourage hypermasculine, aggressive, and antisocial patterns of behavior. This dynamic is explained through the use of peer support. Additional literature theorizes about the nature of group interaction and its "group think identity" effect on individual-level behavior (Sanday, 1990). It is sometimes difficult to conceptually separate individual level behavior from group action. Additionally, individuals within the group will not always choose to follow the paths of least resistance with regard to going against the group identity (Johnson, 1997). For the purposes of this study, however, the distinction between individual and group level action remains undifferentiated. Hegemonic masculinity, however, suggest that, although all males will not adhere to stereotypical definitions of masculinity at all times and places, men in general will respond similarly to masculine expectations at some level that is acceptable within a patriarchal society.

REFERENCES

Adler, C., & Polk, K. (1996). Masculinity and child homicide. *British Journal of Criminology, 36,* 396-411.

Andrews, D., Zinger, I., Hoge, R., Bonta, J., Gendreau, P., & Cullen, F. (1990). Does correctional treatment work? A clinically relevant and psychologically informed meta-analysis. *Criminology, 28,* 369-404.

Austin, J., & Irwin, J. (2001). *It's about time: America's imprisonment binge (3rd ed.).* Belmont, CA: Wadsworth.

Baskin, D., & Sommers, I. (1998). *Casualties of community disorder: Women's careers in violent crime.* Boulder, CO: Westview.

Belknap, J. (2001). *The invisible woman: Gender, crime, and justice (2nd ed.).* Belmont, CA: Wadsworth.

Benda, B. B. (2001). Factors that discriminate between recidivists, parole violators and nonrecidivists in a 3-year follow-up of boot camp graduates. *International Journal of Offender Therapy and Comparative Criminology, 45,* 719-729.

Benda, B. B. (2003). Survival analysis of criminal recidivism of boot camp graduates using elements from general and developmental explanatory models. *International Journal of Offender Therapy and Comparative Criminology, 47,* 89-110.

Benda, B. B., Toombs, N., & Peacock, M. (2002). Ecological factors in recidivism: A survival analysis of boot camp graduates after three years. *Journal of Offender Rehabilitation, 35,* 63-85.

Bohmer, C., & Parrot, A. (1993). *Sexual assault on campus.* New York: Lexington Books.

Bourgois, P. (1996). In search of masculinity: Violence, respect and sexuality among Puerto Rican crack dealers in East Harlem. *British Journal of Criminology, 36,* 412-427.

Brittan, A. (1989). *Masculinity and power.* New York: Basil Blackwell.

Carrabine, E., & Longhurst, B. (1998). Gender and prison organization: Some comments on masculinities and prison management. *Howard Journal, 37,* 161-176.

Christianson, S. (1998). *With liberty for some: 500 years of imprisonment in America.* Boston: Northeastern University Press.

Clark, C., & Aziz, D. (1996). Shock incarceration in New York state: Philosophy, results, and limitations. In D. MacKenzie & E. Herbert (Eds.), *Correctional boot camps: A tough intermediate sanction* (pp. 39-68). Washington, DC: U.S. Department of Justice, National Institute of Justice.

Clark, C., Aziz, D., & MacKenzie, D. (1994). *Shock incarceration in New York: Focus on treatment.* Washington, DC: U.S. Department of Justice, National Institute of Justice.

Cloward, R., & Ohlin, L. (1960). *Delinquency and opportunity: A theory of delinquent gangs.* Glencoe, IL: Free Press.

Cohen, A. (1955). *Delinquent boys: The culture of the gang.* New York: Free Press.

Collison, M. (1996). In search of the high life: Drugs, crime, masculinities and consumption. *British Journal of Criminology, 36,* 428-444.

Correia, M. (1997). Boot camps, exercise, and delinquency: An analytical critique of the use of physical exercise to facilitate decreases in delinquent behavior. *Journal of Contemporary Criminal Justice, 13,* 94-113.

Gendreau, P., & Ross, R. (1987). Revivification of rehabilitation: Evidence from the 1980s. *Justice Quarterly, 4,* 349-407.

Goodstein, L., & Wright, K. (1989). Inmate adjustment to prison. In L. Goodstein & D. MacKenzie (Eds.) *The American prison: Issues in research and policy* (pp. 229-251). New York: Plenum.

Harland, A. (1996). *Choosing correctional options that work: Defining the demand and evaluating the supply.* Thousand Oaks, CA: Sage.

Hatty, S. (1999). *Masculinities, violence, and culture.* Thousand Oaks, CA: Sage.

Haywood, C., & Mac an Ghaill, M. (2003). *Men and masculinities.* Buckingham: Open University Press.

Hearn, J., & Parkin, W. (2001). *Gender, sexuality, and violence in organizations.* London: Sage.

Herbert, T. (2002). *Sexual violence and American manhood.* Cambridge: Harvard University Press.

Humphrey, S., & Kahn, A. (2000). Fraternities, athletic teams, and rape: Importance of identification with a risky group. *Journal of Interpersonal Violence, 15,* 1313-1322.

Jackson, T. (1991). A university athletic department's rape and assault experiences. *Journal of College Student Development, 32,* 77-78.

Johnson, R. (2002). *Hard time: Understanding and reforming the prison* (3rd ed.). Belmont, CA: Wadsworth.

Kempf-Leonard, K., & Tracy, P. (2003). Gender differences in delinquency career types and the transition to adult crime. In R. Muraskin (Ed.), *It's a crime: Women and justice* (pp. 544-569). New Jersey: Prentice Hall.

Kersten, J. (1996). Culture, masculinities and violence against women. *British Journal of Criminology, 36,* 381-395.

Kilmartin, C. (2000). *The masculine self.* Boston: McGraw-Hill.

Krienert, J. (2003). Masculinity and crime: A quantitative exploration of Messerschmidt's hypothesis. *Electronic Journal of Sociology* [issn 1198-3655], 7, 2. Available via Internet at http://www.sociology.org

Johnson, A. (1997). *The gender knot: Unraveling our patriarchal legacy.* Philadelphia: Temple University Press.

Lorber, J. (2001). *Gender inequality: Feminist theories and politics.* Los Angeles, CA: Roxbury.

Lutze, F. (1998). Are shock incarceration programs more rehabilitative than traditional prisons? A survey of inmates. *Justice Quarterly, 15,* 547-563.

Lutze, F. (2001). The influence of a shock incarceration program on inmate adjustment and attitudinal change. *Journal of Criminal Justice, 29,* 255-267.

Lutze, F. (2002). Conscience and convenience in boot camp prison: An opportunity for success. *Journal of Forensic Psychology Practice, 2,* 71-81.

Lutze, F. (2003). The acceptance of ultramasculine stereotypes and violence in the control of women inmates. In B. Zaitzow and J. Thomas (Eds.), *Women in prison: Gender and social control* (pp. 183-203). Denver: Lynne Reinner.

Lutze, F., & Brody, D. (1999). Mental abuse as cruel and unusual punishment: Do boot camp prisons violate the eighth amendment? *Crime and Delinquency, 45,* 242-255.

Lutze, F., & Murphy, D. (1999). Ultramasculine prison environments and inmates' adjustment: It's time to move beyond the 'Boys Will Be Boys' paradigm. *Justice Quarterly, 16,* 709-733.

MacKenzie, D. (1997). Criminal justice and crime prevention. In L. Sherman, D. Gottfredson, D. MacKenzie, J. Eck, P. Reuter, and S. Bushway (Eds.), *Preventing crime: What works, what doesn't, what's promising* (pp. 1-76). Washington, DC: National Institute of Justice.

MacKenzie, D. (2000). Evidence-based corrections: Identifying what works. *Crime & Delinquency, 46*(4): 457-471.

MacKenzie, D., & Souryal, C. (1994). *Multi-site evaluation of shock incarceration: Executive summary.* Washington, DC: U.S. Department of Justice, National Institution of Justice.

MacKenzie, D., Wilson, D., & Kider, S. (2001). Effects of correctional boot camps on offending. *ANNALS, AAPSS, 578,* 126-143.

Marcus-Mendoza, S., Klein-Saffran, J., & Lutze, F. (1998). A feminist examination of boot camp prison programs for women. *Women & Therapy, 21*(1): 173-185.

Messerschmidt, J. (1993). *Masculinities and crime: Reconceptualization of theory.* Lanham, MD: Rowman and Littlefield.

Messerschmidt, J. (1997). *Crime as structured action: Gender, race, class, and crime in the making.* London: Sage.

Messner, M., & Sabo, D. (1994). *Sex, violence, and power in sports: Rethinking masculinity.* Freedom: The Crossing Press.

Miedzian, M. (1993). How rape is encouraged in American boys and what we can do to stop it. In E. Buchwald, P. Fletcher, & M. Roth (Eds.), *Transforming a rape culture* (pp. 154-163). Minneapolis: Milkweed Editions.

Mills, A. (1992). Organization, gender, and culture. In A. J. Mills & P. Tancred (Eds.), *Gendering organizational analysis* (pp. 93-111). London: Sage.

Morash, M., & Rucker, L. (1990). A critical look at the idea of boot camp as a correctional reform. *Crime and Delinquency, 36,* 204-222.

Newton, C. (1994). Gender theory and prison sociology: Using theories of masculinities to interpret the sociology of prisons for men. *Howard Journal, 33,* 193-202.

Parent, D. (2003). *Correctional boot camps: Lessons for a decade of research.* Washington, DC: U.S. Department of Justice, National Institute of Justice.

Parsons, T. (1964). *Social structure and personality.* New York: Free Press of Glencoe.

Petersilia, J. (2003). *When prisoners come home: Parole and prisoner reentry.* Oxford: Oxford University Press.

Pisciotta, A. (1994). *Benevolent repression: Social control and the American reformatory prison movement.* New York: New York University Press.

Pleck, J. (1981). *The myth of masculinity.* London: MIT Press.

Rothman, D. (1971). *The discovery of the asylum: Social order and disorder in the New Republic.* Boston: Little, Brown and Company.

Sanday, P. (1990). *Fraternity gang rape: Sex, brotherhood, and privilege on campus.* New York: New York University Press.

Schwartz, M., & DeKeseredy, W. (1997). *Sexual assault on the college campus.* Thousand Oaks, CA: Sage.

Shakur, S. (1993). *Monster: The autobiography of an L.A. gang member.* New York: Penguin Books.

Sims, J. (1994). Tougher than the rest? Men in prison. In T. Newburn & E. A. Stanko (Eds.), *Just boys doing business? Men, masculinities, and crime* (pp. 100-117). London: Routledge Publishing.

Stinchcomb, J., & Terry, III, W. (2001). Predicting the likelihood of rearrest among shock incarceration graduates: Moving beyond another nail in the boot camp coffin. *Crime & Delinquency, 41,* 221-242.

Sutherland, E., & Cressey, D. (1999).A theory of differential association. In F. Cullen & R. Agnew (Eds.), *Criminological theory: Past to present* (pp. 82-84). Los Angeles, CA: Roxbury.

Sykes, G. (1958). *The society of captives: A study of maximum security prison.* New Jersey: Princeton University Press.

Toombs, N., Benda, B., & Corwyn, R. (2000). Violent youth in boot camps for non-violent offenders. *Journal of Offender Rehabilitation, 31,* 113-133.

Toombs, N., Benda, B., & Tilmon, R. (1999). A developmentally anchored conceptual model of drug use tested among adult boot camp inmates. *Journal of Offender Rehabilitation, 29,* 49-64.

Welch, M. (1997). A critical interpretation of correctional bootcamps as normalizing institutions. *Journal of Contemporary Criminal Justice, 13,* 184-205.

Witz, A., & Savage, M. (1992). The gender of organizations. In M. Savage & A. Witz (Eds.), *Gender and bureaucracy* (pp. 3-62). Oxford: Blackwell.

Zachariah, J. (1996). An overview of boot camp goals, components, and results. In D. MacKenzie & E. Herbert (Eds.), *Correctional boot camps: A tough intermediate sanction* (pp. 17-38). Washington, DC: National Institute of Justice.

Zaitzow, B., & Thomas, J. (2003). *Women in prison: Gender and social control.* Boulder, CO: Lynne Reinner.

Zaplin, R. (1998). *Female offenders: Critical perspectives and effective interventions.* Gaithersburg, MD: Aspen.

AUTHORS' NOTES

Dr. Faith E. Lutze is an associate professor and director of the Criminal Justice Program at Washington State University. Her current research interests include the rehabilitative nature of prison environments, offender adjustment to community corrections supervision, gender and justice, and drug courts. She teaches criminal justice courses related to corrections, violence against women, and gender and justice. Dr. Lutze has published in *Justice Quarterly, Crime and Delinquency, The Journal of Contemporary Criminal Justice, The Journal of Criminal Justice,* and *Corrections Management Quarterly.*

Cortney A. Bell is a doctoral candidate in the Criminal Justice Program at Washington State University. Her research interests include gender and justice, gender theory and masculinity, violence against women, and corrections.

Address correspondence to Dr. Faith E. Lutze, Criminal Justice Program, Washington State University, P.O. Box 644880, Pullman, WA 99164-4880 (E-mail: lutze@wsu.edu).

Gender Differences in the Perceived Severity of Boot Camp

PETER B. WOOD
Mississippi State University

DAVID C. MAY
Eastern Kentucky University

HAROLD G. GRASMICK
University of Oklahoma

ABSTRACT We analyze survey data from 181 male and 224 female inmates serving brief prison terms for nonviolent offenses to examine offenders' perceptions of the severity of boot camp compared to prison. Building on the limited work in this area, we present reasons those offenders feel are important to both avoid and participate in alternative sanctions. Results show that men are more likely than women to choose prison over any duration of boot camp, men identify more strongly than women with reasons to avoid alternatives, and women will serve more boot camp than will men. Binary logistic and OLS regression analyses for the total sample, and by gender, reveal that prior experience serving boot camp increases the likelihood that offenders will enroll in boot camp to avoid one year of imprisonment, as well as the amount of boot camp that offenders are willing to serve. In addition, controlling for potentially relevant factors, women will serve more boot camp than men to avoid imprisonment, and being a parent has a significant, positive impact on the amount of boot camp that women (but not men) are willing to endure to avoid one year of prison. Findings have implications for the use of alternative sanctions (particularly boot camp) in corrections, and for understanding "rational choice" processes among male and female offenders. *[Article copies available for a fee from The Haworth Document Delivery Service: 1-800-HAWORTH. E-mail address: <docdelivery@haworthpress.com> Website: <http://www.HaworthPress.com> © 2005 by The Haworth Press, Inc. All rights reserved.]*

KEYWORDS Ratings of boot camp versus prison, gender differences, rational choice theory

Recent work has noted that a variety of demographic and experiential factors influence offenders' perceptions of the punitiveness of criminal justice sanctions (Apospori and Alpert, 1993; Spelman, 1995; Wood and Grasmick, 1999; Petersilia and Deschenes, 1994a, 1994b; Crouch, 1993, Wood and May, 2003). Specifically, it is claimed that offenders serving identical sanctions may "perceive the severity of their punishment to be very different due to differences in their age, race, sex, prior punishment history, or other factors" (Spelman, 1995 p. 132). Similarly, Wood and Grasmick (1999 p. 22) observe that variation in the perceived severity of sanctions "bears directly on a 'rational' evaluation of costs and benefits by each potential offender." We adopt this assumption, which guides our study of how offenders vary in their perceptions of the severity of correctional boot camp.

Most studies of correctional boot camps focus on the effectiveness of boot camp in rehabilitating offenders and reducing recidivism, and the general consensus appears to be that "There is little research demonstrating the effectiveness of boot camp programs in changing the long-term outcomes of participants" (Gover, Styve, and MacKenzie, 1999, p. 400). A multisite study of the effectiveness of boot camps concluded that "Most of the time, offenders released from the boot camp prison did as well as similar offenders who spent a longer term in prison" (MacKenzie, 1995, p. 404).

While the presumed effectiveness of boot camps for rehabilitation and reduction in recidivism has received considerable study, there has been little work done examining offenders' perceptions of the punitiveness of boot camp compared to imprisonment, and no work examining gender differences in this regard. We offer a look at how males and females view the pros and cons of alternative sanctions in general, and more specifically, why males and females differ in their willingness to serve boot camp to avoid imprisonment as well as the amount of boot camp that they will serve.

It is hoped that findings presented here might inform practitioners with regard to why offenders may avoid or participate in boot camp. In addition, results may help us understand why women may be more amenable to serving boot camp than are men. This second objective is important given that the majority of boot camp participants are male, most boot camps are designed with the male inmate in mind, and boot camps typically do not incorporate components that would address the needs of female offenders (Gover, Styve, and MacKenzie, 1999; MacKenzie and Donaldson, 1996).

SURVEY INSTRUMENT, SAMPLING, AND DATA COLLECTION

The survey instrument was developed with significant input from inmates. In May 1995, the authors spent an afternoon with a focus group of 7 inmates in an Oklahoma correctional center to explore the best way of examining the issue of the punitiveness of alternative sanctions compared to prison. Each of these inmates had served previous prison terms and all had experienced one or more alternative sanctions. One inmate admitted experience with five different alternatives. Based on this meeting a draft instrument was developed, and in June 1995 the survey was pre-tested on 25 other inmates at the same correctional center. After the pre-test, the inmates and investigators engaged in intensive discussion about the wording of specific items, the inclusion of reasons for and against participating in alternatives, and the inmates' own experiences with alternative sanctions. Based on the pre-test and inmates' comments, the survey was revised.

The survey also collected detailed background information including age, gender, education, marital status, number and ages of children, and information about the offenders' experience in correctional settings–their longest sentence served, and the total amount of time they have spent in prisons and jails. We also included a race identification item in the pre-test survey, but were counseled by DOC personnel to delete it. At the time of the survey Oklahoma DOC was conducting a racial balance study of its inmate population. DOC personnel were concerned that race-specific findings might be politically sensitive and might discourage some inmates from participating in the survey. Though the inclusion of race-specific findings was of interest to us, we bowed to their request and removed the race item from the instrument. Finally, based on offenders' comments regarding their reluctance to enroll in alternative sanctions, we included items examining reasons why an offender might participate in an alternative sanction and reasons why an offender might avoid participation.

In October 1995 a sample of 875 inmates (450 men and 425 women) was drawn from DOC automated files. For inclusion in the sample the offender must have been convicted of a nonviolent controlling offense, must not have a history of habitual or violent behavior, and must have received a sentence of five (5) years or less in the Oklahoma correctional system. We used these selection criteria because they roughly identify the population of offenders most likely eligible for some form of alternative sanction, and because inmates meeting these criteria would most likely serve no more than one year actual time in prison. Thus, this group of offenders resembles those most likely to qualify for a range of alternative sanctions.

By the end of 1995 (the year of the survey) there were 17,983 inmates serving time in Oklahoma correctional centers. Approximately 2,800 of these inmates met our selection criteria. Our initial sample of 875 accounts for approximately 31% of these inmates, and approximately 5% of the total inmate population. While the sample consisted of 875 male and female inmates who met our criteria (nonviolent controlling offense, no history of violence, and less than a 5-year sentence), we determined that slightly fewer than 800 inmates were available to participate in the survey. Some inmates had been released by the time the survey was administered, others had been transferred to another institution, and there were inmates who were serving an administrative sanction and were unable to participate in the survey. Many inmates who were eligible simply refused to participate in the survey. We concluded data collection with 415 respondents (181 men, 224 women, and 10 who did not report their gender) representing better than a 50% response rate based on those inmates available for participation. This response rate compares very favorably with other voluntary, self-administered surveys conducted in correctional centers (Wood et al., 1997).

In 1995 Oklahoma claimed the third highest incarceration rate in the nation, and the highest female incarceration rate of all 50 states–a distinction we felt was significant enough to warrant special attention. Further, a review of the published literature on the relative punitiveness of punishments revealed no previous work examining female offenders' perceptions of the severity of alternative sanctions. Consequently, we over-sampled women so they comprised half of our sample and just over 50% of our survey respondents.

The research team met with Case Managers from 8 correction and community correction centers on site in October 1995. Printouts identifying inmates at each facility who met the selection criteria and who had been randomly sampled were distributed to the Case Managers. Case Managers also received detailed instructions regarding administration of the survey, questions to anticipate, and ways to help inmates complete the survey if they required assistance. During October, the survey was administered in classroom settings to small groups of inmates who met the selection criteria, had been randomly sampled, and who voluntarily agreed to participate. All data analysis reported here is based on an initial N of 415 inmates.

BOOT CAMPS IN OKLAHOMA

In 1983, Oklahoma became one of the first states to implement a military-style correctional boot camp, initially termed the Regimented Inmate Discipline program (RID), and Oklahoma's boot camp program was one of those reviewed by MacKenzie and Souryal (1994) in an early NIJ funded multistate evaluation of boot camp effectiveness. Since 1983, Oklahoma has instituted separate correctional boot camps for men and women. The women's boot camp (first labeled the Shock Incarceration Program or SIP but called the Female Offender Regimented Treatment program or FORT at the time of the survey in 1995) was established in 1991. Oklahoma has operated boot camp-style programs for males at different correctional facilities since 1983, including William S. Key Correctional Center, Oklahoma State Penitentiary (discontinued in 1994), and most recently at Bill Johnson Correctional Center.

Correctional boot camps in Oklahoma evidenced considerable variation in programmatic features. The year of the survey (1995) the 45-day program for women at Eddie Warrior Correctional Center (a women's only facility) had no educational or psychological programming, and inmates' time was divided between drill time and work assignments. Women in boot camp were housed separately, but shared other facilities and were not truly segregated from the general inmate population. In contrast, male boot camp programs often average up to 120 days before a court-ordered evaluation. The multiphase drug offender work camp program at Bill Johnson Correctional Center (established in September 1995) begins with a 12-week boot camp of strict regimentation, drill, ceremony, inspections, labor-intensive work, and physical fitness. Inmates then progress through substance abuse treatment and education programs to earn increasing privileges. The program concludes with a one-year aftercare program characterized by intensive supervision and drug testing. In general, male inmates enrolled in boot camp in Oklahoma typically divide their time between work, drill time, education, and therapy. Program offerings for males include Moral Recondition Therapy, Rational Behavior Therapy, Substance Abuse Education, Stress Management and Relaxation Training, Narcotics Anonymous, Alcoholics Anonymous, and the General Equivalency Diploma (GED). The male boot camps averaged about 550 inmates per year through the mid-1990s, while the female boot camp averaged about 150 participants per year. Inmates in Oklahoma are typically eligible to participate in boot camp programs if they have no prior prison stays, have sentences of five years or less, and have not been convicted of sexual or violent crimes. They may have been sentenced to boot camp by a judge, or reclassified (on request) into boot camp on entry into the prison system, depending on space availability (Holley and Brewster, 1996; Marcus-Mendoza, 1995; Holley and Wright, 1995; Holley and Connelly, 1994).

MEASURING RELATIVE SEVERITY

Three means of determining the relative severity of punishments using offender samples have been employed. The comparative judgments method is simplest in that it presents respondents with a series of paired comparisons between two punishments and asks which is more severe. If the set of choices is prepared carefully, a rank ordering of all options is possible. A second method, magnitude estimation, involves presenting the respondent with a standard level of punishment (say 1 year in prison) worth 100 points. The respondent is then asked to assign a score to each of several other punishments compared to the 100 points that are equivalent to 1 year in prison. In this case punishment perceived as half as severe would receive 50 points, while punishment perceived as more severe would receive a score greater than 100. As Petersilia and Deschenes (1994b) suggest, however, the validity of magnitude estimation depends to a great degree on the mathematical aptitude of the respondents, which is often questionable among inmate populations. Petersilia and Deschenes combined this method with a rank-ordering procedure to simplify the task for inmate respondents. The two techniques have strengths and weaknesses, but most recent work on punishment severity has employed comparative judgements or magnitude estimation.

Wood and Grasmick (1999) developed a third method (which we use here) that asks respondents to make realistic comparisons based on their own experiences serving time and participating in alternative sanctions. This method allows a more sophisticated comparison in which the offender chooses the amount (in months) of an alternative sanction he or she would endure to avoid a specified length of actual imprisonment. We call this an "offender-generated equivalency." Since all our respondents know the experience of imprisonment, and have either experienced alternatives personally or have knowledge of alternatives through the experience of acquaintances, offenders are able to make an "educated" comparison and offer their own punishment equivalencies between imprisonment and the alternative in question.

Briefly, in the current study probationers were presented with descriptions of boot camp and nine other "alternative sanctions." After reading the description, probationers were asked to consider 12 months of medium security imprisonment and asked to indicate how many months of boot camp they were willing to endure to avoid serving 12 months of actual imprisonment. If the respondent is willing to serve more than 12 months of boot camp to avoid 12 months of imprisonment, then imprisonment is viewed as more punitive. If a probationer will do fewer than 12 months of boot camp to avoid 12 months of imprisonment, we claim that boot camp is perceived as more punitive than prison. In this way, probationers employ a direct and flexible means of registering their own perceptions of the severity of boot camp compared to one year of imprisonment. The actual survey format of the question appears in Appendix A (Wood and Grasmick, 1999).

SURVEY RESULTS

Aside from the common characteristics of being convicted of nonviolent controlling offenses, and having been sentenced to 5 years or less for their current offense, Table 1 displays some basic descriptive information about the inmate respondents. Just over half of our respondents are women (224 women and 181 men) and in 1995 Oklahoma registered the highest rate of female incarceration in the United States. Overall, the inmate respondents have served an average of 38.64 months total time in prisons, with males averaging 48.36 months and females averaging 28.18 months. The inmates average 32.84 years of age (males average 34.27, females average 31.66), and 11.33 years of education (males average 11.34, females average 11.31). Nearly 80 percent of female inmates and 65.7 percent of males have at least one child. Despite this high rate of parenthood, only 23.4 percent of males and 19.3 percent of females reported being married at the time of the survey.

A significant proportion (34.9 percent) of inmates reported serving in boot camp before the study. A greater percentage of women (36.7 percent) than men (32.7 percent) had served some time in boot camp. Though we asked re-

Table 1: Characteristics of Inmate Respondents: Men, Women, All Respondents

	Men	Women	All Respondents
Number of Cases	181	224	415*
Average Age	34.27	31.66	32.84
Years of Education	11.34	11.31	11.33
Married	23.4%	19.3%	21.0%
Have Kid(s)	65.7%	79.5%	71.8%
Total Time in Prison (Months)	48.36	28.18	38.64
Percent Who Have Served Boot Camp Previously	32.7%	36.7%	34.9%
Percent Who Refuse to Serve Any Boot Camp to Avoid One Year in Prison	25.8%	21.5%	23.4%
Months of Boot Camp R Is Willing to Serve to Avoid 12 Months Prison**	3.24 4.39#	3.92 4.99#	3.63 4.75#
Total Number of Alternatives Served Previously	3.76	3.09	3.39

*Men and women do not add up to 415 due to 10 respondents who did not identify gender.
**Gender difference is significant at .05 (T-Test) for both gender comparisons.
#Mean scores after offenders who refuse to do any boot camp (zero scores) are deleted.

spondents if they had ever served boot camp previously, we did not gather information regarding the characteristics of the boot camp they attended, nor did we determine whether they had completed boot camp, quit on their own, or if they had been "expelled" or revoked back to prison by program administrators. Thus, we lack information regarding the exact nature of offenders' experiences with boot camp.

When offered the option of serving any duration of boot camp to avoid one year of prison, 23.4 percent of all respondents chose prison, though men were more likely to choose prison (25.8 percent) than were women (21.5 percent). Table 1 also presents two measures of the amount of boot camp that offenders will endure to avoid one year of imprisonment. If respondents who refuse to serve any boot camp (zero scores) are included in the calculation, the total sample averages 3.63 months of boot camp to avoid one year of prison, women average 3.92 months, men average 3.24 months, and the gender difference is significant at $p < .05$. When zero scores are deleted, the full sample is reduced to 314 cases and averages 4.75 months of boot camp to avoid one year of prison, women average 4.99 months, men average 4.39 months, and again the gender difference is significant at $p < .05$. Thus, when given the choice to serve some amount of boot camp or one year in prison, men are more likely to choose prison than are women, and women will serve a longer duration of boot camp than men. Finally, inmates in the sample had previously served on average 3.39 of the ten different alternatives examined in the survey (which included a high proportion who had served some duration of county jail), with men averaging about four alternatives and women averaging about three.

Consistent with results reported by Wood and Grasmick (1999), women seem slightly more willing to endure some amount of boot camp than are men, while men appear more likely to choose prison over any duration of boot camp when compared to women. Thus, Table 1 shows that women are more amenable to serving boot camp than are men–that is, a larger proportion of women say they are willing to participate in boot camp.

Gender Differences in Reasons to Avoid and Participate in Alternative Sanctions

The survey included items that represent reasons to avoid and participate in alternatives. It is important to note, however, that the items do not reference any particular alternative sanction, but simply ask about alternatives in general. Therefore, while the items shown in Tables 2 and 3 can be used to demonstrate gender differences in reasons to avoid or participate in alternatives, it would be a mistake to conclude the responses are specific to boot camp. In fact, prior research has noted that boot camp (along with county jail) is viewed as the most punitive of alternative sanctions due to the unique conditions it presents to participants (Wood and Grasmick, 1999; Wood and May, 2003). It is likely, then, that responses to these items might differ considerably if they

Table 2: Response Frequencies for the Eight Reasons to Avoid Alternative Sanctions Items, by Gender

Below is a list of reasons that might cause an inmate to *avoid* an alternative sanction. We want to know *how important* you think these reasons are for *avoiding* an alternative sanction.

Survey Items	Not at All Important Male	Not at All Important Female	Somewhat Important Male	Somewhat Important Female	Pretty Important Male	Pretty Important Female	Very Important Male	Very Important Female
Programs like those in this survey are too hard to complete.	29.1%	32.3%	21.8%	26.0%	24.0%	18.4%	25.1%	23.3%
Program rules are too hard to follow.	26.3%	32.9%	21.8%	22.5%	25.1%	23.4%	26.8%	21.2%
Parole and program officers are too hard on the program participants, they try to catch them and send them back to prison.	17.4%	22.7%	15.7%	19.0%	16.3%	15.3%	50.6%	43.1%
Serving time in prison is easier than the alternatives offered by the DOC.	27.8%	28.3%	20.6%	19.6%	16.7%	21.9%	35.0%	30.1%
If you fail to complete the alternative sanction, you end up back in prison.	13.3%	12.8%	13.3%	14.2%	15.6%	16.1%	57.8%	56.9%
In general, living in prison is easier than living outside prison.	47.8%	49.5%	15.7%	14.2%	12.9%	14.2%	23.6%	22.0%
Inmates are abused by parole and probation officers who oversee the programs.	20.2%	28.5%	16.3%	16.7%	19.1%	18.1%	44.4%	36.7%
Serving time in prison is less hassle because the programs have too many responsibilities.*	33.0%	35.7%	15.1%	23.5%	25.1%	15.4%	26.8%	25.3%

* = Gender difference is significant at .05 (Chi-Square).

Table 3: Response Frequencies for the Six Reasons to Participate in Alternative Sanctions Items, by Gender

Below is a list of reasons that might cause an inmate to *participate in* an alternative sanction. We want to know how *important* you think these reasons are for *participating in* an alternative sanction.

Survey Items	Not at All Important Male	Not at All Important Female	Somewhat Important Male	Somewhat Important Female	Pretty Important Male	Pretty Important Female	Very Important Male	Very Important Female
Alternatives offer a better lifestyle than prison.	8.8%	12.2%	11.6%	14.0%	18.8%	17.2%	60.8%	56.6%
Alternatives allow the inmate to live outside prison.	8.4%	5.5%	6.2%	9.1%	12.9%	16.4%	72.5%	69.1%
Alternatives have a good reputation among inmates.*	19.0%	22.0%	9.5%	19.3%	24.0%	22.5%	47.5%	36.2%
Alternatives successfully rehabilitate the offender.	14.0%	7.8%	13.4%	12.8%	19.0%	20.1%	53.6%	59.4%
Alternatives are easier to complete than a prison term.*	21.5%	17.4%	20.4%	16.9%	15.5%	27.4%	42.5%	38.4%
Alternatives help you get out of prison sooner.*	14.4%	6.8%	12.7%	9.5%	12.7%	18.1%	60.2%	65.6%

* = Gender difference significant at .05 (Chi-Square).

were in reference to boot camp as compared to community service for example.

Table 2 presents gender-specific responses to eight reasons to avoid alternative sanctions. Perhaps the most obvious gender difference is that a higher percentage of males rate each reason to avoid alternatives as "very important" compared to females. In addition, for seven of the eight reasons, a higher percentage of women say that reason is "not at all important" for avoiding alternatives. In general, Table 2 shows that women are less likely to agree with reasons to avoid alternatives. But for both men and women, the most important reasons for avoiding alternatives are "Parole and program officers are too hard on the program participants, they try to catch them and send them back to prison," "If you fail to complete the alternative sanction you end up back in prison," and "Inmates are abused by parole and probation officers who oversee the programs." It appears that both men and women entertain concerns about being revoked back to prison as a result of what they perceive as discriminatory treatment by program officers. As a consequence, they may be less inclined to participate in alternatives, or more inclined to choose a set prison term with no strings attached.

Similarly, Table 3 presents six reasons that might convince an inmate to participate in an alternative sanction. The gender difference is not as clear with regard to reasons to participate, and it appears that men and women are in general agreement that all six reasons are either "pretty important" or "very important" reasons to participate in alternatives. The four most important reasons for men and women are "Alternatives offer a better lifestyle than prison," "Alternatives allow the inmate to live outside prison," "Alternatives help you get out of prison sooner," and "Alternatives successfully rehabilitate the offender."

We use the items in Tables 2 and 3 to develop two scales reflecting the degree to which respondents identify with reasons to avoid or participate in alternative sanctions. Responses to the statements are coded such that offenders who thought the statements were important reasons for avoiding alternative sanctions scored higher on the "avoidance scale" than respondents who felt those statements were not important reasons for avoiding the sanctions. We conducted a factor analysis (varimax rotation) which generated one factor that included all eight avoidance items with an Eigenvalue of 3.990 in which all eight survey items registered factor loadings of .555 or higher. The alpha reliability for the eight-item additive scale was .854. We would expect that those scoring at the high end of the avoidance scale would be less likely to serve any amount of boot camp and therefore more likely to choose prison. In addition, we would expect that among those respondents willing to serve some amount of boot camp, those scoring higher on the avoidance scale would serve less of it. Thus, we expect a negative relationship between the avoidance scale and (1) willingness to serve some boot camp, and (2) the amount of boot camp that those willing respondents will serve. As with the avoidance scale, responses to the six "reasons to participate" items are coded such that inmates with high scores on the "participation scale" identify more strongly with those reasons to participate in alternatives. Again, factor analysis identified one factor that combined the six items with a Eigenvalue of 2.705 and an alpha reliability of .7502. The six items in the participation scale registered factor loadings of .590 or higher. We expect those scoring high on the participation scale will be more likely to choose some amount of boot camp rather than prison. In addition, we expect that among those offenders who are willing to serve some boot camp, those scoring higher on the participation scale will serve more of it.

Regarding differences by gender, given that women are willing to serve more boot camp than men ($p < .05$), and that men are more likely to choose prison over any duration of boot camp compared to women (see Table 1), we would expect women to score lower on the avoidance scale and higher on the participation scale than men. In fact, the gender comparison of mean scores on these scales reveals that men average 21.08 on avoidance while women average 20.19 (mean difference is significant at $p < .10$), and men average 18.91 on participation while women average 19.06 (gender difference is not significant). However, it remains to be seen how these associations present themselves in multivariate analysis.

Multivariate Results

We conducted both logistic and OLS regression analyses for the total sample, and for males and females separately in order to explore (1) what sociodemographic and correctional experience measures might influence offenders' willingness to serve boot camp, and (2) what sociodemographic and correctional experience measures might influence the amount of boot camp offenders are willing to serve. Given that men and women differ with regard to their preference for prison over any duration of boot camp and the amount of boot camp they are willing to endure to avoid one year of prison, we expect that men and women will generate different predictive models in our analyses. Though we likely have too few cases to satisfy the minimal guidelines for regression analysis, we opted to present these results for two reasons. First, we are aware of no other analysis of this sort in the published literature. Second, despite the limited number of cases in the male and female models, results nevertheless reveal important gender differences that can and should be examined with larger sample sizes. Results presented here, then, should be viewed as exploratory and illustrative, rather than conclusive.

Table 4 presents binary logistic regression results for the total sample, men, and women. The dependent variable has been coded 0 for "won't serve any boot camp" and 1 for "will serve some amount of boot camp." Predictors include the following: years of education, age of the respondent, total months spent in prison, total number of alternatives ever served, cumulative scores on the avoidance and participation scales, a female dummy variable (relevant to

Table 4: Logistic Regression, Full Model for Total Sample, Men, Women (0 = Won't Serve Any Boot Camp, 1 = Will Serve Some Amount of Boot Camp).

Predictors	Total Sample (N = 272) b	sig	odds	Men (N = 114) b	sig	odds	Women (N = 158) b	sig	odds
Education	.127	.048	1.136	.203	.037	1.225	.029	.403	1.029
Age	−.036	.047	.965	−.041	.095	.959	−.033	.164	.968
Total Time in Prison (Months)	.000	.488	1.000	.001	.405	1.001	−.002	.395	.998
Total Number of Alternatives Served	.028	.402	1.028	.055	.360	1.056	.002	.495	1.002
Avoidance Scale	−.032	.090	.968	−.026	.242	.974	−.043	.100	.958
Female	.258	.221	1.295	---	---	---	---	---	---
Have Kid(s)	−.287	.298	.750	−.160	.387	.852	−.589	.215	.555
Participation Scale	.060	.058	1.062	.044	.225	1.045	.082	.060	1.085
Married	−.514	.077	.598	−.861	.063	.423	−.147	.386	.864
Served Boot Camp Previously	.703	.043	2.021	.667	.134	1.949	.784	.094	2.190
Chi-square/Sig	23.910/.004			13.165/.078			12.484/.098		

the total sample equations), whether the respondent has any children, whether the respondent is married, and whether the respondent has any prior experience serving boot camp.

Table 4 presents the direction of the association as evidenced by the unstandardized coefficient, the significance of the association, and the odds-ratio. The interpretation of the odds-ratio coefficient is as follows: for the Total Sample equation, a one unit increase in education (years) results in a 13.6 percent increase in the likelihood that the respondent will agree to serve some amount of boot camp. Likewise, a one-year increase in the age of the respondent results in a 3.5 percent decrease in the likelihood of serving any amount of boot camp. Therefore, the Total Sample equation shows that education, age, the avoidance scale, the participation scale, married status, and having served boot camp previously all register a significant impact on the likelihood of serving some amount of boot camp (and conversely on the likelihood of choosing prison over any duration of boot camp). Specifically, respondents who are better educated, identify more with reasons to participate in boot camp, and have served boot camp previously are significantly more likely to do some boot camp rather than one year in prison. Further, respondents who are older, score higher on the avoidance scale, and who are married are significantly less likely to do boot camp. Of those predictors that achieve significance at the p < .10 level, the likelihood of agreeing to serve some amount of boot camp is increased by 102 percent among those who have served boot camp previously. Apparently, personal knowledge of the requirements and conditions of boot camp prepares respondents for doing it again, while those with no prior experience will more likely choose prison instead. Also, there appears to be no significant gender difference in the likelihood of serving boot camp when controlling for other factors, despite that there was a difference (albeit nonsignificant) in the percentage of males versus females who refused to serve any duration of boot camp.

Gender-specific results in Table 4 are hampered by the reduction in cases. Nevertheless, education, age, and being married still retain a significant impact in the male model. The impact of education is significant only among males (i.e., a one-year increase in education results in a 22.5 percent likelihood of serving some amount of boot camp compared to one year in prison). Being married decreases the likelihood of serving boot camp by 57.7 percent among males, but has no impact on females. Having served boot camp previously approaches a significant effect among males, and would likely register a significant impact with a larger sample size.

Higher scores on the participation scale, having served boot camp previously, and higher scores on the avoidance scale particularly influence women's likelihood of serving boot camp. In particular, having served boot camp previously increases women's likelihood of serving some amount of boot camp by 119 percent. It seems probable that a larger female sample size would allow the effect of age to become statistically significant as well.

We present ordinary least squares (OLS) regression results in Table 5. In these models, the dependent variable represents the number of months respondents will serve to avoid one year of prison. Further, respondents who refuse to serve any amount of boot camp (zero scores) are deleted from models presented in Table 5. Unfortunately, this has the effect of even further reducing the number of cases in each model, but we are interested in exploring factors that affect the *amount* of boot camp that respondents are willing to do among offenders who are willing to do some, and felt that the inclusion of zero scores would skew our results since we are asking a different question than that addressed by results in Table 4.

The Total Sample model identifies four predictors that could arguably be considered significant using a liberal p < .10 significance level. These include the participation scale, the avoidance scale, having served boot camp previously, and being female. Total months spent in prison has a borderline significant impact. Specifically, having served boot camp previously, being female, and total months in prison increase the amount of boot camp respondents are willing to serve. The gender difference observed in Table 1 with regard to the amount of boot camp offenders are willing to serve remains even when controlling for other potentially relevant factors. And it appears that inmates with

Table 5: OLS Regression, Full Model for Total Sample, Men, Women (Respondents Refusing to Serve Any Boot Camp Are Deleted)

Predictors	Total Sample (N = 211) Beta	sig	Men (N = 85) Beta	sig	Women (N = 126) Beta	sig
Education	−.055	.276	−.083	.232	.021	.415
Age	−.032	.398	−.091	.224	−.021	.471
Total Time in Prison (Months)	.097	.104	.188	.064	.040	.389
Total Number of Alternatives Served	−.059	.229	−.053	.333	−.049	.311
Avoidance Scale	.115	.057	−.049	.328	.219	.018
Female	.120	.055	---	---	---	---
Have Kid(s)	.000	.498	−.134	.126	.160	.066
Participation Scale	−.127	.037	−.298	.004	−.023	.406
Married	−.021	.386	.007	.477	−.039	.389
Served Boot Camp Previously	.124	.055	.153	.093	.174	.055
R-Square	.060		.164		.061	

significant time in prison may be willing to serve more boot camp than those with less prison experience. Similar to findings in Table 4, having served boot camp previously has a significant positive effect on the amount of boot camp respondents are willing to serve.

Perhaps counterintuitively, in Table 5 the avoidance scale is positively associated with the dependent variable and the participation scale is negatively associated with the dependent variable. We were puzzled with regard to these associations. It is possible that the deletion of zero scores in the dependent variable (which account for 23.4 percent of our sample and contribute to the *predicted* direction of the association between the scales and our dependent variables) results in the reverse associations found in Table 5. And it is true that there is little variation in the number of months of boot camp that offenders are willing to serve (for example, when zero scores are deleted, the number of valid cases drops from 411 to 314, the average number of months increases from 3.63 to 4.75, and the standard deviation declines from 3.056 to 2.623). Thus, perhaps the change in direction of the association is due to these changes in the dependent variable. It is also true that the reasons to avoid or participate in alternatives used in the analysis, and the scales that correspond to them, reflect generalized perceptions of alternative sanctions, and are not targeted toward boot camp in particular. Unlike other alternatives like electronic monitoring, ISP, or community service, boot camp does not allow the offender to live outside prison, typically involves close supervision, military drill activities, strict regimentation, minimal or absent visitation privileges, and a nearly total lack of autonomy on the part of the offender. We suspect that were inmates asked to respond to the avoidance and participation items with specific reference to boot camp, many more would score higher on the avoidance scale and many more would score lower on the participation scale. For example, the notion that boot camp offers a better lifestyle than prison or that boot camp allows an inmate to live outside prison would generate nearly universal disagreement. Previous work has demonstrated that boot camp is viewed as more punitive than any other correctional sanction, including prison, and this holds for male, female, white, and black offenders (Wood and Grasmick, 1999; Wood and May, 2003).

In reference to the avoidance scale, it may be that once offenders who are strongly opposed to alternative sanctions and who are unwilling to invest any amount of time in boot camp are removed from the analysis (about a quarter of all respondents), the equation changes somewhat, because their high scores on the avoidance scale are no longer included in the association. Even though an offender may score high on the avoidance scale, he/she may realize that the time served in boot camp will be shorter than 12 months in prison if he/she successfully completes the sentence and is therefore motivated to serve some amount of boot camp. But only four percent of the sample agreed to do as much as 12 months boot camp to avoid 12 months imprisonment while almost two-thirds (64.8 percent) of the sample said they would do seven months or less to avoid twelve months in prison. In this case, offenders who score low on avoidance also score low on the number of months of boot camp they are willing to serve. Likewise, when asked to indicate the amount of boot camp they would be willing to serve to avoid 12 months imprisonment, offenders who have more favorable views toward alternative sanctions in general are nevertheless unlikely to serve longer durations of boot camp.

Conversations with inmates concerning their views of boot camp reveal that boot camp is highly stigmatized and unpopular, and many inmates feel that only "punks" and young, first-time inmates would allow themselves to be subjected to what one inmate called "institutionalized embarrassment." It seems likely that the negative stigma and conditions that surround boot camp makes it qualitatively different when compared to other alternative sanctions. The statements used to compose the index do not deal directly with any specific alternative sanction; as such, when the inmates were stating their views of alternative sanctions in general, they may not have been thinking about boot camp as one of the alternative sanctions. Consequently, when asked about their willingness to participate in boot camp specifically, they agreed to do so but are not willing to invest a large amount of time in boot camp when compared to the alternative of prison. Among inmates, boot camp likely carries a heavier stigma than prison, and many inmates feel that the "easier time" might be in prison than in boot camp. In analysis not shown here, we substituted community service and regular probation for boot camp, and the predicted negative association between the avoidance scale and number of months inmates are willing to serve was supported, as was the positive association between the participation scale and number of months (May and Wood, 2003). We suspect that the restrictive nature of boot camp and its extremely negative reputation among inmates (such that a quarter of offenders will choose 12 months in prison rather than serve even one month of boot camp) produces a very different association between the measures in our analysis. This explanation is purely speculative, and more work seems warranted to explore these unexpected findings generated by boot camp.

Gender-specific analyses in Table 5 reveal factors that seem important for men versus women. (Again, the number of cases likely violates assumptions necessary for valid multivariate analysis, and we view these results as exploratory while urging researchers to pursue issues discussed here with larger and more representative data sets.) Factors that have a statistically significant ($p < .10$) impact on the number of months of boot camp that men are willing to serve include total months in prison, the participation scale, and having served boot camp previously. Possibly for reasons noted above, the participation scale evidences a negative association with amount of boot camp. Men with more time in prison appear willing to serve more months of boot camp, and those with prior boot camp experience are willing to serve more boot camp than those without such experience.

Findings for women offenders focus on the impact of the avoidance scale, which operates in the counterintuitive manner described above, having served boot camp previously, and having at least one child. As noted in Table 1, only 19.3 percent of women in our sample (who average 31.66 years of age) are married, while 79.5 percent have at least one child. And Table 1 shows that women will serve on average about 21 percent more boot camp than men to avoid one year of imprisonment. Results for women in Table 5 would suggest that women with children are motivated to serve more boot camp than men as an alternative to a year in prison in order to be released sooner so as to minimize the time of separation from children. Moreover, having served boot camp in the past appears to encourage some women to serve it again, and to gamble on a slightly longer duration of it in order to secure early release.

DISCUSSION

The 415 men and women in our sample represent the kind of inmates most likely to be eligible for alternative sanctions, including correctional boot camp. We begin by observing that among other differences, women will serve a significantly longer amount of boot camp than men in order to avoid one year of prison, and that men are more likely than women (25.8 percent vs. 21.5 percent) to choose one year in prison than serve any duration of boot camp. We were also somewhat surprised to note that 34.9 percent of our sample had served some amount of boot camp in the past (32.7 percent of men and 36.7 percent of women), which allowed us to test for an experiential effect.

Women identify more strongly than men with four of the six reasons to participate in alternative sanctions, though a clear majority of both genders rate these reasons as either "pretty" or "very" important reasons to participate (see Table 3). Men seem to identify more strongly with reasons to avoid alternatives, with a higher percentage of men rating each of the eight reasons as "very important," and a higher percentage of women rating seven of the eight reasons as "not at all important" (Table 2). We developed two additive scales (supported by factor and reliability analysis) representing the composite scores for reasons to avoid alternatives and reasons to participate in alternatives, and along with other demographic and correctional experience indicators tried to account for the difference between inmates who will choose prison rather than any amount of boot camp as compared to inmates who will serve some amount of boot camp to avoid one year of prison. Next, we deleted inmates who would not serve any boot camp, and regressed the amount of boot camp the remaining respondents would serve on the same set of predictors. Finally, we developed these models for the full sample, and for men and women separately.

Overall, results demonstrate the importance of having served some boot camp in the past, which significantly increases both the likelihood of serving boot camp again, and the amount of boot camp offenders are willing to serve. As expected, a higher avoidance scale score decreases the likelihood that an offender will do boot camp, and increases the likelihood that an offender will choose prison over any amount of it, while the participation scale works to encourage enrollment in boot camp, and these results hold for both men and women. But once inmates who refuse to serve any boot camp are removed (23.4 percent of the total sample), the scales work in the opposite direction with respect to the number of months of boot camp that the remaining inmates will serve–though the anomalous finding for the avoidance scale is limited to females and is only marginally significant ($p = .10$) and the anomalous finding for the participation scale is limited to men. It is possible that with larger sample sizes these anomalies might resolve themselves, but we suspect the problem is partly due to the unique conditions presented by correctional boot camps, the negative stigma that boot camp carries among inmates, and the items we use to measure reasons to participate and/or avoid alternatives in general. Several reasons to participate in alternatives (offer a better lifestyle than prison, allow the inmate to live outside the prison, are easier to complete than a prison term, etc.) are generally not applicable to boot camp. Unlike other alternatives, boot camp is characterized by institutional confinement, strict discipline and rules, military-style drill, and limited or absent visitation rights. Moreover, we would note that in additional analysis that examined preferences for community service and regular probation compared to prison (not shown), the effects of the avoidance and participation scales are in the predicted directions for both logistic and OLS full sample models.

Older inmates appear less willing to enroll in boot camp, and may agree to serve less of it than younger inmates, and this seems in line with comments noted earlier regarding inmates' attitudes toward boot camp. Older inmates may view those who volunteer for it as "punks" who are willing to subject themselves to "institutionalized embarrassment" and who may be afraid of serving time in the general prison population. Boot camp, therefore, is not only viewed as highly punitive with a strong likelihood of revocation, but it also carries a heavy negative stigma among many inmates. Those with more years of education are apparently more willing to gamble on some duration of boot camp, but are not willing to serve longer durations of it. Married men are less willing to enroll in any amount of boot camp, perhaps because male inmates in general rate a brief prison term as easier than boot camp, they enjoy regular visitation rights in prison but not in boot camp, and they likely count on spouses and relatives to administer child care in their absence.

Finally, while the female dummy variable does not generate a significant impact in the logistic model (Table 4), it does in the OLS model (Table 5). The gender difference noted in Table 1 is supported in multivariate analysis, with women willing to serve more months of boot camp than men even when controlling for potentially relevant demographic and experiential factors. Reasons for this seem to center on whether women have any prior experience with boot camp, and if they have any children living outside prison. And though 65.7 percent of men and 79.5 percent of women report being parents, the parental status measure achieves significance only among women. It appears that though boot camps typically do not cater to the needs of women offenders, women are willing to serve more boot camp than men for reasons noted above (MacKenzie et al., 1996; Wood and Grasmick, 1999).

Logistic and OLS regression results, though vulnerable to the charge of using an insufficient number of cases, point toward potentially important gender differences in factors that may promote avoidance of or participation in alternative sanctions, and that influence the amount of boot camp offenders are willing to serve. Prior research finds that boot camp is viewed by inmates as perhaps the most punitive of correctional sanctions, including prison (Wood and Grasmick, 1999; Wood and May, 2003). As such, it has little in common with less restrictive community- or home-based alternatives like electronic monitoring, ISP, community service, day reporting, and the like, except in that if an offender successfully completes boot camp he/she is returned to the community sooner than if a corresponding prison term were to be served. Both men and women in our sample view boot camp as a significant gamble with a high likelihood of both revocation back to prison and abusive treatment at the hands of boot camp personnel. And they are not willing to serve on average more than four months of boot camp to avoid one year of imprisonment.

We offer several caveats with regard to our findings. First, there are likely other demographic and experiential factors that influence preferences for boot camp that are not included in our analysis. For example, drug offenders may be less likely to enroll in boot camp than nonviolent property offenders due to the strict drug-testing regimen and/or lack of autonomy demanded by boot camp. Further, there may be features of the offender's bond with his/her family or home community that might encourage enrollment in boot camp and return to the community more quickly (the offender may have a job waiting for them, or may have responsibilities that require their attention), or that might encourage them to remain in prison longer (i.e., their lifestyle outside prison might be worse, persons outside prison are waiting to retaliate against them, all their friends are in prison, etc.).

Second, boot camps in Oklahoma are segregated by gender, and over a third of female offenders in our sample have prior experience serving boot camp. Though many programmatic features that are available in male boot camps are missing from the female boot camps examined here, the fact that women in our sample are able to enroll in boot camp that is gender-specific and located in an exclusively female prison may make it more attractive to these women compared to boot camps that integrate men and women. Characteristics of boot camp vary considerably from one program to another, and we are unable to account for these potentially important differences in our data. Third, it appears necessary to employ measures of avoidance and participation that reference specific alternative sanctions. Sanctions differ significantly from one another, and a generalized index that represents reasons to avoid or participate in alternatives may not be accurate for some of them. Fourth, larger data sets are necessary in order to allow multivariate analysis by subgroups and by specific alternative sanctions. Results presented here are plagued by an insufficient number of cases, and should be considered exploratory until replicated and extended using a larger number of respondents and additional potentially relevant predictors. Finally, more research focusing on the unique needs of female inmates is required, particularly if it is established that female inmates are more amenable to alternative sanctions (including boot camp) than are men. A better understanding of factors that motivate or inhibit offenders' willingness to enroll in alternatives may have some value for correctional policy and practice.

REFERENCES

Apospori, E. & Alpert, G. (1993). Research note: The role of differential experience with the criminal justice system in changes in perception of severity of legal sanctions over time. *Crime and Delinquency, 39,* 184-194.

Crouch, B.M. (1993). Is incarceration really worse? Analysis of offenders' preferences for prison over probation. *Justice Quarterly, 10,* 67-88.

Gover, A.R., Styve, G.J., & MacKenzie, R.L. (1999). Evaluating correctional boot camp programs: Issues and concerns. In K.C. Haas and G.P. Alpert (Eds.). *The dilemmas of corrections: Contemporary readings* (4th Ed.) (pp. 384-402). Prospect Heights, IL: Waveland Press, Inc.

Holley, P.D. & Brewster, D. (1996). The women at Eddie Warrior Correctional Center: Descriptions from a data set. *Journal of the Oklahoma Criminal Justice Research Consortium*, Volume 3.

Holley, P.D. & Connelly, M.D. (1994). Oklahoma's Regimented Inmate Discipline (RID) program for males: Preliminary evaluation and assessment. *Journal of the Oklahoma Criminal Justice Research Consortium*, Volume 1.

Holley, P.D. & Wright, D.E. (1995). Oklahoma's Regimented Inmate Discipline program for males: Its impact on recidivism. *Journal of the Oklahoma Criminal Justice Research Consortium*, Volume 2.

MacKenzie, D.L. (1995). Boot camp prisons: Examining their growth and effectiveness. In K.C. Haas and G.P. Alpert (Eds.). *The dilemmas of corrections: Contemporary readings* (3rd Ed.) (pp. 396-405). Prospect Heights, IL: Waveland Press, Inc.

MacKenzie, D.L. & Donaldson, H. (1996). Boot camp for women offenders. *Criminal Justice Review*, 21, 21-43.

MacKenzie, D.L., Elis, L.A., Simpson, S.S., & Skroban, S.B. (1996). Boot camps as an alternative for women. In D.L. MacKenzie and E.E. Hebert (Eds.). *Correctional boot camps: A tough intermediate sanction* (pp. 233-244). Washington, DC: U.S. Department of Justice. Office of Justice Programs.

MacKenzie. D.L. & Souryal, C. (1994). *Multisite evaluation of shock incarceration.* Washington, DC: U.S. Department of Justice, Office of Justice Programs.

Marcus-Mendoza, S.T. (1995). A preliminary investigation of Oklahoma's shock incarceration program. *Journal of the Oklahoma Criminal Justice Research Consortium*, Volume 2.

McClelland, K.A. & Alpert, G. (1985). Factor analysis applied to magnitude estimates of punishment seriousness: Patterns of individual differences. *Journal of Quantitative Criminology*, 1, 307-318.

May, D.C. & Wood, P.B. (2003). What influences offenders' willingness to serve alternative sanctions? Unpublished Manuscript. Paper Presented at the Southern Criminal Justice Association Annual Meeting. Nashville, TN.

Petersilia, J. (1990). When probation becomes more dreaded than prison. *Federal Probation*, 54, 23-27.

Petersilia, J. & Deschenes, E.P. (1994a). What punishes? Inmates rank the severity of prison vs. intermediate sanctions. *Federal Probation*, 58, 3-8.

Petersilia, J. & Deschenes, E.P. (1994b). Perceptions of punishment: Inmates and staff rank the severity of prison versus intermediate sanctions. *The Prison Journal*, 74, 306-328.

Spelman, W. (1995). The severity of intermediate sanctions. *Journal of Research in Crime and Delinquency*, 32, 107-135.

Wood, P.B., Gove, W.R., Wilson, J.A., & Cochran, J.K. (1997). Nonsocial reinforcement and habitual criminal conduct: An extension of learning theory. *Criminology*, 35, 335-366.

Wood, P.B. & Grasmick, H.G. (1999). Toward the development of punishment equivalencies: Male and female inmates rate the severity of alternative sanctions compared to prison. *Justice Quarterly, 16,* 19-50.

Wood, P.B. & May, D.C. (2003). Race differences in perceptions of sanction severity: Comparison of prison with alternatives. *Justice Quarterly, 20,* 605-631.

AUTHORS' NOTES

Peter B. Wood is an associate professor of Sociology, Director of the Program in Criminal Justice and Corrections, and a research fellow at the Social Science Research Center at Mississippi State University. His interests include the study of positive and negative reinforcers and rational choice processes among convicted offenders, and issues related to correctional policy and practice. His work has appeared in *Criminology, Justice Quarterly, Punishment and Society,* and *Journal of Research in Crime and Delinquency.*

David C. May is an associate professor and School Safety Fellow in the Department of Correctional and Juvenile Justice Services at Eastern Kentucky University. His interests include juvenile delinquency, fear of crime, gun ownership among male delinquents, and issues related to offenders' perceptions of the severity of criminal justice sanctions. His work has appeared in *Deviant Behavior, Youth and Society, Adolescence,* and *Justice Quarterly.*

Harold G. Grasmick is a professor of Sociology at the University of Oklahoma. Among his many interests are the extension of deterrence/rational choice theory to include informal sanctions, issues related to social disorganization theory, and the study of the link between religion and public opinion concerning punishment and justice. He has published extensively in journals such as *Criminology, Social Forces, Journal of Quantitative Criminology,* and *Justice Quarterly.*

This work was funded through the Edna McConnell Clark Foundation State-Centered Program and sponsored by the Oklahoma Department of Corrections. Appreciation goes to the many DOC personnel who aided in the project, particularly Dan Lawrence.

Address correspondence to Dr. Peter B. Wood, Department of Sociology, Anthropology, and Social Work, P.O. Box C, Mississippi State University, Mississippi State, MS 39762 (E-mail: wood@soc.msstate.edu).

☐ ***Appendix A***

Boot Camp. Boot camp is for a shorter time than you would have been sent to prison. But boot camp can be more unpleasant in many ways than living in prison. Boot camp is like basic training for the army. You live with about a hundred other people in one big room. There is regular drill instruction like in the military and you are pushed physically and psychologically to perform beyond your capabilities. You experience sleep deprivation. You are required to become physically active and fit. You are constantly supervised by drill instructors who watch you closely. You are generally required to participate in an education program. Virtually all your time and activities are controlled. You are subject to random UA and can be sent back to prison if you fail to obey the rules.

Think about 12 months actual time spent in a medium security correctional center.

What is the maximum number of months of boot camp you would take to avoid serving 12 months actual time in prison? (Put an X on the line below to indicate your answer)

0 1 2 3 4 5 6 7 8 9 10 11 12 13 14 15 16 17 18

Months of Actual Time Spent in Boot Camp

The X is equal to _____ months of boot camp. (Write the number)

Have you personally ever served time in a boot camp?

   1. Yes
   2. No

Native American Ethnicity and Childhood Maltreatment as Variables in Perceptions and Adjustments to Boot Camp vs. "Traditional" Correctional Settings

ANGELA R. GOVER

University of Florida

ABSTRACT A sample of 302 juveniles confined in two separate correctional facilities in a Western plains state was assessed to examine the relationship between child maltreatment and other delinquency risk factors, and Native American ethnicity on perceptions of the institutional environments and psychological adjustment in a boot camp and traditional facility. The results indicate few differences between Native and non-Native American youth's perceptions of institutional environments. Youth institutionalized in the boot camp, however, differed significantly from those in the traditional facility in their perceptions of institutional activity, control, justice, and freedom. Child maltreatment and other risk factors were related to psychological adjustment for all youth. In addition, the boot camp facility significantly reduced anxiety for Native American youth. The implications of this research for boot camps and juvenile justice policy are discussed. *[Article copies available for a fee from The Haworth Document Delivery Service: 1-800-HAWORTH. E-mail address: <docdelivery@haworthpress.com> Website: <http://www.HaworthPress.com> © 2005 by The Haworth Press, Inc. All rights reserved.]*

KEYWORDS Native American youth, delinquency, boot camps, childhood maltreatment, conditions of confinement

INTRODUCTION

There is a gap in the criminological literature as to the causes, extent, and experiences of Native Americans in the juvenile justice system (Armstrong, Guilfoyle, & Melton, 1996). One barrier to identifying trends, patterns, and prevalence rates of delinquency using Native American samples at the national level is complicated by the various cultures, customs, and traditions associated with different tribes. Numerous researchers have acknowledged the lack of empirical studies on crime and delinquency among Native American youth (Black & Smith, 1980; Forslund & Cranston, 1975; Jensen, Stauss, & Harris, 1977; O'Brien, 1977; Robbins, 1985). However, the small amount of research that has been conducted on Native American offenders has primarily focused on adults; thus, research on Native American delinquency is limited (Jung & Rawana, 1999; Micozzi, 1985). Additionally, little research exists that examines the experience of Native American youth in the juvenile justice system.

Early research focused on disparity in sentencing between Native American offenders and White offenders, and differences in arrest rates and parole decisions between these two ethnic groups (Bynum, 1981; Hall & Simkus, 1975). This research showed that Native Americans had higher incarceration rates than Whites (Kickingbird, 1976), and that Whites were more likely to receive deferred sentences (Hall & Simkus, 1975). Supporting this earlier research, Armstrong et al. (1996) indicated that Native American youth were overrepresented in the criminal justice system from the initial state of arrest to the last stage of incarceration (National Council of Juvenile and Family Court Judges, 1990). Other studies have documented the fact that Native American youth are incarcerated at rates second to African Americans (Krisberg, Schwartz, Fishman, Eisikovits, Guttman, & Joe, 1987) and that they are incarcerated at more than twice the rates of Whites (Poupart, 1995). Camp and Camp (1991) examined the number of Native American youth confined within eleven juvenile residential facilities compared to their makeup in the population and found that Native Americans were disproportionately confined in all facilities. All of these studies support the historical pattern of the overrepresentation of Native American youth within training schools and other types of correctional facilities.

Little research has been conducted on the experience of Native American youth within the juvenile justice system. As a result, we know very little about how Native youth perceive and adjust to correctional environments compared with non-Native youths. Given that Native youth are at greater risk for involvement in the justice system, it is important to examine their experience within institutional environments. There are a number of reasons to suspect that Native American youth may adjust differently to correctional environments than non-Native Americans.

Native American and Western Culture Conflict

While there is little evidence regarding the extent to which Native Americans have accepted and conformed to the culture of the Western society, the literature has well documented the differences and incompatibility between the two cultures (Robbins, 1985). According to Kickingbird (1976), "The prison environment, in which a disproportionate number of Native Americans find themselves, given the selective and discriminatory law enforcement system, is one in which they find especially hostile and alien. Indians are greatly over-represented in prison populations, yet often lack a voice in their operation" (p. 19). It has been suggested that Native American offenders who are incarcerated in correctional institutions are struggling with being caught between two cultures: their traditional native culture and the dominant White culture (French, 1980). To assist Native Americans in their adjustment within the correctional environment, an Indian-run prison (minimum security) in South Dakota implemented the federally funded 'Swift Bird Project' to assist Native Americans in their correctional survival by strengthening their self-images and teaching inmates skills necessary to survive in both cultures (French, 1980).

Longclaws, Barbes, Grieve, and Dumoff (1980) examined juvenile problem drinking among the Brokenhead Ojibwa tribe and attributed the problem to a breakdown in family ties and traditional Indian norms. Robbins (1985) suggests that certain behaviors are part of the 'Indian experience' for Native youth, which results in Native youth not responding to the same institutional attachments as non-Native youth. Sellers, Winfree, and Griffiths (1993) proposed that drug and alcohol use would be higher among transient Indians, which are individuals who do not have ties to their own culture, in order to insolate them from the impact of modernization. These researchers found that the modernization effect and cultural breakdown perspective was having an impact on attitudes and behaviors towards drugs and alcohol for Indian youth, but these findings varied by tribe and residence on a reservation (Sellers et al., 1993). Interestingly, however, when comparing the strength of the cultural perspective between Native youth and non-Native youth, the "norm qualities appear to transcend cultural barriers: the Indian youths respond to the norm qualities of their peers in very similar fashion to non-Indians" (Sellers et al., 1993, p. 508).

Needs of Native American Offenders

Some researchers have suggested that Native American offenders have special needs that should be responded to in a more sensitive manner, compared with offenders from other ethnic backgrounds (Hann & Harman, 1993; Starr,

1978). Specifically, juveniles living in reservation settings are faced with many stressors that can culminate in many emotional and psychological problems (Duclos, Beals, Novins, Martin, Jewett, Duclos, & Manson, 1998). Most reservations do not have appropriate resources to deal with problems that adolescent Natives face.

Empirical research has documented the fact that the Native American population is at a disadvantage for heath problems and that Native youth show signs of distress before adulthood (Cummins, Ireland, Resnick, & Blum, 1999). Specifically, several studies have suggested that the prevalence of mental health problems among youth within reservation settings are higher than mental health problem that youth face in the general population (Beals, Piasecki, Nelson, Jones, Keane, Dauphinais, Red-Shirt, Sack, & Manson, 1997; Duclos et al., 1998; Jones, Dauphinais, Sack, & Somervell, 1997). Specifically, studies have found higher rates among Native American youth for suicide, depression, conduct disorder, anxiety, trauma-related symptoms, and alcohol and drug abuse (Beals et al., 1997; Beauvais, 1996; Cummins et al., 1999; Duclos, LeBeau, & Elias, 1994; Fischler, 1985; Jones et al., 1977; May, 1989; May and Van Winkle, 1994; Oetting, Goldstein, & Garcia-Mason, 1985; U.S. Congress, 1990; Yates, 1987). Thus, Native youths who enter the juvenile justice system are likely to have higher rates of mental health problems compared to other youth (Duclos et al., 1998).

Childhood Maltreatment Among Native American Youth

Although research on childhood maltreatment among Native American youth is growing, what exists in the literature remains limited (DeBruyn, Chino, Serna, & Fullerton-Gleason, 2001).[1] For numerous methodological reasons, the few empirical studies that have been conducted to date do not accurately represent the prevalence of maltreatment in Indian Country.[2] Regardless of these limitations, the literature supports the finding that childhood maltreatment is a serious problem among Native American youth and is as prevalent among Natives as among non-Natives (Fischler, 1985).

A survey of 1,155 Native American children and adolescents from reservations in Albuquerque, New Mexico, and Phoenix, Arizona, found 67% of the sample to be neglected or abused (Piasecki, Manson, Biernoff, Hiat, Taylor, & Bechtold, 1989). Neglect was most prevalent among boys while abuse was most prevalent among girls. Lower rates of maltreatment were reported in a study by Blum, Harmon, Harris, Bergeisen, and Resnick (1992). Blum and associates examined physical and sexual abuse among a sample of thirteen thousand youth in the seventh through twelve grades attending school on reservations. Their findings indicated that the rate of physical and sexual abuse experienced by these youth were twice as high as rates reported by rural youth in Minnesota. However, 13% of the Native American sample reported physical abuse and 10% reported sexual abuse. In contrast, a retrospective study of childhood sexual abuse (experienced before the age of 15) among three southwestern reservations revealed rates of childhood sexual abuse for Native American women (49%) and men (14%) comparable to Whites (Robin, Chester, Rasmussen, Jaranson, & Goldman, 1997).

Research has documented the relationship between childhood maltreatment among Native Americans and alcoholism. For example, according to a study by White and Cornley (1981), 17% of non-Native child maltreatment cases were found to be alcohol related compared to 50% of child abuse and 50% to 80% of native child neglect cases. Childhood maltreatment is a well-documented risk factor for later behavioral problems, such as delinquency. In addition, research has found a relationship between childhood maltreatment and later psychiatric problems in a Southwestern American Indian tribe (Robin et al., 1997).

Boot Camp for Juvenile Offenders

Boot camp institutions for juvenile offenders became popular during the early 1990s, after the proliferation of boot camp institutions for adults during the early 1980s. It has recently been estimated that there are currently more than 75 boot camp institutions operating for juveniles in 39 states across the country (Rogers, 2002). Boot camp facilities were originally designed as a correctional option for less serious offenders who would serve shorter sentences compared to the average sentence served in a non-boot camp.

Traditional boot camps incorporate a 'military model' within their correctional programming. Several elements of the military model include drill and ceremony, rigorous physical fitness activities, challenge programs, staff and juveniles being required to wear military-style uniforms, youth entering the facility in squads or platoons, the requirement for juveniles to march to class, meals, and other activities, and having formal graduation ceremonies upon juveniles' release from the institution (see reviews, Gover, MacKenzie, & Styve, 2000; Zhang, 1998). Youth typically adhere to a rigorous daily schedule of activities that include educational and treatment programming. Compared to a traditional correctional facility for juveniles, such as a training school, boot camps model their correctional philosophy after basic training in the military.

Researchers and policy makers have debated the appropriateness and purposes of boot camps for juvenile offenders for over a decade (Anderson, Dyson, & Burns, 1999; Benda, 2001; MacKenzie & Parent, 1992; Morash & Rucker, 1990; Zhang, 1998). Many opponents of the military philosophy have questioned the programming emphasis placed on treatment and that the confrontational nature of the military model is antithetical to treatment (Andrews, Zinger, Hode, Bonta, Gendreau, & Cullen, 1990; Lipsey, 1992). However, advocates of these programs suggest that the military atmosphere creates a productive and structured environment for rehabilitation to occur (Bottcher & Isorena, 1994;

Cowles & Castellano, 1995). Despite the long-time debate, empirical research that has examined recidivism among offenders released from boot camps have not found positive results for reductions in later criminal activity (Anderson et al., 1999; MacKenzie, Brame, McDowall, & Souryal, 1995; Peters, Thomas, & Zamberlan, 1997). However, recent studies have recognized the importance of offenders' perceptions of the institutional environment as pertinent factors in predicting institutional adjustment and recidivism after release (Benda, 2001; Benda, Toombs, & Peacock, 2002; Gover et al., 2000; Lutze, 1998).

Conditions of Confinement

Factors within the correctional environment that influence offenders' adjustment during institutionalization have received considerable attention in the research literature (Ajdukovic, 1990; Gover et al., 2000; Johnson & Toch, 1982; MacDonald, 1999; Styve, MacKenzie, & Gover, 2000; Wright, 1985; Wright & Goodstein, 1989; and see Zamble & Porporino, 1990, for a similar comparison to adult inmates). The Office of Juvenile Justice and Delinquency Prevention assessed conditions of confinement within numerous juvenile detention centers and institutions and recommended that further research be conducted on how these environmental conditions influence juveniles during their confinement (OJJDP, 1994). Lutz (1998) suggests that although boot camps have basic conditions of confinement such as safety, structure, and activity, there still may be insufficient programming to foster rehabilitation.

MacKenzie, Gover, Armstrong, and Mitchell (2001) conducted a national study that compared the environments of 27 juvenile boot camps with the environments of 22 traditional facilities. These researchers developed measures of the correctional environment in order to quantify conditions of confinement within each facility.[3] Overall, juveniles in boot camps had more favorable perceptions of their institutional environments compared to juveniles in traditional facilities. Four conditions of confinement scales from the MacKenzie et al. (2001) study are used in the current research (activity, control, justice, and freedom) to measure whether Native American youth perceive their institutional environments differently in a boot camp compared to a traditional training school.

PRESENT STUDY

The prior literature on Native American youth suggests that they come from environments that place them at heightened risk for involvement in the juvenile justice system and mental health problems. Native American youth enter the juvenile justice system with a greater risk of cultural conflicts, prior histories of substance abuse, and childhood maltreatment. These risk factors may increase the likelihood that Native American youth will perceive their correctional experience as harsh, alien, and unjust. Also, the risk factors that

Native American youth in the juvenile correctional system face may increase the likelihood that they will have difficulty adjusting to the correctional environment and be at an increased risk for mental health problems like anxiety and depression. However, little is known about how Native Americans perceive and adjust to the environments of juvenile correctional institutions. Additionally, no research has examined if a boot camp environment has a unique effect on institutionalized Native American youth and those with histories of childhood maltreatment. Given the concern that some have with exposing youth from highly disadvantaged social and cultural backgrounds to the strict disciplinary approach and military philosophy of boot camps, it would be prudent to investigate whether boot camps have a negative effect on institutionalized Native Americans. If Native American youth have special needs that are negatively affected by the boot camp experience, then juvenile justice systems should be careful about placing these youth in a boot camp environment. To date, however, the literature has not examined these issues.

In the present study four research questions are examined to address these issues: (1) Do Native American youth perceive their conditions of confinement differently from non-Native Americans? (2) Does Native American ethnicity have a significant independent effect on psychological adjustment to the correctional institution? (3) Do Native American youth with histories of child maltreatment differ significantly from non-Native American youth in their adjustment to the correctional institution? (4) Do perceptions of confinement and psychological adjustment differ for Native Americans in the boot camp setting compared to a traditional institution?

PROCEDURE

This study used a series of individual self-reported measures provided by 308 youth confined in two correctional facilities located in a Western plains state. One facility surveyed was a state-run boot camp and the other facility was a traditional state-run training school. The traditional facility was selected as a comparison institution because it was the secure residential facility that the juveniles in the boot camp would have been institutionalized at if the boot camp did not exist. The survey questionnaire included 266 questions that asked youth about their social history (e.g., prior delinquent involvement, family criminality, and delinquent peer association), their perceptions of the conditions of confinement, and their current level of psychological well-being. Surveys were administered in small groups of 15 to 20 youth in a classroom setting. A videotaped presentation of the survey was shown during survey administration to assist youth with reading disabilities and ensure consistency in administration (see MacKenzie, Gover, Armstrong, & Mitchell, 2001, for a discussion of the national study).

MEASURES

This study used six measures to examine the relationship between the boot camp and Native American ethnicity on perceptions of confinement and psychological well-being.

Conditions of confinement. The following four individual-level composite measures were used to examine the youths' perceptions of their institutional environment: activity, control, justice, and freedom. Activity measured the perceptions of the level and variety of activities available to youth and was comprised of 8 Likert-scale items (with five response choices from never to always). The internal consistency of this scale was high (alpha = .79). Control measured the perceptions of the level of security exerted over the juveniles' daily activities and security used to keep residents in the facility. The control scale was constructed from 11 Likert-scale items. The internal consistency of this scale was adequate (alpha = .66). Justice measured the perceived fairness of disciplinary procedures for misconduct and was comprised from 11 Likert-scale items. For example, youth were asked to indicate whether there were adequate procedures for filing grievances. The internal consistency of this scale was high (alpha = .76). Freedom measured the provision of activities and movement of residents and was constructed from 11 Likert-scale items. For instance, youth were asked to indicate if they were encouraged to make their own decisions. The internal consistency of this scale was adequate (alpha = .74). Higher scores on these four scales indicated higher perceptions of the named condition of confinement.[4]

In addition to the perceptual measures of the conditions of confinement, the level of anxiety and depression were included as dependent variables to measure these youths' psychological well-being. Anxiety was measured using six dichotomous (yes-no) items that assessed state anxiety. These measures were drawn from Spielberger, Gorsuch, and Luschebe (1970). This scale measured the level of stress and anxiety among youth. The internal consistency of this scale was high (alpha = .78). Higher scores on this scale indicated higher levels of anxiety. Depression was measured using five Likert-type items. These measures were adapted from the Beck Depression Inventory (Beck, Ward, Mendelson, Mock, & Erbaugh, 1961) and the Jesness Inventory (Jesness, 1983). These questions were intended to measure characteristics of a depressed mood. Higher scores on this scale indicated higher levels of depression. The internal consistency of this scale was high (alpha = .76).

Native Americans. The primary demographic variable of interest in this study was race and was dummy coded to equal '1' if a youth identified himself as Native American and '0' otherwise.

Type of correctional institution. The type of correctional institution was dummy coded to equal '1' if a youth was residing in the boot camp and '0' if they resided in the traditional facility.

Delinquency risk factors. To control for the influence of delinquent risk factors on juveniles' perceptions of the conditions of confinement and psychological state, several measures of these youths' social history were included in the present study. Prior literature has also noted that Native Americans are at an increased risk for a number of these risk factors related to psychological well-being and delinquency including: substance abuse, peer criminality, family criminality, prior delinquency behavior, and child maltreatment. Substance abuse (drug and alcohol) was measured according to a 10-item scale with dichotomous responses ("yes" or "no") that asked youth about their past history of drug and alcohol use. Responses were summed and divided by 10. Higher scores indicate higher levels of substance abuse. The internal consistency of this scale was high (alpha = .77) (see Gover & MacKenzie, 2003, for details of scale items). Peer criminality was measured with four Likert-type items that captured the extent to which the youth's friends were involved in crime, gangs, or had been incarcerated. Higher scores indicate higher levels of peer criminality. The internal consistency of this scale was adequate (alpha = .71). Family criminality was measured according to a 4-item scale ("yes" or "no") that asked youth to indicate whether their family members had been incarcerated, were involved in illegal behavior or gangs, or had been treated for alcohol and drug abuse. Higher scores indicate higher levels of family criminality. The internal consistency of this scale was high (alpha = .74). Two open-ended self-report measures were used to assess prior delinquency: the number of reported prior arrests and prior institutional commitments. Child maltreatment was measured with a 9-item Likert-type scale that asked youth to indicate the extent to which in the past they had experienced neglect, physical abuse, sexual abuse, or witnessed family violence in their homes (see Gover & MacKenzie, 2003, for further details of scale construction). Higher scores on this scale represent higher levels of child maltreatment. The internal consistency of the child maltreatment scale was high (alpha = .84).

Control measures. To control for the potential differences in perceptions of the institutional environments and psychological adjustment caused by differences in the time youth spent in a boot camp versus a traditional institution, a measure of the length of stay was included. Juveniles were asked in an open-ended question to indicate how many months they had been in the facility at the time of the survey administration. Age was also included as a control variable and was measured on a continuous scale.

RESULTS

Descriptive statistics for the measures of the institutionalized juveniles are displayed in Table 1. The average age of the juveniles in this sample is 15.8 years (*SD* = 1.39). Approximately 28.2% (N = 87) of the sample identified themselves as Native American.[5] Juveniles reported having an average of 8.4

($SD = 7.9$) prior arrests and an average of 4.1 ($SD = 4.5$) prior commitments to juvenile institutions. In terms of commitment offenses, 32.7% reported that they were committed for a property offense, 29.4% for a probation violation, 18.3% for a violent offense,[6] 10.6% for a drug offense, and the remaining juveniles were committed to the institutions for other miscellaneous offenses.[7]

Differences by Type of Institution

Approximately 57.5% (N = 50) of Native American juveniles were incarcerated in the boot camp. A t-test indicated that Native American youth represented a significantly ($t = 1.90$; $p < .05$) larger proportion of youth in the overall sample in the boot camp facility (35.2%) compared with Native American youth in the traditional facility (24.6%). Also, juveniles confined in the traditional facility were significantly ($t = 2.63$; $p < .05$) younger ($M = 15.5$; $SD = 1.76$) than juveniles in the boot camp ($M = 16$; $SD = 1.12$). On average, juveniles in the traditional facility had a significantly ($t = 4.48$, $p < .05$) higher

Table 1: Characteristics of Sample (N = 308)

Measures	Mean (SD)
Conditions of Confinement	
Control	4.04 (.74)
Activity	4.18 (.70)
Justice	3.10 (.73)
Freedom	1.99 (.80)
Psychological Adjustment	
Anxiety	1.47 (.33)
Depression	3.05 (.95)
Risk Factors	
Child maltreatment	1.67 (.74)
Substance abuse	1.39 (.27)
Number of prior commitments	4.07 (4.46)
Number of prior arrests	8.44 (7.95)
Family criminality	1.43 (.36)
Peer criminality	3.37 (1.06)
Age	15.83 (1.39)
Length of time in facility	2.98 (2.85)
Boot camp	65.9%
Native American	28.2%

number of prior arrests ($M = 10.74$; $SD = 8.28$) than did juveniles in the boot camp ($M = 6.91$; $SD = 6.41$). At the time of the survey, residents in the boot camp had been confined for a significantly ($t = 11.599$; $p < .05$) shorter period of time (months) ($M = 1.84$; $SD = 1.32$) compared to residents in the traditional facility ($M = 5.19$; $SD = 3.64$). A t-test comparison of facility type indicated that juveniles did not significantly differ on their average number of prior commitments. In terms of Native American youth, the number of prior arrests was significantly greater ($t = 2.20$; $p < .05$) for Native juveniles who resided in the traditional facility ($M = 12.59$; $SD = 8.41$) compared with Native youth institutionalized in the boot camp facility ($M = 8.76$; $SD = 7.47$). Overall, these descriptive statistics indicate that there are some differences in the average length of stay and the seriousness of prior delinquent histories in the two institutions. These findings are not surprising, given that the boot camp facility was more selective in determining who was eligible for participation. In the following section, therefore, these differences between the two groups are controlled for in a series of multivariate models.

ANALYSIS

Ordinary least squares regression was used to assess the independent influence of Native American ethnicity and the boot camp setting on juveniles' perceptions of the correctional environment and psychological adjustment.[8] An interaction term also was added to each model to measure the influence of being Native American and residing in a boot camp on the perceptions of the institutional environment and psychological adjustment. The results from the conditions of confinement models are displayed in Table 2. Only family criminality and the boot camp setting are significantly related to juvenile's perceptions of institutional control. Juveniles whose families were more involved in crime reported significantly lower perceptions of institutional control ($b = -.243$; $p < .05$). In contrast, juveniles who were residing in boot camps reported significantly higher perceptions of institutional control compared to juveniles in the traditional facility ($b = .943$; $p < .05$). These findings indicate that Native American youth do not have significantly different perceptions of institutional control. The interaction term of Native American youth and the boot camp setting indicates no significant relationship. In other words, there is no unique relationship between being Native American and being institutionalized in the boot camp and the perception of institutional control. Family criminality, boot camp setting, and the length of time in the facility are significantly related to juveniles' perceptions of institutional activity. Juveniles with greater levels of family criminality were less likely to view the institutional environment as active ($b = -.292$; $p < .05$). In contrast, youth in the boot camp ($b = .665$; $p < .05$) and those who had been residing in the institution for a longer period of time ($b = .047$; $p < .05$) perceived greater amount of institutional activi-

Table 2: Effects of Native American Ethnicity, Facility Type, and Other Factors on Perceptions of Environment

	Activity	Control	Justice	Freedom
Child maltreatment	.085 (1.51)	−.003 (−.072)	.069 (1.08)	−.020 (.41)
Substance abuse	−.031 (.20)	−.225 (1.77)	−.136 (.78)	−.338* (2.51)
Number of prior commitments	.009 (.61)	−.012 (−1.07)	.002 (.12)	.010 (.80)
Number of prior arrests	−.000 (−.02)	.000 (.01)	.004 (.62)	.002 (.50)
Family criminality	−.292* (−2.36)	−.243* (−2.38)	−.155 (−1.11)	−.130 (−1.20)
Peer criminality	.023 (.62)	.041 (1.29)	−.066 (−1.54)	−.012 (−.36)
Age	.032 (1.09)	.023 (.97)	.036 (1.10)	.032 (1.25)
Length of time in facility	.047* (2.72)	−.024 (−1.72)	.031 (1.64)	.029* (1.97)
Boot camp	.665* (6.35)	.943* (10.90)	−.229* (−1.94)	−1.17* (12.88)
Native American	.067 (.75)	−.034 (−.47)	.172 (1.71)	.070 (.91)
Native American * Boot camp[a]	.084 (.46)	−.020 (−.13)	.202 (.98)	.137 (.87)
R^2	.18	.51	.08	.53

Note: T-scores are displayed in parentheses.
a. For ease of interpretation only the interaction coefficient is displayed in these models.

ties. There was not a significant relationship between Native American youth and activity. Similar to the findings for control, there was no statistically significant interaction between Native American youth and the boot camp institution on perceptions of institutional activities. In terms of perceptions of justice in the facilities, the findings indicate only one significant relationship. Youth residing in the boot camp facility perceived significantly less justice than those in the traditional institution ($b = -.229; p < .05$). There was no relationship between Native American youth and perceptions of justice. An interaction effect was not found between Native American youth and boot camps on perceptions of institutional justice. The findings indicate that substance abuse, time in the facility, and the boot camp setting are significantly related to perceptions of institutional freedom. Youth with greater levels of prior substance abuse had lower perceptions of institutional freedom ($b = -.338; p < .05$). Juveniles who had spent more time in the facility had significantly higher perceptions of freedom ($b = .029; p < .05$). In contrast, youth in the boot camp setting had significantly lower perceptions of freedom ($b = -1.17; p < .05$). There is no significant relationship between Native American youth and perceptions of justice. Also, Native American youth and non-Native American youth in boot camps do not differ significantly from one another in their perceptions of institutional justice.

Overall the results from the conditions of confinement models indicate that the boot camp environment is perceived as more controlled and active, and as having less justice and freedom than the traditional facility environment. Importantly, the results indicate that Native American perceptions do not vary significantly by the type of facility setting. In other words, Native American youth institutionalized in a boot camp setting do not have distinctly different perceptions of the correctional environment than similarly situated youth of other ethnic groups. This is an important finding because it suggests that the military setting of a boot camp does not have a unique cultural impact on disadvantaged Native American youth. Therefore, any concern with increasing victimization among this population by placing them in facilities with high levels of military related activity and control appears to be overstated.

The results for the models estimating juveniles' anxiety and depression levels are presented in Table 3. Age, childhood maltreatment, prior substance abuse, and number of prior arrests are significantly related to self-reported levels of anxiety. Older juveniles report significantly less anxiety ($b = -.030; p < .05$). Juveniles with significantly higher levels of past childhood maltreatment reported significantly higher levels of anxiety ($b = .073; p < .05$). Youth with more previous arrests reported significantly lower levels of anxiety ($b = -.007; p < .05$). There was no direct relationship between Native American ethnicity or the boot camp facility and self-reported anxiety. However, the interaction term of Native American ethnicity and boot camp facility has a statistically significant relationship with anxiety. Native American youth in the boot camp reported significantly lower levels of anxiety than all other groups

Table 3: Effects of Native American Ethnicity, Facility Type, and Other Factors on Psychological Adjustment

	Anxiety		Depression	
Child maltreatment	.073* (2.54)	--	.217* (2.74)	--
Substance abuse	.168* (2.13)	--	.420* (1.94)	--
Number of prior commitments	.001 (.19)	--	.030 (1.50)	--
Number of prior arrests	−.007* (−2.43)	--	−.020* (2.39)	--
Family criminality	.010 (.16)	--	.350* (1.99)	--
Peer criminality	−.018 (−.92)	--	−.061 (−1.33)	--
Age	−.030* (−2.06)	--	−.026 (−.66)	--
Length of time in facility	−.008 (−.94)	--	.023 (.99)	--
Boot camp	−.016 (−.30)	--	−.242 (−1.64)	--
Native American	−.076* (−1.68)	--	−.057 (−.45)	--
Native American * Boot camp[a]		−.198* (−2.16)		−.269 (−1.05)
Native American * Child maltreatment		.042 (.71)		.080 (.49)
R^2	.07	.09	.09	.13	.12

Note: T-scores are displayed in parentheses.
a. For ease of interpretation only the interaction coefficient is displayed in these models.

($b = -.198; p < .05$). The findings for depression indicate it is significantly related to childhood maltreatment, prior substance abuse, and family criminality. Youth with greater levels of past childhood maltreatment reported significantly higher levels of depression ($b = .217; p < .05$). Native American youth who experienced child maltreatment, however, were not significantly more depressed than their non-Native American counterparts. Additionally, youth with higher levels of family criminality ($b = .350; p < .05$) and higher levels of prior substance abuse ($b = .420; p < .05$) reported significantly higher levels of depression. There was not a significant independent relationship between Native American youth and boot camp on self-reported depression.

The results for psychological adjustment indicate that children who come from neglectful and abusive environments are significantly more anxious and depressed. These findings are consistent with research previously published on a national sample of juveniles in boot camps and traditional institutions (see Gover & Mackenzie, 2003; MacKenzie et al., 2001). There is, however, no significant interaction between child maltreatment and Native Americans on anxiety or depression. In other words, Native American youth that have experienced childhood maltreatment are not more anxious or depressed than their non-Native American counterparts. The boot camp environment also appears not to have any negative influence on Native American adjustment. In fact, the boot camp environment significantly decreased the level of anxiety for Native American youth. These findings exist even when controlling for the length of time juveniles spent in the facilities and a variety of other risk factors. Therefore, these findings suggest that the experience of the boot camp environment may actually have some positive influence on psychological adjustment for Native American youth.

CONCLUSION

Little research attention has been devoted to studying Native Americans in the juvenile and criminal justice systems. For example, a survey of 12 introductory criminal justice textbooks during the 1980s found that the problem of crime among Native Americans was not even acknowledged (Young, 1990). However, in recent years scholars have recognized the need to study crime among Native Americans and research has increased. Empirical literature indicates that disadvantaged reservation environments place Native American youth at a greater risk for a number of delinquency risk factors including: child maltreatment, exposure to alcoholism and other forms of substance abuse, and the association with delinquent peers (OJJDP, 2003). Less is known about how these risk factors influence Native American delinquents who come under the supervision of the juvenile justice system. Key to successful rehabilitation is providing juvenile delinquents with correctional programming that can promote proper adjustment and positive change.

One would expect that the disadvantaged social and cultural backgrounds that Native American juvenile offenders face would influence their perceptions of the correctional environment. This study, however, indicates few differences between Native and non-Native American delinquents' perceptions of the level of activity, control, freedom, and justice in two separate correctional facilities. Native American ethnicity also appears to have little direct bearing on psychological adjustment. Rather, it appears that negative psychological adjustment (e.g., depression) is not distinct among Native American youthful offenders and has more to do with prior childhood maltreatment, substance abuse, and coming from families that are involved in criminal behavior. This is not to argue that one should discount the importance of studying Native Americans and other ethnic minorities' experience in the juvenile correctional system. Rather, these findings suggest that within a highly selected sample of institutionalized youth, Native American ethnicity no longer remains a major factor in explaining either one's perceptions of the conditions of confinement or psychological adjustment.

Critics suggest that the dogmatic boot camp environment may be detrimental to juveniles' perceptions of the correctional experience and adjustment to the conditions of confinement. Results from this study indicate that there are distinct differences in how juveniles perceive the boot camp versus the traditional training school environments. Juveniles in the boot camps are more likely to see their environment as controlled and active, but are less likely to perceive that they can be treated fairly and are given freedom to make their own choices. These findings are not surprising given the highly structured and controlled environment of the boot camp compared to the training school. Some would suggest that highly controlled and active institutional environments are more conducive to effective rehabilitation (Styve et al., 2000). Interestingly, findings from this study suggest that the controlling environment of the boot camp appears to alleviate anxiety for Native American youth. Therefore, this study offers little support for the idea that the boot camp environment is detrimental for youth in general or for Native American youth.

The site visit researchers made to this boot camp also affirms these findings (MacKenzie et al., 2001). The boot camp placed a particular emphasis on team building and self-esteem enhancement among youth. Juveniles in this facility were encouraged to engage in challenge-related activities that promoted increased self-confidence. Youth spent a great deal of time engaging in outdoor activities and challenge courses that were built on a teamwork model, where a youth's accomplishments were praised by staff and other juveniles. In addition, the boot camp also had a higher ratio of staff per inmate (compared to the staff per inmate ratio in the traditional facility) that permitted increased individualized attention from staff.

There are, however, a number of limitations to this research that suggest caution in interpreting the findings. The comparison of the boot camp versus training school environments was limited to only two facilities. The analysis of the perceptions of the conditions of confinement and psychological adjustment are, therefore, limited to only Native and non-Native Americans residing in these two facilities in a single state. As a result, one cannot generalize these findings to the experiences of other Native American youth institutionalized in boot camps and training schools in other locations. It is possible, for example, that boot camps run by other staff in other states may have a detrimental influence on Native Americans' perceptions of their environment and psychological adjustment. Therefore, it is important for future research to explore Native American delinquents' experiences in the juvenile correctional environment in other states.

NOTES

1. It has been suggested that uncooperative relationships among Native American reservations and departments of social services, health, and legal agencies have contributed to the lack of attention given to the examination of child maltreatment among Native Americans (White & Cornley, 1981). Many Native Americans argue that claims of childhood maltreatment are efforts of the dominant White culture to marginalize the minority Native culture and that the claims of abuse are untrue (Fischler, 1985). Native Americans view the removal of children from their native families as abuse by the White culture. Furthermore, the different styles of communication between Native Americans and Whites contribute to the distrust of representative of White agencies, such as those from the criminal justice system and social service agencies (Horejsi, Craig, & Pablo, 1992). For example, the Indian Child Welfare Act of 1978 acknowledged blatant discrimination when it was found that approximately 30% of all Native American children were removed from their families during the 1960s and 1970s and placed in White families or institutions such as boarding schools due to accusations of maltreatment (Fischler, 1985).
2. The primary methodological limitation results from varying definitions of maltreatment across studies (DeBruyn et al., 2001).
3. Conditions of confinement scales were developed by adapting the following models previously used for assessing environments of juvenile correctional facilities: OJJDP's Conditions of Confinement Study by Parent (1993); Quality of Confinement indices (Logan, 1990); the Prison Environment Inventory (Wright, 1985); the Correctional Facilities Environment Scale (Moos, 1974); and others such as the Correctional Program Evaluation Inventory (Gendreau & Andrews, 1994), and the Prison Social Climate Survey used by the Federal Bureau of Prisons (Brooks, Brustman, Gilman, Schoppet, & Styles, 1991).
4. The individual items and factor scores are available from the author.
5. Of the non-Native youth, 59.3% were White, 2.9% were Hispanic, 2.0% were African American, 0.7% were Asian, and 6.8% identified themselves as being of 'other' race.
6. Violent offenses include assault, weapons-related offenses, sexual assault, and robbery.
7. Miscellaneous offenses consisted of a few minor offenses such as CHINA (children in need of supervision), status offenses, and AWOL (N = 3).
8. Variance inflation factor estimates for all models were below the conventional value of 4.0, indicating that multicollinearity was not present in these analyses.

REFERENCES

Ajdukovic, D. (1990). Psychosocial climate in correctional institutions: Which attributes describe it? *Environment and Behavior, 22,* 420-432.

Anderson, J. F., Dyson, L., & Burns, J. C. (1999). *Boot camps: An intermediate sanction.* New York, NY: University Press of America.

Andrews, D. A., Zinger, I., Hode, R. D., Bonta, J., Gendreau, P., & Cullen, F. T. (1990). Does correctional treatment work? A clinically relevant and psychologically informed meta-analysis. *Criminology, 28,* 369-404.

Armstrong, T. L., Guilfoyle, M. H., & Melton. (1996). Native American delinquency: An overview of prevalence, causes, and correlates. In M. O. Nielson & R. A. Silverman (Eds.), *Native Americans, crime, and justice* (pp. 75-95). Boulder, CO: Westview Press.

Beals, J., Piasecki, J., Nelson, S., Jones, M., Keane, E., Dauphinais, P., Red-Shirt, R., Sack, W., & Manson, S. (1997). Psychiatric disorder in a sample of American Indian adolescents: Prevalence in Northern Plains youth. *Journal of the American Academy of Child & Adolescent Psychiatry, 36,* 1252-1259.

Beauvais, F. (1996). Trends in drug use among American Indian students and dropouts, 1975 to 1994. *American Journal of Pubic Health, 86,* 1594-1598.

Beauvais, F., Oetting, E. R., & Edwards, R. W. (1985). Trends in drug use of Indian adolescents living on reservations: 1975-1983. *American Journal of Drug and Alcohol Abuse, 11,* 209-229.

Beck, A. T., Ward, C. H., Mendelson, M., Mock, J., & Erbaugh, J. (1961). An inventory for measuring depression. *Archives of General Psychiatry, 4,* 561-571.

Benda, B. B. (2001). Factors that discriminate between recidivists, parole violators, and nonrecidivists in a 3-year follow-up of boot camp graduates. *International Journal of Offender Therapy and Comparative Criminology, 45,* 711-729.

Benda, B. B., Toombs, N. J., & Peacock, M. (2002). Ecological factors in recidivism: A survival analysis of boot camp graduates after three years. *Journal of Offender Rehabilitation, 35,* 63-85.

Black, T. E., & Smith, C. P. (1980). *A preliminary assessment of the numbers and characteristics of Native Americans under 18 processed by various justice systems.* Sacramento, CA: National Juvenile Justice System Assessment Center, American Justice Institute.

Blum, R. W., Harman, B., Harris, L., Bergeisen, L., & Resnick, M. D. (1992). American Indian-Alaska Native youth health. *Journal of the American Medical Association, 267,* 1637-1644.

Bottcher, J., & Isorena, T. (1994). *LEAD: A boot camp and intensive parole program: An implementation and process evaluation after the first year.* Sacramento, CA: California Department of the Youth Authority.

Brooks, T., Brustmas, P., Gilman, E., Schoppet, R., & Styles, S. (1991). Summary of results from the 1990 Prison Social Climate Survey. *Research Forum, 1,* 1-8.

Bynum, T. (1981). Parole decision-making and Native Americans. In R. L. McNeely & C. E. Pope (Eds.), *Race, crime, and criminal justice* (pp. 75-87). Newbury Park, CA: Sage.

Camp, G., & Camp, C. (1992). *The corrections yearbook–juvenile corrections.* South Salem, MA: Criminal Justice Institute.

Cowles, E., & Castellano, T. (1995). *"Boot camp" drug treatment and aftercare intervention: An evaluation review* (NCJ 153918). Washington, DC: National Institute of Justice.

Cummins, J., Ireland, M., Resnick, M. D., & Blum, R. W. (1999). Correlates of physical and emotional health among Native American adolescents. *Journal of Adolescent Health, 24,* 38-44.

DeBruyn, L., Chino, M., Serna, P., & Fullerton-Gleason, L. (2001). Child maltreatment in American Indian and Alaska Native communities: Integrating culture, history, and public health for intervention and prevention. *Child Maltreatment, 6,* 89-102.

Duclos, C. W., Beals, J., Novins, D. K., Martin, C., Jewett, C. S., & Manson, S. M. (1998). Prevalence of common psychiatric disorders among American Indian detainees. *Journal of the American Academy of Child and Adolescent Psychiatry, 37,* 866-873.

Duclos, C. W., LeBeau, W., & Elias, G. (1994). American Indian adolescent suicidal behavior in detention environments: Cause for continued basic and applied research. *American Indian and Alaska Native Mental Health Research, 4,* 189-221.

Fischler, R. S. (1985). Child abuse and neglect in American Indian communities. *Child Abuse & Neglect, 9,* 95-106.

Forslund, M. A., & Cranston, V. A. (1975). A self-report comparison of Indian and Anglo delinquency in Wyoming. *Criminology, 13,* 193-198.

French, L. (1980). An analysis of contemporary Indian justice and correctional treatment. *Federal Probation, 44,* 19-23.

Gendreau, O., & Andrews, D. A. (1994). *The correctional program evaluation inventory.* Unpublished manuscript.

Gover, A. R., & MacKenzie, D. L. (2003). Child maltreatment and adjustment to juvenile correctional institutions. *Criminal Justice and Behavior, 30,* 374-396.

Gover, A. R., MacKenzie, D. L., & Styve, G. J. (2000). Boot camps and traditional correctional facilities for juveniles: A comparison of the participants, daily activities, and environments. *Journal of Criminal Justice, 28,* 53-68.

Hall, E., & Simkus, A. (1975). Inequality in the types of sentences received by Native Americans and Whites. *Criminology, 13,* 199-222.

Hann, R. G., & Harman, W. G. (1993). Predicting release risk for Aboriginal penitentiary inmates (User Report 1993-12). Ottawa, Canada: Ministry of the Solicitor General of Canada.

Horejsi, C., Craig, B. H. R., & Pablo, J. (1992). Reactions by Native American parents to child protection agencies. *Child Welfare, 71,* 329-342.

Jensen, G., Stauss, J., & Harris, V. W. (1977). Crime, delinquency, and the American Indian. *Human Organization, 36,* 252-257.

Jesness, C. (1983). *The Jesness Inventory.* Palo Alto, CA: Consulting Psychologists Press.

Johnson, R., & Toch, H. (1982). *The pains of imprisonment.* Beverly Hills, CA: Sage.

Jones, M. C., Dauphinais, P., Sack, W. H., & Somervell, P. (1977). Trauma-related symptomatology among American Indian adolescents. *Journal of Traumatic Stress, 10,* 163-173.

Jung, S., & Rawana, E. P. (1999). Risk and need assessment of juvenile offenders. *Criminal Justice and Behavior, 26,* 69-89.

Kickingbird, K. (1976). In our image . . . after our likeness: The drive for the assimilation of Indian court systems. *American Criminal Law Review, 13,* 675-700.

Krisberg, B., Schwartz, I., Fishman, G., Eisikovits, Z., Guttman, E., & Joe, K. (1987). The incarceration of minority youth. *Crime and Delinquency, 33,* 173-205.

Lipsey, M. (1992). Juvenile delinquency treatment: A meta-analytic inquiry into the variability of effects. In T. Cook et al. (Eds.), *Meta-analysis for explanation: A casebook.* New York, NY: Sage.

Logan, C. H. (1990). *Private prisons: Pros and cons.* New York, NY: Oxford University Press.

Longclaws, L., Barnes, G., Grieve, L., & Dumoff, R. (1977). Alcohol and drug use among the Brokenhead Ojibwa. *Journal of Studies on Alcohol, 41,* 21-36.

Lutze, F. (1998). Are shock incarceration programs more rehabilitative than traditional prisons? A survey of inmates. *Justice Quarterly, 15,* 547-556.

MacDonald, J. M. (1999). Violence and drug use in juvenile institutions. *Journal of Criminal Justice, 27,* 33-44.

MacKenzie, D. L., Brame, R., McDowall, D., & Souryal, C. (1995). Boot camp prisons and recidivism in eight states. *Criminology, 33,* 327-357.

MacKenzie, D. L., Gover, A. R., Armstrong, G. S., & Mitchell, O. (2001). A national study comparing the environments of boot camps with traditional facilities for juvenile offenders (NCJ 187680). Washington, DC: National Institute of Justice.

MacKenzie, D. L., & Parent, D. (1992). Boot camp prisons for young offenders. In J. Byrne, A. Lurigio, & J. Petersilia (Eds.), *Smart sentencing: The emergence of intermediate sanctions* (pp. 103-122). Newbury Park, CA: Sage.

May, P. (1989). *Alcohol abuse and alcoholism among American Indians: An overview.* Springfield, IL: Charles AC. Thomas.

May, P. A., & Van Winkle, N. (1994). Indian adolescent suicide: The epidemiologic picture in New Mexico. *American Indian and Alaska Native Mental Health Research, 4,* 5-34.

Moos, R. H. (1974). *Correctional Institutional Environment Scale Manual.* Palo Alto, CA: Consulting Psychological Press.

Morash, M., & Rucker, L. (1990). A critical look at the idea of boot camp as a correctional reform. *Crime and Delinquency, 36,* 204-222.

National Council of Juvenile and Family Court Judges. (1990). Minority youth in the juvenile justice system: A judicial response. *Juvenile & Family Court Journal, 41,* 1-71.

O'Brien, M. (1977). Indian juveniles in the state and tribal courts of Oregon. *American Indian Law Review, 5,* 343-367.

Oetting, E. R., Goldstein, E. R., & Garcia-Mason, V. (1985). Drug use among adolescents of five southwestern Native American tribes. *International Journal of Addictions, 15,* 439-445.

Office of Juvenile Justice and Delinquency Prevention. (2003). Juvenile justice partners in Indian Country. *OJJDP News At A Glance, 4,* 1-3.

Parent, D. G. (1993). Summary of the conditions of confinement study. *Prison Journal, 73,* 237-245.

Peters, M., Thomas, D., & Zamberlan, C. (1997). *Boot camps for juvenile offenders: Program summary*. Washington, DC: Office of Juvenile Justice and Delinquency Prevention.

Piasecki, J. M., Manson, S. M., Biernoff, M. P., Hiat, A. B., Taylor, S. S., & Bechtold, D. W. (1989). Abuse and neglect of American Indian children. *American Indian & Alaska Native Mental Health Research, 3*, 43-62.

Poupart, L. M. (1995). Juvenile justice processing of American Indian youths: Disparity in one rural county. In K. K. Leonard, C. E. Pope, & W. H. Feyerherm (Eds.), *Minorities in juvenile justice* (pp. 179-200). Thousand Oaks, CA: Sage.

Robbins, S. P. (1985). Commitment, belief, and Native American delinquency. *Human Organization, 44*, 57-62.

Robin, R. W., Chester, B., Rasmussen, J. K., Jaranson, J. M., & Goldman, D. (1997). Prevalence, characteristics, and impact of childhood sexual abuse in a southwestern American Indian tribe. *Child Abuse & Neglect, 21*, 769-787.

Rogers, D. (2002). Juvenile boot camps. *Law Enforcement Technology, 29*, 88-95.

Sellers, C. S., Winfree L. T., & Griffiths, C. T. (1993). Legal attitudes, permissive norm qualities, and substance use: A comparison of American Indian and non-Indian youth. *The Journal of Drug Issues, 23*, 493-513.

Spielberger, C. D., Gorsuch, R. L., & Lushebe, R. E. (1970). *Manual for the State-Trait Anxiety Inventory*. Palo Alto, CA: Consulting Psychological Press.

Starr, F. M. (1978). Indians and the criminal justice system. *Canadian Journal of Criminology, 20*, 317-323.

Styve, G. J., MacKenzie, D. L., Gover, A. R., & Mitchell, O. (2000). Perceived conditions of confinement: A national evaluation of juvenile boot camps and traditional facilities. *Law and Human Behavior, 24*, 297-308.

U.S. Congress. (1990). *Indian adolescent mental health*. Washington, DC: Office of Technology Assessment.

White, R., & Cornley, D. (1981). Navajo child abuse and neglect study: A comparison group examination of abuse and neglect of Navajo children. *Child Abuse & Neglect, 5*, 9-17.

Wright, K. N. (1985). Developing the prison environment inventory. *Journal of Research in Crime and Delinquency, 22*, 257-277.

Wright, K. N., & Goodstein, L. (1989). Correctional environments. In L. Goodstein & D. L. MacKenzie (Eds.), *The American prison: Issues in research and policy* (pp. 253-270). New York, NY: Plenum Press.

Yates, A. (1987). Current status and future directions of research on the American Indian child. *American Journal of Psychiatry, 144*, 1135-1142.

Young, T. (1990). Native American crime and criminal justice require criminologists' attention. *Journal of Criminal Justice Education, 7*, 111-116.

Zamble, E., & Porporino, F. (1990). Coping, imprisonment and rehabilitation: Some data and their implications. *Criminal Justice and Behavior, 17*, 53-70.

Zhang, S. X. (1998). In search of hopeful glimpses: A critique of research strategies in current boot camp evaluation. *Crime & Delinquency, 44*, 314-334.

AUTHOR'S NOTE

Angela R. Gover, PhD, is affiliated with the Center for Studies in Criminology and Law at the University of Florida.

This research was supported in part by Grant No. 96-SC-LX-0001 from the National Institute of Justice, Office of Justice Programs, U.S. Department of Justice, to the University of Maryland. Points of view in this document are those of the author and do not necessarily represent the official position of the Department of Justice.

Address correspondence to Angela R. Gover, PhD, Center for Studies in Criminology and Law, P.O. Box 115950, 201 Walker Hall, University of Florida, Gainesville, FL 32611-5950 (E-mail: agover@crim.ufl.edu).

Ruminating About Boot Camps: Panaceas, Paradoxes, and Ideology

JAMES O. FINCKENAUER

Rutgers University

ABSTRACT The editors invited the author, a leading authority on "shock prisonization" regimens generally and on that "imperfect panacea," the Scared Straight program, in particular, to consider the research in this volume from the perspective of more than two decades of scientific inquiry and analysis undertaken by himself and his colleagues. Particular focus is placed on studies reported in this volume that link ideology and empirical evidence. *[Article copies available for a fee from The Haworth Document Delivery Service: 1-800-HAWORTH. E-mail address: <docdelivery@haworthpress.com> Website: <http://www.HaworthPress.com> © 2005 by The Haworth Press, Inc. All rights reserved.]*

KEYWORDS Scared Straight, shock prisonization, boot camps, ideology, evidence, policy implications

The editors have invited me to "ruminate" about the focus of this volume, which is on boot camps. Synonyms I looked up for ruminate include ponder, muse, and think–each referring to an activity that is obviously a whole lot easier than actually doing something! I regard this as a very loose mandate, and thus will feel free to range over a number of subjects here. These will include theory, ideology, empiricism, symbolic politics, interest groups, policy, practice, evaluation, and panaceas and paradoxes. My ultimate aim is to try to link all this to the subject of boot camps.

To begin, I will return to my work on Scared Straight, which started more than two decades ago (Finckenauer, 1982). After all, Scared Straight is, in many ways, a logical ancestor of correctional boot camps.

THE PANACEA PHENOMENON

From my initial examination of Scared Straight, I was struck by what appeared to be exemplified especially starkly in the various iterations of that program, namely a seemingly strong desire to find quick, simple solutions to the complex problems of crime and criminality. There indeed seemed to be a strong undercurrent of searching for silver bullets, for cure-alls. This, I believed, led to what I called then the panacea phenomenon, which I described as follows in the context of dealing with youth crime.

> First, a certain approach is posed as a cure-all or becomes viewed and promoted as a cure-all–as an approach that will have universal efficacy and thus be appropriate for nearly all youths. The approach may be promoted and sold as the all-encompassing solution to the delinquency problem. Think big! is the catchword. Each promoter/salesperson believes, or at least behaves as if, his or her idea is effective in saving youths and "hypes" it accordingly. Unfortunately, the approach, no matter what it is, almost always fails to deliver. It fails to live up to the frequently unrealistic or unsound expectations raised by the sales pitch. As this failure slowly becomes apparent, frustration usually sets in and the search for the next panacea or "answer" begins anew. (Finckenauer & Gavin, 1999:13)

The reasons for the belief in an idea, for creating unrealistic expectations with respect to its impact, and for its ultimate failure to work, are all quite complex. Because most of my ruminating to follow will be with respect to understanding the reasons supporting the belief, let me just briefly mention the expectations and outcomes issues. With respect to expectations, in a world of fierce competition for ideas and especially for resources, modest predictions for outcomes, or so-called deliverables, even though entirely appropriate, tend to get pushed aside. To get attention and funding, one must promise much and promise loudly. Modesty is usually not rewarded.

Then, with respect to outcome and impact, "Murphy's Law" is usually in evidence. Much can go wrong, and very frequently does. Assumptions are not borne out, implementation breaks down, unforeseen problems arise, and so on. One need only consider recent policy developments on the world scene to see that this is so. Under those sorts of circumstances, even "good" ideas that are adequately funded cannot and will not work.

With 20/20 hindsight, my description of the panacea phenomenon those years ago was clearly itself entirely too simplistic. Patricia Gavin and I recognized this in our 1999 book that revisited Scared Straight. We said then that we regarded the panacea depiction as "incomplete" because it implied that ostensibly failed panaceas were discarded and rejected. Because there had accumulated considerable evidence in the interim that a demise of policies/programs did not necessarily follow from their failure to empirically demonstrate success, we were faced with what we regarded as a puzzling development. It seemed paradoxical that practices that had been evaluated and deemed to be ineffective would nevertheless continue, and even expand (Finckenauer & Gavin, 1999:216-217).

THE POLICY PARADOX

Attempting to explain this paradox, we needed to think about what might account for an endurance of seemingly failed initiatives. Gavin and I offered a number of potential explanations that we saw as possibly working in concert. Especially important among these is the political climate. In this case, we see the political climate that has prevailed in the United States over the past 25 years as being one that demands "get tough" action against crime. Along with this demand is the often accompanying belief that alternatives to getting tough on criminals do not work, and more important from a symbolic perspective, are perceived as being soft on crime. Ironically, tough although of questionable effectiveness appears preferable to soft and of questionable effectiveness! I will come back to this issue.

Next, there also seems to be a kind of inertia factor at work. Once programs and policies are created, they tend to take on a life of their own. It is thus often easier to continue them and avoid angering their constituents than it is to stop them. To some degree, of course, this depends upon who the constituents and the interest groups are. We will return to this as well.

Third is the media factor. Programs, practices, and policies that have visual appeal, compelling stories, and good sound bites have greater odds of survival. Positive media coverage helps build and maintain constituents. In the case of Scared Straight, the media has been especially influential in its continuation.

Fourth, there is the information gap between researchers and policy-makers. On the research side, evaluators may be more interested in communicating with their peers in the academic community than with practitioners. After all, publication in peer-reviewed journals gets one tenure and promotion. On the policy side, research results may be rejected because of a general practitioner suspicion of social science, with its complicated analyses, hedged conclusions, conflicting findings, and general lack of timeliness.

Finally, administrators and officials–for many of the reasons just cited– might not try to find or even care about the information that might be available to them. They know what they want to do and why, and they do not want nor seek to be dissuaded.

Rethinking all this today, and pondering what it means with respect to boot camps, these possible explanations in this case of why boot camps might continue despite what seems to be overwhelming evidence that they do not work still look quite reasonable. Admittedly, as is pointed out in several of the articles in this volume, approximately one-thirds of boot camps have been closed, and their closure may well have been the result of negative evaluations. Two-thirds, however, continue to operate, and indeed new ones may be opening. Additionally, where there were closures, these may well have occurred for reasons other than their poor results.

That programs and policies can and do continue in the face of negative evidence of their effectiveness seems to be borne out by the boot camp example. Given this state of affairs, I would therefore like to go somewhat further with the proffered explanations for why this might be. Some elaboration and further discussion is in order, but more importantly, there may in fact be a common thread or theme that runs through each of these ideas, and I want to develop an argument that indeed there is. If I can make that case, we may then have an overall answer to the paradox outlined above. We may also have a sense of what will be the future of boot camps and why.

RESEARCH AND POLICY

Gloria Laycock is one of those who has long been thinking about the role that social science plays or does not play in the making of social policy. She is currently the director of the Jill Dando Institute in England, where she is attempting to put her thinking about crime prevention into practice. A few years ago, in her final report from her Visiting Fellowship with the National Institute of Justice, Gloria described how multiple factors, including what she called simply "science," can affect policy decisions (Laycock, 2003). That there are multiple factors is important to keep in mind, because it forces us to confront the reality that science research is not only not the sole influential factor, it may in fact be far down the list or not on the list at all in terms of actual influences on policy and practice. Laycock's list of multiple factors include budgeting, precedent, the media, politics, pressure groups, public perceptions, and legislation at the policy level; and additionally, they include training, culture, the role and persona of the local manager/leader, and the specific expectations, at the local or practice level (Laycock, 2003:23).

What does this mean? Simply, that policies and programs arise for multiple reasons that may have little or nothing to do with "scientific" knowledge about the problem to which the policy or program is a response. And, that once policies and programs are in place, they may continue again for reasons having little or nothing to do with science. This will not come as a surprise to people who have looked at these issues. We researchers should obviously not kid ourselves that our work somehow significantly influences or is going to influence policy and practice. Does that mean it has no influence? No! But, it does mean we must be realistic, must not take things for granted, and that we must work much harder at bringing our influence to bear. How to do so is in fact much of the thrust of Laycock's report.

Laycock cites two sources whose words about politics and policy are worth pondering in this context. Chelimsky (1997:55) writes that the ability of researchers to serve policy "depends as much on what we understand about how politics works as it does on the quality and appropriateness of our methods." Then there is Brereton (1996) who says: "Research findings tend to be assessed for their practical and symbolic value, rather than their inherent intellectual worth. Consequently, whether a research study is embraced, ignored, misrepresented, or attacked is likely to be contingent on how various players in the policy process see that research fitting into their own political agendas." These conclusions support the important, even overarching, role of the political climate in influencing policy.

This view is also echoed in the work of Barbara Stolz (2002) on criminal justice policy-making. The framework she uses to explain policy-making includes the roles of symbolic politics, interest groups, the political culture, and implementation. Symbolic politics refers to the idea that political acts are really mostly symbols, and that it is the perception of the acts, rather than their substance, that is their more important feature. Actions policies that reassure, educate, and provide a moral direction are most politically palatable and viable. Political culture, which refers to attitudes and behavior with respect to specific public policies, is also an important influence, according to Stolz.

Laycock and Stolz likewise agree on the key role of interest or pressure groups in shaping criminal justice policy. Because they share common goals, are organized, know the players in the policy arena, and know how to take action, members of interest groups are much more important to the policy-making process than is everyone else. They are also much more likely to be very committed to a particular set of beliefs than is the average person, and their particular beliefs about what should be done about crime and criminals thus assume special significance.

Among the other possible explanations for the policy paradox offered earlier is the information gap between researchers and policy-makers. Laycock (2003:29) addressed this issue as well.

> [P]olicy-advisors need to be able to understand the results of a research project. Research papers that are written in obscure technical language, permeable to the chosen few, and covering reams of paper, are less likely to influence policy than a concise, crisp few pages which summarize the

important points and spell out the implications for policy. Some researchers are distinctly uncomfortable with this scenario, particularly the idea that they should perhaps go somewhat beyond their data in spelling out the policy implications of what they have done. This latter point is contentious. Whether or not researchers articulate what they think or believe, on the basis of their research experience, rather than what they feel they know, on the basis of the conclusions of their work, a policy decision will probably be made, or some practical steps will be taken ... there will be occasions when the researcher knows more than anyone about the subject of the research, and is therefore in a good position to influence the policy-making or practical process. "Opinion giving," should not be problematic, if it is made clear at all stages the status of the advice as opinion.

Leaving aside the topic of "opinion giving" for another day, clearly policy-makers must be able to quickly grasp the essence of a research or evaluation report if they are going to pay it any heed at all. We might ask how many of the extant research studies of boot camps have been specifically targeted at decision-makers, versus how many have been targeted at academic publication.

Moving ahead, is there a common theme that can bring together political climate, program support from interest groups including the inertia factor, media support, and receptivity of policy-makers to research? Yes, I think there is.

IDEOLOGY AND POLICY

Musing about the effects of beliefs, politics, symbolic politics, and political culture on policy-making with respect to boot camps has led me to look for a kind of umbrella that can cover these factors. That umbrella, that common theme, that linking element is, I believe, ideology. A number of scholars have thought and written about ideology and public policy, including crime policy (see, e.g., Bartollas & Miller, 1998; Bennett, 1980; Bernard, 1992; Edelman, 1977; Scheingold, 1984), so I am not claiming any dramatic revelations here. Instead, I simply want to try to locate boot camps, specifically, into this larger discussion.

What I mean by ideology in this context was stated quite well by Walter B. Miller more than 30 years ago. Thinking about ideology and criminal justice policy, Miller defined ideology as referring "to a set of general and abstract beliefs or assumptions about the correct or proper state of things, particularly with respect to the moral order and political arrangements, which serve to shape one's positions on specific issues" (Miller, 1973:141). Elements of ideology, according to Miller, include assumptions that are preconscious rather than explicit, presumptions that are unexamined, and a strong emotional charge to the particular beliefs. Ideology encompasses a deep and abstract set of beliefs about who commits crime and why Stolz (2002:19), and further, about what should be done about it and those who do it.

Thinking as social scientists, all this should immediately strike us as being quite different from theory as an explanation of a phenomenon. Theory, a set of plausible assumptions about causes and effects that are subject to empirical testing, is very much rational-empirical in nature. The assumptions or propositions composing a theory are subject to operational definition, to rigorous testing, and ultimately to support or refutation. Such is not true of ideology. Rather than rational-empirical, ideology is emotional-belief in nature. It is derived from a conglomeration of attitudes and beliefs formed over a lifetime of experiences and learning, not all elements of which may be consciously known to the believer. Unlike theory, ideology is not subject to refutation. We should keep this in mind when we think about the role of science and research in influencing policy and practice.

The ideology that has held sway with respect to crime policy over the past two decades–one that stresses getting tough on crime and criminals–is an ideology that supports a belief in personal responsibility and accountability, a belief that leniency and permissiveness are bad, and a belief that offenders need discipline and a respect for authority. Criminal behavior is a rational choice, according to this ideological stance, and criminals need to learn that making that choice is bad and produces bad consequences for them. It is not a great leap to see that boot camps would be very appealing to persons holding these beliefs. And that brings me to my final ruminations.

IMPLICATIONS FOR BOOT CAMPS

As editor Brent Benda indicates in his introduction to the boot camp articles in this volume, boot camps were not conceived with any systematic theory in mind. There was and is no explicit theoretical base for them. True, if one thinks about it and some folks have, you can discern some implicit theoretical underpinning for boot camps, e.g., social learning, deterrence, and so on. But boot camps were not created and did not evolve from an explicit theoretical model. There were no rigorous, controlled experiments to test the components of that model, perhaps through a series of pilot tests, to determine what worked, with whom, and why. Instead, they were created full-blown, with a mixed bag of programmatic components, usually determined by the jurisdiction, the resources, and especially the ideological perspective of those doing the creating.

The evaluations of boot camps have thus been–and have had to be–very much after the fact concoctions. What I refer to as a "mixed bag of programmatic components" has been treated pretty much as a kind of black box. Some efforts have been made to do before/after studies, and some have included various kinds of quasi-experimental designs with matching, etc. Desegregating and examining what is in the black box–admittedly very difficult–has, however, not been done. As a result, when studies, with all their limitations, conclude, as most have, that boot camps do not work, we should think about what is actually meant by "work."

Have they produced empirically sound evidence of effectiveness in preventing or reducing the recidivism of criminal offenders? No, they have not. Given the reality of how they were developed and how they operate, we should probably not be surprised by that. But, does that mean they do not work?

Again, Benda says here that "boot camps might be labeled 'Teflon programs' because they seemingly are resistant to damaging evidence–empirical criticism simply does not stick." This is the policy paradox to which I referred earlier. I propose to you that the empirical evidence does not stick because it is *irrelevant*. We deal with offenders in certain ways in order to uphold the integrity of a particular ideological stance, of particular ideological beliefs. That is the end being sought, and to the degree that programs and policies achieve that end, to that extent they "work." They are thus not only not theory-based, they are not utilitarian, at least as that is determined through empiricism. Rather, they are ideological.

The article by Cullen and his associates in this volume argues that what those authors call common sense fulfills very much the role I am attributing to ideology. For them, common sense trumps science, is a socially constructed reality that resists falsification, is true virtually by definition, etc. These, I am arguing, are just so with ideology. For me, common sense–the kind of common sense that teaches one not to touch a hot stove–is too simple a notion to capture the deep-seated, emotionally charged beliefs that comprise ideology. Scientific evidence might indeed win the battle with common sense, as Cullen et al., suggest, but ideology, it seems to me, is a different kettle of fish.

Both public officials, including correctional administrators, and the public, find satisfying, policies and practices that fit their ideological perspective with respect to crime and criminals. Ideology is something to be clung to, and to be protected and defended–not discarded. We all try to avoid cognitive dissonance. So what if boot camps do not produce glowing results in reducing recidivism? Maybe they were not implemented properly? Maybe they were not tough enough? Even if they deter one or a few criminals, maybe that is worthwhile? Maybe the experience will have delayed effects? Whatever! The science, such as it is in this case, does not shake the beliefs–the ideology–that offenders need to assume personal responsibility for their crimes, that they need to be held accountable, that they should not be treated leniently, and that they need discipline and to be taught to respect authority.

I find myself in considerable agreement with the arguments put forth by Stinchcomb in this volume. She says that those with a vested interest in boot camps are unlikely to curb their support merely because of negative evaluations, and that this vested interest is one that has a "secure niche" in the prevailing political ideology and "patriotic symbolism." To this I would simply say: Hear, hear!

REFERENCES

Bartollas, C., and S.J. Miller. 1998. *Juvenile Justice in America*. Englewood Cliffs, NJ: Prentice-Hall.

Bennett, William. 1980. *Public Opinion in American Politics*. New York: Harcourt Brace Jovanovich.

Bernard, T.J. 1992. *The Cycle of Juvenile Justice*. New York: Oxford University Press.

Brereton, David. 1996. Does criminology matter? Politics and the policy process, *Current Issues in Criminal Justice, 8,* 1.

Chelimsky, Eleanor. 1997. The political environment of evaluation and what it means for the development of the field. In Eleanor Chelimsky and William R. Shadish (eds.), *Evaluation for the 21st Century*. New York: Sage Publications.

Edelman, J.M., 1977. *Political Language: Words That Succeed and Policies That Fail*. New York: Academic Press.

Finckenauer, James O. 1982. *Scared Straight and the Panacea Phenomenon*. Englewood Cliffs, NJ: Prentice-Hall.

Finckenauer, James O., and Patricia W. Gavin. 1999. *Scared Straight and the Panacea Phenomenon Revisited*. Springfield, IL: Waveland Press.

Laycock, Gloria. 2003. *Social Research–Getting It Right for Practitioners and Policy Makers*, Unpublished report prepared for the U.S. Department of Justice, April; available from NCJRS at <http://www.GloriaLaycockNIJRpt#199361.pdf>.

Miller, Walter B. 1973. Ideology and criminal justice policy: Some current issues, *Journal of Criminal Law and Criminology, 64,* 2.

Scheingold, S., 1984. *The Politics of Law and Order: Street Crime and Public Policy*. New York: Longman.

Stolz, Barbara Ann. 2002. *Criminal Justice Policy Making*. Westport, CT: Praeger.

AUTHOR'S NOTE

James O. Finckenauer, PhD, is a professor in the School of Criminal Justice at Rutgers University, Newark. On leave from Rutgers, he served between 1998 and 2002 as founding Director of the International Center at National Institute of Justice in Washington. His research interests include juvenile justice, organized crime, crime and justice in the former Soviet Union, gun control politics, the death penalty, and the politics of crime and criminal justice. Dr. Finckenauer's books include the landmark *Scared Straight! and the Panacea Phenomenon* as well as *Organized Crime in America, Russian Youth: Law, Deviance, and the Pursuit of Freedom,* and *Russian Mafia in America: Immigration, Culture, and Crime*. He served as editor of the *Journal of Research in Crime and Delinquency* and presently serves as editor of *Trends in Organized Crime*.

Address correspondence to Dr. James Finckenauer, School of Criminal Justice, Rutgers–The State University, Newark, NJ 07052 (E-mail: finckena@andromeda.rutgers.edu).

Index

In this index, page numbers in *italic* designate figures; page numbers followed by the letter "t" designate tables.

Abbreviated time concept, 40-41
Abuse. *See also* Abuse history
   childhood in Native Americans, 180-181
   in drug counseling groups, 17-18
   of female inmates, 15-16
Abuse history, 102,147
   antisocial behavior and, 102-104,106-107
   gender differences, 91-92,92
   measures, 97,122
   Native Americans and, 176-195. *See also* Native Americans
Academic education, 74
Addiction Severity Index, 96-97, 121-122
Adjustment to prison, 144-145
Aftercare, 66
Age/aging
   as predictor of recidivism, 127
   recidivism and, 142-144
Aggressivity, as communication, 139-140
Aging-of-organism theory. *See* Life-course theory
Ameliorating experiences, 119-120,128-129
   antisocial behavior and, 106
   gender differences, 93
   military service as, 59-60
Antisocial attitudes, 14-15,71-86
   attrition, 78-79,79t
   background and principles, 72-73

Cox's proportional-hazards model, 100-105,101t,103t,104t
   data collection, 77-79,79t
   discussion, 83-84,105-108
   eligibility criteria for study, 75-76
   findings, 99-105,*100*,101t,103t,104t
   life table methods (survival curves), 99-100,*100*
   measures, 79
   method, 76-79
   program descriptions, 73-75
   random assignment procedure, 76-77
   results: post-program comparisons, 81-83,82t,83t
   results: research sample, 80-81,82t
   statistical analyses, 99
(University of) Arkansas: Little Rock, 1-25,87-113
Athletic activity, 140-141
Attachments, 89. *See also* Life-course theory
   measures, 97,122
   peer, 97-98
   sexual abuse and, 92-93
Attrition, 78-79,79t
Authoritarianism, 57-58

Bankruptcy of rehabilitation theme, 9-11
Boot camps
   authoritarian nature of, 57-58

benefits, 18-19,98
common sense as approach to, 53-70
conclusions and observations, 12-16
contradictory goals, 41
disadvantages of, 19-20
fall of, 64-65
five-year follow-up on self-control, 115-132
historical context, 7-12
hypermasculine behaviors and, 133-152
as immediate sanctions, 56-61
inmate perceptions. *See* Perceptions
justification of military model, 30
life-course theory and, 89-113
Maryland antisocial attitude study, 71-86
Native Americans and abuse history, 176-195. *See also* Native Americans
observations and recommendations, 16-20
in Oklahoma, 156-157. *See also* Perceptions
panacea phenomenon and, 200-201
popularity of idea, 37
program concept, 2-4
program goals and objectives, 4-7
public policy and, 27-52,199-207
Break down/build up concept, 60-61, 146-147

Caregiver monitoring, 97,122
(University of) Cincinnati, 53-70
Common sense approach, 53-70
 appeal of boot camps, 56-61
 background and principles, 54-55
 conclusions and recommendations, 65-66
 cost of, 63-64
 dangers of, 61-64,66
 intermediate sanction idea, 56-58

Moneyball: Winning an Unfair Game (Lewis) and, 61-64
Communication, through aggressivity and confrontation, 139-140
Confrontation, as communication, 139-140
Congruity, extent of, 44
Coping, mature, 145
Corporal punishment, 140,146
Cost reduction, as goal, 6-7
Cox's Proportional-Hazards Model, 123-127,124t,126t,127t
Crime boom period, 8-9
Criminal male accomplishment, 137
Crowding, 56

Delinquency, history of previous, 59-60
Deterrence, 4-5,35. *See also* Recidivism
Drug counseling groups, sexual abuse/harassment in, 17-18
Drug education, 74
Drug treatment programs, 146-147
Drug use. *See* Substance abuse

Eastern Kentucky University, 153-174
Education
 academic, 74
 drug, 74
 gender difference in risk and, 89
 physical, 140-141
Employment, as ameliorating experience, 128-129
Empowerment vs. power, 145-146
Equality of services, 18
Evidence-based corrections, 54-55, 62,65
 lack of empirical findings, 58
Expedience, 99
Extent of congruity, 44

Family visitation, 16-17, 141, 142
Femininity, defined, 135
(University of) Florida, 176-195
Florida Atlantic University, 27-52

Gang membership, 93, 94-95
  predictive value, 102
Gender, choice of boot camp and, 17
Gender differences
  in antisocial behavior, 102-104
  life-course theory and, 87-113. *See also* Life-course theory
  in Oklahoma program, 157
  self-control, 125
Gendered organizations, 137-138
Gender research, on organizations, 137-138
Gender roles, 135-136. *See also* Hypermasculine behaviors
Get tough period, 11
Glueck study (1939-1950), 59
Goals and objectives, 4-7
  contradictory, 41
  cost reduction, 6-7
  deterrence, 4-5
  incapacitation, 6
  life-course study, 90-92
  overcrowding reduction, 6-7
  punishment, 6
  rehabilitation, 5-6
Great Society programs, 7-8

Herman L. Toulson Boot Camp, antisocial attitude study, 71-86
Historical context, 7-12
Homophobia, 141-142
Hot stove concept, 58
Humiliation tactics, 15
Hypermasculine behaviors. *See also* Masculinity
  boot camps as masculine organizations, 127-132
  as communication, 139-140
  conclusion, 147
  corporal punishment and, 140
  crime and, 135-136
  as homophobia, 141-142
  physical activity as, 140-141
  physical (hard) labor and, 141
  prison adjustment and, 144-145
  prison studies, 134-135
  recidivism and, 142-144
  recommendations for change, 144-147
  separation from women and, 141

Ideology, and public policy, 204-205
Incapacitation, as goal, 6
Inertia factor, in public policy, 201
Infractions, reporting of, 123
Inmate perceptions. *See* Perceptions

Job training needs, of women, 17
Justice model, 29-30, 41

Life-course theory, 89-113, 125
  background and principles, 88-89
  description, 88-89
  discriminant analysis and, 14
  gender differences, 92-93
  masculinity and, 143-144
  method, 94-99
  outcome dependent variable, 96
  procedure and data, 94
  questionnaires and prediction measures, 94-99
  sample, 94, 95t
  of self-control, 119-120
  study goals and objectives, 90-92

Male bonding, prison culture as, 139
Maltreatment, 15-16

Mandatory minimum sentencing, 32
Marriage
  antisocial behavior and, 105-106
  difference in risk and, 89-90
Martinson, R.M., 9-11
(University of) Maryland, 71-86
Maryland antisocial attitude study, 71-86
Masculinity, 133-152. *See also* Hypermasculine behaviors
  defined, 135
  as learned behavior, 136
  life-course and, 143-144
Mature coping, 145
Media, public policy and, 201
Medical model, 41
Metropolitan Transition Center, antisocial attitude study, 71-86
Military service, research on impact, 59
Mississippi State University, 153-174
Moneyball: Winning an Unfair Game (Lewis), 61-64
Mutual Agreement Program (MAP) contracts, 76, 78

National Supported Work Demonstration, 89
Native Americans, 176-195
  boot camp history and, 181-182
  childhood maltreatment among, 180-181
  conclusion, 191-193
  conditions of confinement, 182
  differences by type of institution, 185-187
  measures, 184-185
  needs of offenders, 179-180
  notes, 193
  results, 185-188, 186t
  sample, 186t
  statistical analysis, 187-191, 188t, 190t
  study background and principles, 178-179
  study design, 183
  Western culture in conflict with, 179
(University of) Nevada: Las Vegas, 71-86
(University of) New Brunswick at St. John, 53-70
N of 1 phenomena, 60

(University of) Oklahoma, 153-174
Oklahoma severity perception study, 154-176. *See also* Perceptions
Organizational preservation tendency, 43
Organizations, gendered, 137-138
Outcome evaluation, 42-44
Overcrowding, 6-7

Pains of imprisonment, 139
Panacea phenomenon, 200-201
Parenthood, choice of boot camp and, 17
Patriarchy, 136
Peer association
  measures, 122
  self-control and, 118
Peer attachment, 97-98. *See also* Gang membership
Perceptions
  background and principles, 154-155
  of change, 98-99
  data collection, 156
  discussion, 169-172
  gender differences in participation decisions, 160-164, 161t, 162t
  measurement of, 98-99
  measuring relative severity, 157-158
  multivariate results, 164-169, 165t, 167t

recidivism and, 93
sample, 155-156,159-160,159t
of severity, gender differences,
   153-174. *See also*
   Perceptions
survey instrument, 155
survey results, 159-169
Physical education, 140-141
Physical (hard) labor,
   hypermasculinity and, 141
Physical vs. social science, 42-44
Plea bargaining, 32-33
Political issues. *See* Public policy
Power vs. empowerment, 145-146
Prisons, masculinity stripped in,
   137-138
Professionalism, lack of, 55
Profiling, of recidivists, 14
Program design, hypermasculinity and,
   133-152. *See also*
   Hypermasculine behaviors
Program restructuring, 145-146
Public policy, 27-52,199-207
   disillusionments in, 32-33
   empirical evidence countering,
      30-32
   gender considerations in, 107
   ideology and, 204-205
   implementation, 39-42
   implications for boot camps,
      205-207
   inertia factor, 201
   justice model, 29-30
   legislative action, 36-37
   media factor, 201
   outcome evaluation, 42-44
   panacea phenomenon, 200-201
   paradox of, 201-202
   policy conceptualization, 34-36
   policy-making process, 33-34,*34*
   political vs. empirical basis, 31-32
   popularity of concept, 28-29
   research and, 202-204
   strategic development, 37-39
   summary and conclusions, 45-47

Punishment
   as goal, 6
   immediate, 57

Quackery, in corrections field, 55
Quasi-experimental designs, as
   problematic, 19-20

Rational choice theory, 153-174. *See also* Perceptions
Recidivism, 65. *See also* Recidivists
   age as predictor, 127
   criteria for determining, 12-13
   empirical evidence on, 30-32
   gender differences in predictors, 91
   hypermasculine behavior and,
      142-144
   inmate perceptions and, 93
   religiosity and, 14
   research prospects, 15
   social bonds and, 14
Recidivists. *See also* Recidivism
   discriminate analysis, 14
   distinguishing personal factors,
      13-14
   profiling, 14
Rehabilitation, bankruptcy of, 9-11
Rehabilitation goal, 5-6
Religiosity, 14
Rutgers University, 199-207

Science, physical vs. social, 42-44
Self-Appraisal Questionnaire, 79
Self-control, 115-132
   background and principles, 116-118
   Cox's Proportional-Hazards Model,
      124-127,124t,126t,127t
   description of low, 117
   developmental consequences,
      117-118
   discussion, 127-129

findings, 124-127,124t,126t,127t
measures, 122-123
method, 119-124
outcome or dependent variable, 121
procedure and data, 119-121
questionnaire and prediction
    measures, 121-122
sample, 119,120t
statistical analyses, 123-124
study goals and objectives, 119
Self-efficacy, 14
Self-esteem, 14
Sentencing, mandatory minimum, 32
Sentencing Project, 32
Severity, gender differences in
    perceptions, 153-174. See
    also Perceptions
Sexual abuse. See Abuse; Abuse
    history
Shock incarceration concept, 29-30
Social bonding, 16-17
Social controls, 105-106
Social control theory, 88. See also
    Life-course theory
Social vs. physical science, 42-44
Staff, perceptions of, 98
Staff support, 98
Substance abuse, 41
    Addiction Severity Index, 96-97,
        121-122
    measurement, 98
    recidivism and, 142-144
    treatment programs, 146-147

Three strikes policy, 32
Transforming personal experiences.
    See Ameliorating experience;
    Life-course theory

Turning points. See Ameliorating
    experiences; Life-course
    theory

University of Arkansas: Little Rock,
    1-25,87-113,115-132
University of Cincinnati, 53-70
University of Florida, 176-195
University of Maryland, 71-86
University of Nevada: Las Vegas,
    71-86
University of New Brunswick at St.
    John, 53-70
University of Oklahoma, 153-174

Vietnam War era, 59
Virginia Department of Corrections,
    71-86
Vision vacuum concept, 35
Visitation, family, 16-17,141,
    142

War on Crime, 8-9
Washington State University, 133-152
Weapons carrying, predictive value,
    102
Women. See also Gender
    job training needs, 17
    psychological toll on, 17
    as receptive to boot camp, 17

BOOK ORDER FORM!

Order a copy of this book with this form or online at:
http://www.haworthpress.com/store/product.asp?sku=5515

Rehabilitation Issues, Problems, and Prospects in Boot Camp

___ in softbound at $29.95 ISBN: 0-7890-2822-0.
___ in hardbound at $39.95 ISBN: 0-7890-2821-2.

COST OF BOOKS _____

POSTAGE & HANDLING _____
US: $4.00 for first book & $1.50 for each additional book
Outside US: $5.00 for first book & $2.00 for each additional book.

SUBTOTAL _____
In Canada: add 7% GST. _____

STATE TAX _____
CA, IL, IN, MN, NJ, NY, OH, PA & SD residents please add appropriate local sales tax.

FINAL TOTAL _____
If paying in Canadian funds, convert using the current exchange rate, UNESCO coupons welcome.

❏ **BILL ME LATER:**
Bill-me option is good on US/Canada/Mexico orders only; not good to jobbers, wholesalers, or subscription agencies.

❏ **Signature** _____

❏ **Payment Enclosed: $** _____

❏ **PLEASE CHARGE TO MY CREDIT CARD:**
❏ Visa ❏ MasterCard ❏ AmEx ❏ Discover
❏ Diner's Club ❏ Eurocard ❏ JCB

Account # _____

Exp Date _____

Signature _____
(Prices in US dollars and subject to change without notice.)

PLEASE PRINT ALL INFORMATION OR ATTACH YOUR BUSINESS CARD

| Name |
| Address |
| City   State/Province   Zip/Postal Code |
| Country |
| Tel   Fax |
| E-Mail |

May we use your e-mail address for confirmations and other types of information? ❏ Yes ❏ No We appreciate receiving your e-mail address. Haworth would like to e-mail special discount offers to you, as a preferred customer. **We will never share, rent, or exchange your e-mail address.** We regard such actions as an invasion of your privacy.

Order from your **local bookstore** or directly from
The Haworth Press, Inc. 10 Alice Street, Binghamton, New York 13904-1580 • USA
Call our toll-free number (1-800-429-6784) / Outside US/Canada: (607) 722-5857
Fax: 1-800-895-0582 / Outside US/Canada: (607) 771-0012
E-mail your order to us: orders@haworthpress.com

For orders outside US and Canada, you may wish to order through your local sales representative, distributor, or bookseller.
For information, see http://haworthpress.com/distributors

(Discounts are available for individual orders in US and Canada only, not booksellers/distributors.)
Please photocopy this form for your personal use.
www.HaworthPress.com

BOF05